Understanding
Child Sexual
Maltreatment

SAGE SOURCEBOOKS FOR THE HUMAN SERVICES SERIES

Series Editors: ARMAND LAUFFER and CHARLES GARVIN

Recent Volumes in this Series

Kathleen Coulborn Faller

Understanding Child Sexual Maltreatment

SAGE SOURCEBOOKS FOR THE HUMAN SERVICES SERIES 12

SAGE PUBLICATIONS
The International Professional Publishers
Newbury Park London New Delhi

To Lincoln B. Faller,
my husband of 25 years
and source of support and criticism for longer.

For information address:

SAGE Publications, Inc.
2455 Teller Road
Newbury Park, California 91320

SAGE Publications Ltd.
6 Bonhill Street
London EC2A 4PU
United Kingdom

SAGE Publications India Pvt. Ltd.
M-32 Market
Greater Kailash I
New Delhi 110 048 India

Printed in the United States of America

Library of Congress Cataloging-in-Publication Data

Faller, Kathleen Coulborn.
    Understanding child sexual maltreatment / Kathleen Coulborn
Faller.
        p.   cm. -- (Sage sourcebooks for the human services series ;
12)
    Includes bibliographical references and index.
    ISBN 0-8039-3841-1. -- ISBN 0-8039-3842-X (pbk.)
    1. Child molesting.   I. Title.   II. Series: Sage sourcebooks for
the human services series ; v. 12.
HQ71.F35   1990   90-8632
362.7'6--dc20   CIP

SECOND PRINTING, 1991

Sage Production Editor: Kimberley A. Clark

CONTENTS

PREFACE

Despite the increased awareness of sexual maltreatment, of both professionals and the public, in the last ten years, most institutions training mental health practitioners offer little or no material in their regular curricula on child sexual victimization. It is still up to the individual professional to educate her- or himself, by reading articles and books or going to specialized workshops and seminars. This kind of self-education tends to be piecemeal. Further, because sexual maltreatment is a multifaceted, multidisciplinary problem, it is often difficult to find or acquire the material that is relevant to one's own profession.

The purpose of this book is to serve as a resource for mental health professionals who must address the problem of child sexual abuse. Relevant research and clinical material to assist mental health practitioners in performing their various roles in sexual abuse cases has been assembled and integrated. The book relies both on my clinical experience and research in sexual maltreatment during the past 14 years, and on written work and consultation with other practitioners and researchers.

Because sexual maltreatment of children is a problem that requires the input and collaboration of professionals from many different disciplines—law enforcement, attorneys, judges, physicians, nurses, and teachers—to name those most frequently involved—the book will also be of interest to professionals other than those in the mental health field. The material should be useful both to those who have little background in sexual abuse and to those whose background is considerable. This is so because sexual maltreatment is a field in which knowledge is developing at a very rapid rate and is likely to continue to do so for a number of years. Thus the changing nature of the field means the book contains new insights and content in old areas.

In addition, in an effort to make the book as useful as possible, I have employed charts, protocols, and case examples wherever they seem to add clarity. The examples are drawn from actual cases and may cause some readers discomfort. However, it is my view that professionals who cannot bear to hear or read about what children have experienced will not be able to help them. An additional reason for including case examples is that they may serve to desensitize readers so that they can respond in a helpful and professional manner, rather than an emotional one, when confronted with a case of sexual abuse.

It is hoped that the book will serve as a useful reference for mental health professionals and others making assessment and intervention decisions in cases of child sexual maltreatment.

ORGANIZATION OF THE BOOK

The book is divided into four sections. The first consists of two chapters and intends to orient the mental health professional to the problem of child sexual maltreatment. The first chapter describes a victim-centered approach, provides information about incidence and prevalence of the problem, and discusses indicators of sexual maltreatment. The second chapter gives a definition of sexual abuse with relevant examples, differentiates among types of sexually abusive relationships, and lays out a theory for understanding why adults sexually abuse children.

Part II describes the roles of protective services, the police, lawyers, and the courts and provides guidelines for mental health professionals who interact with these agents and institutions, including advice about giving testimony in court.

Part III addresses issues of diagnosis and case decision making. Chapter 5 examines the issue of how to decide whether or not sexual abuse has occurred, providing a protocol to assist mental health professionals in this endeavor. Chapter 6 furnishes guidelines for determining the severity of sexual abuse, the harm it is likely to have caused, whether separation of the victim and offender is indicated, and treatment prognosis.

The final section of the book, Part IV, deals with sexual abuse in three particular contexts. These are in divorce cases, in foster care, and in day care. Mental health professionals are frequently required to handle sexual abuse allegations in these situations. Characteristics that differentiate sexual maltreatment in these contexts from more general patterns of sexual abuse are covered.

THE INTERDISCIPLINARY PROJECT ON CHILD ABUSE AND NEGLECT

Much of the material relied on to produce this book has been accumulated from my work under the auspices of the Interdisciplinary Project on Child

Abuse and Neglect (IPCAN). IPCAN is made up of faculty from the School of Social Work, the law school, and the medical school, including psychiatry and pediatric psychology, at the University of Michigan.

IPCAN faculty teach material relevant to maltreated children within the three professional schools and to practitioners in the community whose charge is to provide services to maltreated children. All faculty are involved in practice relevant to their particular disciplines in the child welfare field. Faculty also offer consultation to state and local agencies related to child welfare policy and practice. In addition, faculty engage in research and writing related to child maltreatment and welfare. Over the years, IPCAN has received support from a variety of sources to engage in its work, including private foundation funding, state contracts, and federal grants.

The character of this book is in considerable part determined by my experiences and activities as a faculty member of IPCAN.

ACKNOWLEDGMENTS

A number of people have given me invaluable assistance by reading chapters and offering advice. Especially helpful have been the suggestions of Lisa D'Aunno, a lawyer and a fellow IPCAN faculty member; David Corwin, a child psychiatrist doing important work in the sexual abuse field; and Patricia Ryan, a sociologist and a colleague from Eastern Michigan University Institute for the Study of Children and Families.

As well, I would like to acknowledge the support of the School of Social Work, particularly two colleagues, Rosemary Sarri and Dean Harold Johnson.

However, probably most important has been the contribution of the IPCAN secretary, Alice Auer, who proofed all of the chapters and corrected my grammar, spelling, and punctuation.

PART I

What Constitutes
Sexual Maltreatment?

Chapter 1

MENTAL HEALTH PROFESSIONALS AND CHILD SEXUAL MALTREATMENT

As recently as 40 years ago, sexual maltreatment of children was thought to be extremely uncommon. Thus, in 1955, Weinberg, in a landmark work on incest, estimated that the rate of incest among children in the United States was only about one per million. Today, experts in sexual abuse believe that as many as one in three American females and one in six males are sexually abused during their childhoods (Faller, 1988).

These recent findings lead to the conclusion that most mental health professionals, regardless of the situations in which they practice, can expect to encounter cases of child sexual abuse. Certainly those involved with children can anticipate coming in contact with numerous cases. Children will present to medical social workers when they come to be examined for physical evidence of sexual abuse. Mental health professionals working in child welfare—protective services, foster care, adoption, and institutional care—will encounter many sexually abused children.

The effects of sexual abuse bring children to mental health outpatient settings as well as to psychiatric facilities. Furthermore, adults who were victimized as children, who never revealed their maltreatment and/or never received treatment, are coming to mental health settings complaining of a wide range of sequelae of sexual abuse—sexual dysfunction, problems in intimate relationships, substance abuse, depression and suicidal ideation, and problems of self-esteem.

Often, children who have been sexually abused require intervention by mental health professionals and others working in school settings. Cases are usually discovered when children reveal their abuse to persons whom they trust, often in school. In addition, child protection workers, wanting to interview children about possible sexual abuse away from the influence of their families, typically come to the child's school to do this. Moreover, the sequelae of sexual abuse often require intervention by mental health professionals and teachers in school.

Mental health professionals involved in cases of divorce need to be aware of the dynamics of sexual abuse as well as the possibility of false allegations. Finally, persons in the mental health field who have responsibilities related to criminal courts need to know about sexual abuse because increasing numbers of these cases are being criminally prosecuted.

Information that will assist mental health professionals in these various capacities will be provided in the coming chapters. In this first chapter, the major concerns will be describing a philosophical orientation to sexual abuse that gives priority to the victim's best interest, providing information on the incidence and prevalence of sexual abuse, and discussing indicators of sexual abuse.

A VICTIM-CENTERED APPROACH

A major dilemma for mental health professionals and others attempting to intervene in sexual maltreatment is the intensely competing interests in a sexual abuse case. In many cases, what is good for the victim is absolutely opposed by the family. The alleged offender may launch a multifaceted campaign against the victim and all those who support her,[1] including professionals involved. Conflicting interests are particularly acute in intrafamilial sexual abuse cases.

The stakes are very high. Children are often removed from their parents' care; families are broken up; parental rights may be terminated; multimodal, long-term treatment can be imposed upon the family; reputations may be ruined; offenders and sometimes their accomplices are criminally prosecuted, and these people may go to jail or prison.

Moreover, in the course of professional intervention, additional damage can be done to the victim and sometimes to the family. Of serious concern is the fact that victims may be mistreated by the system. They may be disbelieved by professionals, when they are telling the truth; they may be subjected to repeated interviews; they may receive a medical exam from someone who is insensitive or inexperienced; they may be inadequately protected from the abuser or the family; they may be removed from their homes unnecessarily or put in unsuitable placements; they may feel traumatized and humiliated by the court process, which requires them to describe to others their sexual abuse and often to submit to brutal cross-examination; and, finally, they may receive inadequate or unskilled treatment.

It is critical for mental health professionals to adopt a stance that can help them cope with the pressures of the competing parties in a sexual maltreatment case and assure that the victim is not additionally traumatized by the intervention. I advocate a *victim-centered approach*. This approach dictates that all case management decisions and intervention be handled according to what is in the victim's best interest.

To act in the victim's best interest, the mental health professional starts by ascertaining the victim's wishes, that is, what the victim wants to happen. However, what the victim wants may not be synonymous with her best interest. For example, a child may wish to return to her mother, when it is clear that the mother will not or cannot at the time protect the child from further sexual abuse. In addition, the younger the victims, the less they may be able to judge what is in their best interest. Therefore, to summarize, best interest requires professional judgment but takes into account the victim's wishes.

Thus, when it is initially determined that the child has been sexually abused, she should be asked what should happen. If the child says the offender should get help, that should result in a therapeutic approach to the abuser. If the child says the offender should go to jail, this desire should lead to a more punitive response. Of course, the victim may change her mind, and these changes also need to be considered.

There are additional steps to be taken in the victim's best interest. Although several people may need to know from the child what happened, the number of people interviewing the child should be minimized. This can often be effected by videotaping the initial interview with the child or having professionals who need information from the victim behind a one-way mirror while the child is being interviewed.

In addition, mental health professionals may need to play a leadership role in developing appropriate community resources to support a victim-centered approach. Physicians with knowledge about sexual abuse and sensitivity to the needs of victims need to be located, so that children are not retraumatized by the medical exam nor important medical evidence overlooked. As will be discussed in Chapter 9, sexually abused children have particular placement needs. Communities need to develop and support specialized facilities for sexually abused children. Finally, the role of the mental health professional is probably most central in developing adequate treatment resources, so that the damage to victims can be alleviated and, in cases where it is appropriate, families can be reunited.

Therefore, although it is important that individual mental health professionals adopt a victim-centered approach, it is necessary also that adequate community resources be available and that all the professionals involved also adhere to a victim-centered approach. Only then will there be minimal retraumatization of the victim from intervention and maximum rehabilitation of the victim and the victim's family.

INCIDENCE AND PREVALENCE

It is difficult to ascertain the extent of a phenomenon that occurs in secrecy, surrounded by shame. To add to the problem of identification is the fact that sexual abuse usually leaves no physical traces. Therefore, information about how widespread sexual maltreatment is comes from the mouths of victims, witnesses, and perpetrators.

There are two main kinds of data used to study the extent of sexual abuse: reports of sexual maltreatment to professionals who have some responsibility for intervention and studies of populations that may contain victims.

Incidence Rates of Child Sexual Maltreatment

Reported cases usually yield estimates of incidence rates, that is, how many cases of sexual abuse occurred within a given time frame, usually a year. By taking the number of reports and comparing that with the number of children in the population during the target year, a rate of sexual abuse for the child population can be calculated. The best national statistics collected in the United States today come from accumulated reports to child protection agencies across the country. These cases go into a central data bank sponsored by the National Center on Child Abuse and Neglect (NCCAN), an agency of the federal government. Since 1976, the data have been analyzed yearly by the American Humane Association (American Association for the Protection of Children, 1985-89).

There are other institutions that collect statistics about cases, but they are not so useful. Police reports yield less reliable information because there are literally thousands of police agencies in the United States. They do not have uniform practices for collecting information about sex crimes, and there is no central data collection. The only national law enforcement statistics come from the FBI, but their data only include cases where a federal statute has been violated. Hospitals, courts, diagnostic, and treatment agencies may collect statistics about their cases. Their findings can be enlightening, but they suffer from being restricted to one institution and, therefore, are not very generalizable.

Despite the fact that child protection agency data are the most comprehensive, even they have limitations. First, most child protection agencies only handle cases where a parent is involved in the maltreatment.[2] The parent must be the perpetrator or must be neglectful by not protecting the child from sexual abuse.[3] As will be elucidated later in the book, many sexual abusers of children are not parents. In addition, although NCCAN has developed a national data collection form, many states and localities do not systematically collect the required information. Further, there are differences in how cases are defined and handled that affect statistics. Finally, the funding for the data analysis has dwindled over the years, so that the published findings have become progressively more sparse and currently are based upon projections from information on a small number of states.

Nevertheless, the findings shed considerable light on the incidence of sexual abuse as reflected in reported cases. What they indicate is an increase in the absolute number of sexual abuse cases over the years, an increase in the rate per 10,000 children, and an increase in the proportion of all abuse and neglect cases represented by child sexual abuse. Thus, in 1976, only 6,000 cases of sexual abuse were reported and they were only 3% of all cases of maltreatment. The rate per 10,000 children was .86. By 1986, this figure had climbed to 132,000 cases and represented 15% of all cases of maltreatment. The rate per 10,000 children was 20.89 (American Association for the Protection of Children, 1988).[4]

A final limitation of these findings is that they only refer to reported cases, obviously a much smaller number than actual cases of sexual maltreatment. An innovative attempt to avoid this limitation is the National Incidence Study (U.S. Department of Health and Human Services, 1981, 1988), first conducted in 1980 and then again in 1986. The National Incidence Study was also sponsored by NCCAN. The researchers examined records of child protective services in 29 counties chosen to be representative of the country as a whole. In addition, they collected information from professionals in those counties who are mandated reporters (law enforcement, school personnel, hospital staff, treatment providers, court staff). They were interested in the proportion of cases falling within the definition of child maltreatment, that were actually referred to child protection agencies by professionals required to report. In addition, one of the purposes of repeating the study was to determine whether there had been changes in the rates at which mandated reporters were complying with requirements to report, and whether there had been any changes in the proportions of various types of cases being identified by professionals.

Briefly, the findings from both studies are as follows: The first study indicates that only about a fifth of cases that should be reported are in fact referred. The second study demonstrates no statistically significant increase in professional compliance with their reporting requirements. Moreover, one of the most controversial and troubling findings of this study is the absolute increase in the number of physical and sexual abuse cases professionals are identifying, a threefold increase in the number of sexual abuse cases (U.S. Department of Health and Human Services, 1981, 1988).

The Prevalence of Child Sexual Maltreatment

Accounts of having being sexually maltreated during childhood give an estimate of the prevalence of sexual abuse, that is, how many people experience sexual abuse while growing up. Such studies are generally conducted by collecting data from adults who recount their sexual maltreatment as children. Information is gathered in a variety of ways: by telephone, by having participants fill out questionnaires, or by face-to-face interview with respondents. In addition, different samples are surveyed: (1) volunteers; (2) special populations, such as persons seeking treatment or college students; and (3) representative samples of the general population.

Because studies are conducted in different ways, using different populations, and with varying definitions of sexual abuse, their results differ. A seminal study was that conducted by Finkelhor (1979) of men and women from six New England colleges and universities. He found that 19.2% of women and 8.9% of men had experiences of sexual abuse during their childhoods. It is assumed that proportions in a college population would be lower than those in the general population, because the sequelae of sexual abuse can affect academic performance. Finkelhor's results startled the child welfare community and led to an appreciation of the seriousness of the problem of child sexual abuse.

Later research found that even higher proportions of Americans had been sexually victimized. Research yielding the highest proportions of the population acknowledging sexual victimization as children are studies involving face-to-face interviews with adult women. Russell (1983), whose subjects consisted of a representative sample of 930 women from the San Francisco area, found that 54% had experienced sexual abuse before the age of 18. When the definition is narrowed to only include those situations involving sexual contact, the percentage is 38. The proportions of women found by Wyatt (1985) to have been sexually abused is even higher, 62%; 45% being subjected to contact sexual abuse. Her sample was a stratified probability sample of 248 black and white women from the Los Angeles area.

These two studies involved only women and both surveyed California populations. Research on the sexual abuse of men has not been as extensive and has consistently found that lower proportions of men than women were victimized. However, two recent studies provide interesting information. A study of close to 3,000 males attending institutions of higher education in the United States by Risin and Koss (1987) noted that 7.3% of them experienced some form of sexual abuse before the age of 14. The definition employed in this study included noncontact as well as contact sexual abuse and required that there be a significant age discrepancy between the victim and the offender, that some form of coercion be present, and that the offender be a care giver or authority figure. Boys are more likely than girls to be victimized by someone outside the home and to be victimized by women.

Fromuth and Burkhart's (1987) sample was also college-aged men, theirs coming from two universities and totaling 582 subjects. They varied the definition of sexual abuse and found that this affected the proportion of men defined as sexually abused. Factors that were varied included the maximum victim age, whether there need be an age differential between a victim and offender, whether coercion must be present, whether noncontact behaviors were included, and whether the victim had to experience the sexual abuse as negative. Proportions of male subjects defined as sexually maltreated varied from 4% to 24% with these manipulations in definition.

Finally, a recent telephone survey conducted by the *Los Angeles Times* (Crewdson, 1988) is notable because it was large (involving 2,627 persons), it included both men and women, and it consisted of a national sample. The *Los Angeles Times* survey noted that 22% of respondents reported sexual victimization as children—27% of women and 16% of men.

What these findings indicate is that sexual abuse is a significant problem for children and adults in our country. It is not a rare occurrence. Therefore, mental health professionals need to know about sexual maltreatment and how to intervene to help victims, offenders, and their families.

INDICATORS

Children who have been sexually abused may show symptoms of these traumatic experiences. In this discussion of indicators, symptoms will be divided into two general categories: sexual symptoms and nonsexual indicators of possible sexual abuse.[5] In addition, asymptomatic children will be considered. An essential point is that sexual symptoms are much more likely to be related to sexual abuse than are nonsexual symptoms.

Sexual Symptoms

Children who demonstrate sexual *behavior*, possess sexual *knowledge*, and make *statements* about sexual activities need to be evaluated for possible sexual abuse. Such symptoms cause particular concern in young children. They are not old enough to have received any sex education and are unlikely to have sexually active or knowledgeable peers who might have exposed them to sexual material.

(1) Sexual behavior. There are six different types of sexual behavior that signal possible sexual abuse: (1) excessive masturbation, (2) sexual interaction with peers, (3) sexual aggression toward younger or more naive children, (4) sexual accosting of older people or adults, (5) seductive behavior, and (6) promiscuity.

(a) Excessive masturbation. When is masturbation excessive? Most children, and indeed most adults, masturbate. This is developmentally normal behavior for children. Generally, they discover that it feels good to touch or rub their genitals as they explore their bodies. Because it feels good, they will repeat the activity. Therefore, it is important not to automatically assume a masturbating child has been victimized. The appropriate adult response to encountering a child masturbating is to acknowledge that it feels good but to explain to the child that masturbation is an activity to be done in private.

Signs that a child is excessively masturbating are as follows: (1) compulsive masturbation, that is, the child cannot stop; (2) inflicting injury while masturbating (also an indication that this is compulsive behavior); (3) masturbating several times in a day; and (4) masturbating when upset and feeling vulnerable.

Illustrative of excessive masturbation is the following case example:

Case example: Ms. T brought her 3-year-old daughter, Sally, to be evaluated for possible sexual abuse. The major symptom the mother complained of was masturbation. She said that she would catch Sally masturbating and tell her to stop. Sally would then go into the bedroom and her mother would catch her again. The mother said that the child would seem mesmerized.

When the evaluator interviewed Sally, Sally told her that she was bad. The evaluator asked what she did that was bad. Sally replied "riding." The evaluator asked what "riding" was. Sally proceeded to demonstrate. She straddled the arm of a chair and, placing one hand on the seat of the chair and holding on to the back with the other, she rocked back and forth on the chair arm, masturbating, for several minutes. She appeared transfixed. She then got off and proceeded to "ride" the other arm of the chair. There were three other chairs with arms in the playroom and she asked if she could "ride" them as well. She took off her jeans and underpants, saying it was better that way. She appeared red from her mons veneris to her anus, apparently from "riding."

When asked where she learned about "riding," she said her grandmother taught her. She then described a range of sexual activity involving both of her grandparents.

In this case, the mother's description suggests excessive masturbation, but, before seeing Sally, the evaluator wondered if perhaps the mother's punitive response was responsible for the masturbation. However, clearly what the child demonstrated in the session was excessive masturbation, and Sally then revealed the source of her "riding" behavior.

A final caution should be raised with regard to excessive masturbation. It appears that some deprived children will masturbate excessively. Because of a lack of stimulation and nurturance in their environment, they resort to self-stimulation and self-comfort in the form of masturbation. Moreover, there is the possible cause considered in the case example above. Children who have been caught and punished for masturbating may develop a pattern of furtive masturbation, which can become preoccupying to the point that the behavior is excessive.

Therefore, to conclude, when there are reports of masturbation, the mental health professional first needs to determine whether the behavior is within normal limits and, second, should look for the cause of the behavior, taking into account that something other than sexual abuse might be the source of excessive masturbation.

(b) Sexual interaction with peers. Some children who have been sexually abused will engage in sexual activity with peers. In cases where this is the child's reaction to sexual abuse, generally the dynamic is that the child has been sexually overstimulated and as a consequence is sexually precocious. But there are cases in which the sexual interaction may also have a compulsive quality to it, reflective of the traumatic aspect of the sexual abuse.

However, again, it is important to differentiate developmentally normal behavior from that which is more likely to be indicative of sexual abuse. Children of 3, 4, or 5 generally discover not only that touching themselves feels good but also that other people have genitalia, some of which are different from theirs (i.e., boys and girls are different). These discoveries may occasion looking at one another's genitals and touching one another. Because the touching feels good, it may be repeated. Furthermore, if children observe adults engaged in sexual activity, they may try these acts themselves. And, as children become older and learn about various forms of sexual activity, they may experiment.

Nevertheless, when children are discovered engaging in sexual activity with one another, it is important to inquire where they learned about these things. Furthermore, they are likely to gain general knowledge about sex acts and information about the more common sexual behaviors from observation or education. For example, when children observe intercourse, they are unlikely to know that the penis goes in the vagina, unless they observe from very close. And, in that case, the question of whether the children were allowed or required to watch must be explored. Therefore, when young children imitate intercourse, commonly it is by lying on top of one another and moving up and down or around. Of course, older children may have learned that the penis goes in the vagina, as part of sex education or from other children. Therefore, when they attempt intercourse, it may well involve penetration.

In addition, children are more likely to observe or learn about fondling or intercourse than fellatio, cunnilingus, analingus, or anal intercourse, simply because the latter are less common and less universally accepted sexual behaviors. Thus engaging in the latter types of behavior is more likely to be a symptom of sexual abuse than engaging in the former.

The following case example is one where sexual interaction is a clue that the children have been sexually abused.

Case example: Nannette, 6, and Dottie, 5, typically spent several weeks during the summer with their paternal grandmother. She saw little of them during the school year because she worked as a teacher's aide.

She had fixed up their father's room for them with bunk beds. (He was residing in the state prison for armed robbery.) She noted that they would usually be in the lower bunk together in the morning. She asked why they did not stay in their separate bunks, and they giggled and said that they were scared of the dark. She put a night light in the room, but still would find them together in the morning. She became concerned when she noted that sometimes they had taken their pajamas off. When she queried about this, they again giggled and told her it was hot.

One night as she passed their door, she heard talking and entered the room. She found both children naked. Nannette was on her hands and knees with her buttocks up in the air, and Dottie had her finger in Nannette's anus. As the grandmother entered the room, Dottie said, "Now it's your turn to do it to me."

Their grandmother was very upset, told the girls to put their pajamas back on and go down to the living room. She then questioned them about what they were doing and where they had learned to do it. They told her that they had figured it out themselves. She made Nannette sleep on the couch and sent Dottie back to the bedroom. Because of some training she had received as a teacher's aide, she doubted their story.

The next day, thinking that the sexual play was something that their mother or her new boyfriend had instigated, she called protective services. Eventually, the children told the child protection worker that their dad used to sleep with them when their mother was at work. He would put his fingers in their "pussies" and their "butts." The part with the "pussy" hurt, but if you put a finger in the "butt" and wiggled it around, it felt good.

In this case, the behavior was of the sort unlikely for children to discover spontaneously, nor would it be something they might observe. The fact that they chose to repeat the activity they reported felt good suggests that this sexual interaction was a reaction to the sexual overstimulation aspect of their abuse.

(c) Sexual aggression toward younger or more naive children. Another possible symptom of sexual abuse is sexual aggression toward younger or vulnerable children. The dynamic here is somewhat different from that related to sexual interaction with peers. The child who has been victimized identifies with the sexual aggressor as a way of dealing with the trauma of his or her victimization. That is, the child becomes a perpetrator in order to achieve mastery over his or her own sense of vulnerability.

Children as young as 4 have been found to exhibit this aggressive response (Cavanagh-Johnson, 1988). This kind of reaction to sexual abuse is more common in boys than in girls. Sexual aggression is much more likely to be related to previous sexual abuse than the two types of sexual symptoms already described.

Such a pattern may be an acute response to the trauma of sexual maltreatment and disappear of its own accord. However, in a number of cases, the sexual aggression becomes chronic. In the latter instances, these aggressive acts may be merely defined as sexual play when the child is young, but, as the child becomes older, especially during adolescence, the child is relabeled as a perpetrator. Sadly, if the significance of the problem had been recognized earlier and adequately treated, the child might not have become an adolescent sex offender. In yet other instances, there is minimal or no sexual aggression following the sexual abuse, and sexual aggression as a response to earlier sexual maltreatment does not begin until adolescence. This syndrome is sufficiently common to be labeled "the victim to offender cycle." It argues for early treatment of sexual abuse, especially among boys, even if the child appears asymptomatic, and for vigilance on the part of caretakers in order to detect later hypersexual behavior.

In the following case example, sexual aggression was the outcome of sexual victimization.

Case example: Martin, 5, and his sister, Sarah, 3, were sexually abused by their adolescent cousin, Henry. Sarah disclosed her sexual abuse to her mother, and both children were brought to treatment. Initially, Martin denied anything had happened to him and said Henry was a really nice guy. He said he wanted to be like Henry when he grew up. In the next session, Martin said that he knew something had happened to Sarah, but not to him. Sarah then described Henry requiring both her and Martin to fellate him, saying that she had to tell for Martin because he was too scared.

Martin still did not admit to any abuse, but after the session in which Sarah told about his victimization, he got in her bed at night and put his hands inside her pants. She began having nightmares, but it took her several days to tell her mother what Martin had done.

When the children's mother confronted Martin, he began to tell her about his victimization by Henry. He also began to discuss this in treatment. He said that at first it was fun being with Henry. Henry would toss him up in the air, and Martin would land on the bed. Then Martin described his surprise when Henry told him to take his shirt off and rubbed his penis on his chest. Then Henry put his penis in Martin's mouth. Martin became very upset when he described this to the therapist, saying he couldn't make him stop. Even more distressing to Martin was having to watch Henry put his penis in Sarah's mouth and in her vagina while she cried for him to stop. Martin said he couldn't protect himself or his sister.

There was one subsequent incident in which Martin tried to pull Sarah's pants down, and she kicked him. In contrast to his aggression with his little sister, Martin was very nonassertive with male peers. In treatment, the therapist helped Martin talk about how awful it was to be tricked by someone you looked up to and not be able to do anything to stop him when he mistreated you. In addition, treatment focused on how Sarah must feel when Martin sexually abuses her. Martin was helped to be more assertive with his peers and was enrolled in a karate class.

Before the sexual maltreatment, Martin seems to have very much identified with Henry. Therefore, in the early stages of treatment, he could not acknowledge that his cousin betrayed him or directly express his anger and sense of vulnerability. This identification and denial appears to result in his victimizing the only person in his environment he could dominate, his little sister. Focusing on Martin's own feelings, as well as those of his sister, and teaching him more appropriate ways of achieving a sense of mastery and expressing aggression were important techniques in reducing the likelihood of repeated sexual aggression.

  (d) Sexual accosting of older people. Behavioral or verbal sexual advances to older persons are another symptom of possible sexual abuse. In such instances, the dynamics are somewhat different from those cited in other types of sexual interaction. The child has been socialized both to expect adults to be sexual and often to view sexual interaction as a way adults and children show they care about one another. Thus children who have been previously sexually maltreated may invite people whom they like or value to be sexual with them. So, for example, a 4-year-old victim, who had been required to fellate a number of men, liked her uncle, and said to him, "Take down your pants so I can see your penis." It is my clinical experience that girls are more likely to engage in this kind of behavior than boys. Like sexual aggression, sexually accosting older people is quite a compelling indicator of having been sexually victimized. (See Chapter 7 for a discussion of this phenomenon in foster care.)

  In the following case, a child demonstrated the symptoms of sexual abuse in foster care.

Case example: Diane, 3, was removed from the home of her mother and mother's boyfriend after the boyfriend severely physically abused one of her older brothers. She was initially placed with her brothers but had to be moved because her brothers were attempting intercourse with her.

In her new placement, she was the youngest child. Her foster mother initially had no knowledge about possible sexual abuse and was quite surprised at the large size of Diane's vaginal opening. She did nothing about this observation.

She became concerned when Diane kept asking her older foster brothers and sisters to rub her "tu-tu." Diane would stretch the elastic of her underpants open in the front and say, "Touch down here," or she would take the older child's hand and try to put it on her genitalia.

The foster mother became very worried at a family gathering and finally reported her suspicions to the child welfare worker. A grandfatherly friend of the family's was on the floor playing with the children. He was lying on his back, and Diane came and sat on his face and rubbed her vagina back and forth across it. Diane looked quite surprised when the man jumped up and told her she was a bad girl. She began to cry.

Eventually, it was learned that Diane's father, her mother, and the mother's boyfriend had all been involved in sexual abuse of the three children in the family.

In this case, there were symptoms that actually preceded Diane's sexual advances to both her foster siblings and the family friend. Her invitations were both behavioral and verbal.

This type of overt sexual invitation is more characteristic of younger children who do not fully appreciate the inappropriateness of their actions. However, it may also be found in emotionally disturbed children who may be much older.

(e) Seductive behavior. Older children who have been sexually abused are more likely than younger ones to know that overt sexual invitations are inappropriate. They learn this from the admonitions the offender may use to prevent disclosure as well as from reactions to such invitations and other information sources. Nevertheless, like their younger counterparts, they have been socialized at an early age to be sexual beings. They are likely to persist in more subtle behaviors that may be perceived as seductive.

It is important for mental health professionals and others, who observe children acting in this manner, to realize that this is learned behavior, a result of how their abuser(s) taught them to act. Therefore, it is important not to blame the victim for these patterns but, instead, to appreciate that their source is the perpetrator. Often victims are quite unaware that their actions are viewed as seductive. They may believe they are ugly or otherwise unappealing and are bewildered by the responses they elicit from others.

The following case example illustrates this type of symptom:

Case example: Ursula, 15, ended up in foster care because of intense conflicts with her mother. She blamed her mother for the fact that her mother had lost custody of four younger siblings and for marrying two men who sexually abused Ursula.

Soon after placement, her first foster mother demanded that she be removed. The foster mother was vague about what the problems were, but did say that she didn't like the way her husband responded to Ursula.

After Ursula had been in her second foster home about two weeks, she called her worker in a panic. She said she got along fine with the foster mother and liked the foster father, but she felt very anxious when she was left alone in the house with him.

Her worker went to the home to see if she could understand what the problems were. She had a meeting with Ursula and the foster parents. Ursula was dressed in very tight jeans and a tight sweater. She was a very statuesque 15-year-old. Although it was a cold, rainy day, about 10 minutes into the meeting, Ursula declared she was hot and left the room, returning in a few minutes in a pair of very short cutoff jeans. She sat with one leg draped over the arm of the chair and the other on the coffee table. Her foster father was facing her, essentially being forced to look at her crotch.

The worker quickly sensed what the problem was. She decided that she needed to talk to Ursula separately. When she spoke later with Ursula about how she was sitting, noting that this might be misinterpreted by the foster father and lead to a sexual advance, which would make Ursula feel uncomfortable, she was quite surprised. Ursula said she didn't understand how the foster father could think she was sexy because her face was too fat. She then went on to relate similar trouble with both the owner of the restaurant where she was working and his son. Both had been grabbing her sexually and the son had tried to force her to have sex with him in his car.

Further work with Ursula helped her to decrease behaviors that were interpreted as sexual invitations.

In Ursula's case, her previous sexual abuse by both a father and a stepfather resulted in an exaggerated style of behavior that was perceived as a sexual invitation. Not only had this led to a reaction by the foster father in her second foster home that made her uncomfortable, but it had resulted in sexual aggression by both her boss and his son. Moreover, probably the request for her removal by her first foster mother was a consequence of this woman's interpretation of Ursula's behavior as an attempt to seduce her husband.

(f) Promiscuity. When a sexually abused girl reaches early adolescence, a consequence of her victimization may be promiscuity. She has learned at an early age that her body is for the use of others. This pattern of relating to others that was imposed when she was younger becomes a voluntary or

quasi-voluntary one as she becomes older. Ironically, these victims of sexual abuse may experience little or no sexual pleasure. Many of them are actually frigid. Moreover, some adolescent victims have poor self-images as a consequence of the sexual maltreatment, and being promiscuous reinforces this self-image. For example, one victim said, "I feel like a slut, so I act like a slut."

Of course, not all promiscuous teenagers have been sexually abused. Other dynamics can lead to promiscuity. Some girls resort to sex as a way of gaining acceptance and achieving relationships. In addition, children who have not been nurtured as they have grown up may use sex as a way of relating because they are deficient in skills for developing other kinds of close relationships. Finally, for some adolescents, promiscuity is a way of rebelling, often against their parents.

Promiscuity may be manifested as or develop into adolescent prostitution. A survey of adolescent prostitutes concluded that 90% of them had been sexually abused as children (Carlson and Riebel, 1978). A common sequence is for an adolescent victim of sexual abuse to run away to escape the sexual abuse and other problems at home, and then to be faced with the need to support herself. There are few jobs that underaged girls can find that allow them to support themselves and remain on the street. Therefore, for lack of alternatives, they resort to prostitution. Often these runaways are befriended by men whose intention is to use them as prostitutes.

The case example presented here is illustrative.

Case example: Darlene first ran away from home when she was 12. She was placed in a group home. She intended to stay in the group home, but one afternoon on her way to the dentist, she met a man who offered her some cocaine. She got high with him, and when she was sober again, she had missed her dentist appointment and decided she could not return to the group home. So she went with the man. He turned out to be a pimp, who kept her and three other teenagers. He became her lover before he persuaded her to prostitute for him. However, she had little overt negative reaction to prostituting, using the term "making money" to describe the prostitution, and declaring she didn't see anything wrong with it.

Darlene came to the attention of protective services at the age of 14. At the time, her pimp was in prison for rape and she was five months pregnant. She also had a severe case of venereal warts. Despite her circumstances, her major concern was that the baby might not be her pimp's.

Her description of her family background helped explain why she had run away and gotten herself in her current situation. She said that her mother was "always bitching" at her. Further exploration revealed that the "bitching" was about Darlene's relationship with her stepfather. He had begun sexually abusing Darlene when she was about 6. This abuse continued until Darlene ran away. Despite the stepfather's sexual abuse, he was the more nurturing, caring parent. Darlene's mother had always perceived her as a competitor and a threat. Darlene did not initially tell her mother about the sexual abuse because her stepfather told her that her mother would throw him out. When she did finally tell her mother at 10, her mother blamed her. Then, in the face of the stepfather's denial, Darlene's mother decided Darlene was lying and was just trying to make trouble between the parents. Over the next two years, Darlene's mother vacillated between accusing the stepfather of sexual abuse, accusing Darlene of seducing him, and accusing Darlene of lying about it. At no time did she show any empathy for Darlene.

At 14, Darlene had a hard time conceptualizing what her stepfather had done as abuse and did not think it had negatively affected her.

Because of her family background, Darlene was quite vulnerable to relationships in which she perceived herself as being cared for yet was being exploited. There are parallels between Darlene's perception of the sexual abuse by her stepfather and her perception of being used by her pimp as a prostitute—that is, she minimized their exploitive nature.

(2) Sexual knowledge. One indication of possible sexual abuse in young children is sexual knowledge beyond what would be expected for their developmental stage.

Therefore, when young children know about digital penetration, that adult males get erections, about ejaculation, that the penis goes in the vagina during intercourse, what intercourse feels like, what fellatio and cunnilingus are, about anal intercourse, what fellatio and cunnilingus feel like, what anal intercourse feels like, and what semen looks or tastes like, the possibility of sexual abuse needs to be explored. It is necessary to find out where the children learned this information.

It is possible for them to learn about some of these aspects of sex in ways other than participation. As noted earlier, they may observe sexual activity. However, as also noted, usually they learn about the more common types of activity, fondling and intercourse, and will lack detail. In addition, they may be exposed to pornography. However, pornography that is shown on cable television is soft core; that is, no penises are shown entering vaginas, no cunnilingus or fellatio is shown, and no ejaculation occurs. In addition, when children say they saw these acts on television, it is important to consider the possibility that children have been allowed to view pornography as a prelude to sexual abuse. Moreover, most professionals would regard having children watch pornography as inappropriate and perhaps abusive.

Finally, there are certain types of sexual knowledge that children cannot gain without actual participation. These include what semen tastes like, what anal or vaginal intercourse feels like, what fellatio feels like, and what cunnilingus feels like.

The following example illustrates advanced sexual knowledge.

Case example: Ellen, 8, was alleging sexual abuse by her father and one of his friends. She said first her father had abused her. Then he invited his friend over and let him do it, too.

Her father said that, when she is allowed to visit her maternal grandparents, she gets to do anything she wants. He knew that the grandparents rented pornographic movies, and she had probably gotten her ideas about sexual abuse from watching the movies.

Ellen refused to talk to the police officer who tried to interview her, saying she didn't like men. Men do bad things to girls. She was sent to a female expert in sexual abuse.

During the course of the interview, the evaluator asked her again about her feelings about men. She repeated that they do bad things to girls. As to what these were, she said "with their dick." She was asked what they do with their dick, and she showed vaginal intercourse, using an anatomically explicit girl and adult male doll, adding, "That can really hurt your pussy." When asked if they do anything else, she put the male doll's penis in the girl doll's mouth. She was asked if anything comes out of the penis, and she nodded. As to what color it was, she said "white." As to what it tastes like, she said "salt."

She then went on to describe the specific acts her father committed and those his friend had engaged in.

In this case, Ellen demonstrates a great deal more sexual knowledge than one might expect of an 8-year-old. It is not too unusual that she is aware that the penis goes in the vagina during intercourse, but her knowledge of fellatio, ejaculation, and the color of semen are very abnormal for her age. Moreover, her awareness that intercourse can hurt and that semen tastes like salt is information she could only acquire through direct experience and not from watching movies at her grandparents' house.

(3) Sexual statements. As will be discussed in detail in Chapter 5, the diagnosis of sexual abuse is usually made based upon the child's statements

(verbal or behavioral). Consequently, when a child makes a statement indicating she has been sexually abused, this requires careful investigation.

Sometimes these statements are made inadvertently, for example, in response to a particular situation or naively, because the child does not know anything is wrong with the sexual abuse. For example, while moving his bowels, a 4-year-old boy said to his baby-sitter that his "bum" hurt because his grandpa put his "wiener" in it. In another case, a 3-year-old girl told her mother, who was assisting her in a bath, that when she visits her daddy, she helps him wash his "dinky," and that he likes this.

In other instances, the child is more cognizant of the inappropriateness of the sexual maltreatment and may have been threatened with negative consequences for telling. When the child does tell, there is typically a delay of weeks to years between the onset of the sexual abuse and the child's disclosure. Often a crisis for the victim, such as the offender demanding to engage in more intrusive sexual behavior, the victimization of a younger sibling, or a change in family circumstances such as a parental separation, precipitates disclosure. Some victims do not tell until they reach adolescence—a time when they may feel less dependent upon the offender and wish to engage in age-appropriate peer relationships, such as dating. Even when children have decided they want to tell, they may be quite hesitant and tentative. In some cases, the information comes out slowly, the child revealing the least traumatic acts first. Furthermore, victims who have been sexually abused may nevertheless retract their assertions, either because of pressure from the perpetrator or family, embarrassment and shame, or some of the other consequences of telling.

It is quite rare for a child to make a false claim of abuse. The best research on this issue to date is a study conducted by Jones and McGraw (1987) of almost 600 child protection reports of sexual abuse. They found that only 2% of unfounded reports (6 cases) were false assertions of sexual abuse by children. (This piece of research and issues related to false allegations are further discussed in Chapters 5 and 7.)

Despite the fact that children's assertions are rarely false, it is, nevertheless, important to have ways to assure that allegations are valid. There are characteristics of children's statements that are indicative of a true allegation (Corwin, 1988; Faller, 1988; Jones and McQuiston, 1986). The mental health evaluator should be looking for explicit descriptions of sexual acts, told from a child's viewpoint, as well as a characteristic noted earlier, sexual knowledge beyond that expected for the child's developmental stage. In addition, the evaluator should expect the child to be able to give some contextual detail, for example, where and when the abuse occurred, what was said, where other people in the family were, what the victim was wearing, and what the offender was wearing. Moreover, most children will show some emotional reaction to describing the sexual abuse. Emotions commonly experienced are reluctance to disclose, fear, anger, embarrassment, disgust, anxiety, and, in some cases, sexual arousal. These are the hallmarks of a true allegation. (For a further discussion of assessing children's assertions that they have been sexually abused see Chapter 5.)

In the following case example, the child provides a statement consistent with a true allegation of sexual abuse.

Case example: Evelyn, age 3½, was taken to the doctor by her mother because of a red vagina. The doctor suspected sexual abuse, based on the medical findings and the child's reaction to the exam. However, her mother, a nurse, said she was pretty sure Evelyn was red because she didn't wipe herself correctly. Two months later the mother returned to the doctor because Evelyn's vagina was still red and she was having nightmares.

At that point the doctor made a referral to protective services, who asked the mother to take Evelyn to an expert in sexual abuse. The mother was very concerned and made the appointment right away.

During the course of the interview, the evaluator asked Evelyn if her peepee hurt. She became agitated and hid behind the doll house. The evaluator asked her if she was upset and she said yes. She then was asked what upset her, and she said, "My peepee. It hurted." At that point she did not respond when the evaluator asked her how it got hurt.

A little later the evaluator introduced anatomically explicit dolls to Evelyn. As she showed Evelyn the little girl doll's vagina, Evelyn said, "Don't put your finger in; it's hurted." The evaluator asked Evelyn how it got hurt, and she replied, "It gets poked lots of times." However, she did not reply when asked who poked it. When asked if it was a man or a woman who poked it, she said a man. As to whether this was a big man or a young man or a boy, she said a big boy. She could not name the big boy. However, when asked whose big boy he was, she said Janice's (her baby-sitter). She was then asked where this happened, and she said in the basement. As to where Janice was, she said outside. She was asked whether it happened before lunch or after lunch, and she replied "at nap time." The evaluator asked Evelyn whether Janice's boy said anything, and she said, "He said, don't tell or I'll put it in your mouth." Evelyn was then asked what it was, and she said "his thing," and pointed to the penis on the adult male doll.

Later, having learned from Evelyn's mother that Janice, the baby-sitter who looked after Evelyn while her mother was at work, had a retarded adolescent son named Spike, the evaluator asked Evelyn if Janice's big boy was named Spike, and she said yes. The evaluator also asked Evelyn if it was her peepee that he had poked, as she had been referring to the doll earlier, and Evelyn said, "Sure, he always wants to poke into my peepee as far as he can get his thing."

The first statement Evelyn makes that is a good indication of possible sexual abuse is "it gets poked lots of times," referring to the doll's vagina. Later on, she identifies his "thing" as what does the poking, and, in the second interview, she gives the explanation, "Sure, he always wants to poke into my peepee as far as he can get his thing." Together these statements are explicit descriptions of sexual abuse. The terms "poked," "peepee," and "thing" are all ones a 3½-year-old might use, supporting a finding that the description is from a child's viewpoint. The fact that Evelyn knows about the penis going into the vagina indicates unusual sexual knowledge for her age. In addition, she is able to give a lot of information about the context of the maltreatment, stating it happened in the basement, at nap time, when Janice was outside. Further, she describes how Spike threatened her should she tell. Her emotional reactions—distress and reluctance to respond to questions—are also consistent with a true allegation.

Nonsexual Indicators of Possible Sexual Abuse

Children may display a wide range of nonsexual symptoms when they are being or have been sexually abused. However, these symptoms can also be responses to other types of trauma, for example, physical abuse, parental disharmony, parental divorce, alcoholism in the family, the birth of a sibling, the death of a family member, moving, or even a natural disaster. This symptomatology by itself should never be considered conclusive of sexual abuse. Positive findings in any of these areas only indicate the child is upset but do not necessarily indicate the source of the distress. Unfortunately, some of the literature and training material on sexual abuse has cited these nonsexual indicators of stress as indicators of sexual abuse.

These nonsexual symptoms can be subdivided into the following categories: (1) disorders of functions, (2) emotional problems, (3) behavior problems, and (4) developmental lags/school problems.

(1) Disorders of functions. Disorders of functions include sleep problems, bowel and bladder problems, and eating problems. Children, who are experiencing or have experienced sexual abuse, may have nightmares, be unable to sleep, be afraid of the dark, walk in their sleep, or talk in their sleep. They may come into their parents' bed at night. Children who are toilet trained may become enuretic, during the day or night or both, or encopretic. Encopresis is sometimes associated with anal penetration. Loss of appetite may be a

response to the onset of sexual abuse. Children may also become picky eaters or refuse certain foods. Adolescent female victims may become anorectic or bulimic. However, some eat excessively so as to be physically unattractive to potential abusers.

(2) Emotional problems. Some observers report personality change in children with the onset of sexual abuse. One mother described her daughter as a "motor mouth" prior to the onset of fondling and cunnilingus by her best friend's father. Afterward, she said her daughter was very quiet and would hardly talk to her.

Children may become depressed, preoccupied, hyperactive, or anxious as a consequence of sexual abuse. In some cases, this anxiety is manifested in phobias. These phobias may relate to the threats the offender uses to prevent disclosure. For example, in a day-care center case, one perpetrator threatened to kill the children's parents if they told. A number of children became phobic about being separated from their parents. In other instances, phobias are long-standing and are associated with the sexual activities of the maltreatment. For example, a victim as an adolescent or adult may become overwhelmed and frightened when asked by a partner to engage in the sexual activities that were the ones inflicted by the abuser.

(3) Behavior problems. A wide range of behavior problems can result from sexual abuse. These may vary based on victim age and sex. They include physical aggression toward younger children, peers, or even older persons, including parents, and other types of difficulties getting along with others. As adolescents, female victims may run away, become suicidal, or become involved in drug or alcohol abuse. Victims may also act out by becoming incorrigible, violating curfew, and stealing. Male victims may engage in cruelty to animals and become fire-setters, but some female victims will also set fires.

(4) Developmental lags/school problems. A possible effect of sexual maltreatment is interference with cognitive development. One of the outcomes of sexual abuse is an undermining of basic trust, a fundamental prerequisite for later development, including cognitive development. Thus young children who experience sexual abuse, and usually other maltreatment, may suffer delays in speech, fine motor control, and even gross motor development. More common are problems in concentration and school performance in older victims of sexual abuse. Often lower grades are reported coincident with the onset of sexual abuse. In addition, in adolescence, victims of sexual abuse, as part of their more pervasive acting out, may become truant from school or defiant in the school setting.

Asymptomatic Children

A bewildering phenomenon is that some children can be currently experiencing sexual maltreatment, or could have been sexually victimized in the past, but do not manifest overt signs of the trauma. Conte and Berliner (1988) studied 369 victims of sexual maltreatment who resided in the community and found that 21% of the children were asymptomatic, according to their social workers. Furthermore, most mental health professionals have had the experience of working with children who were experiencing ongoing sexual abuse but who did not demonstrate any observable signs.

It is tempting to believe that these children were not harmed by their maltreatment. However, it is more likely that the effects are subtle or are delayed or that the child has been well socialized by the offender, and in some cases by the family, not to reveal signs of her or his distress. In addition, symptoms—particularly if they are mild—may be interpreted as consequences of other experiences (as they could be) or as developmentally normal. For example, many 3- and 4-year-olds have nightmares without having suffered any specific trauma. Therefore, nightmares that could be a consequence of sexual abuse may be judged to be characteristic 3- or 4-year-old behavior. Finally, it is important to appreciate that there are children who are being sexually abused who do not disclose when asked or even when evaluated by a skilled mental health professional.

SUMMARY

This first chapter is an introduction for mental health professionals who are to be involved in child sexual abuse cases. A victim-centered approach, which advocates making the victim's best interest paramount in case decisions, is presented. The extent of the problem, as reflected in research on the incidence and prevalence of child sexual maltreatment, indicates that we can expect as many as 150,000 sexually abused children to be reported to child protection agencies annually, and that between one-fourth and half of the female population and one-tenth to one-fourth of the male population are sexually abused during childhood. Finally, indicators of possible sexual abuse are discussed, with an important distinction made between sexual symptoms, which are very likely to be a result of sexual maltreatment, and nonsexual symptoms, which could indicate sexual abuse but are equally likely to be reflective of other types of trauma.

NOTES

1. Although it is recognized that a substantial minority of identified victims are male, the female pronoun will usually be employed for stylistic reasons. Similarly, although between 5% and 15% of perpetrators of sexual offenses are female, the masculine pronoun will generally be employed to refer to offenders.

2. Some child protection agencies cover cases in which caretakers are not necessarily parents, for example, day-care center cases, sexual abuse in foster care, sexual maltreatment of children in institutions, and abuse by school personnel.

3. Of course, child protective agencies handle all kinds of maltreatment, not merely sexual maltreatment.

4. The most recent statistics are for 1986 because, after that time, the American Humane Association no longer produced breakdowns by type of maltreatment.

5. In addition to these indicators that mental health professionals are likely to note, there are, of course, medical indicators. For a discussion of medical indicators, see Steinberg and Westhoff in Faller (1988).

REFERENCES

American Association for the Protection of Children. 1985-89. *Highlights of Official Child Neglect and Abuse Reporting* (1983, 1984, 1985, 1986, 1987). 5 vols. Denver: American Humane Association.

Carlson, Noel and J. Riebel. 1978. *Family Sexual Abuse: A Resource Manual for Health Services Professionals.* Minneapolis: University of Minnesota, Department of Family Practice and Community Health.

Cavanagh-Johnson, T. 1988. "Child Perpetrators—Children Who Molest Other Children: Preliminary Findings." *Child Abuse and Neglect: The International Journal* 12(2):219-29.

Conte, J. and L. Berliner. 1988. "The Impact of Sexual Abuse." In *Handbook on Sexual Abuse of Children*, edited by Lenore Walker. New York: Guilford.

Corwin, David. 1988. "Early Diagnosis of Child Sexual Abuse: Diminishing the Lasting Effects." In *Lasting Effects of Child Sexual Abuse*, edited by G. Wyatt and G. Powell. Newbury Park, CA: Sage.

Crewdson, John. 1988. *By Silence Betrayed.* New York: Harper & Row.

Faller, Kathleen Coulborn. 1988. *Child Sexual Abuse: An Interdisciplinary Manual for Diagnosis, Case Management, and Treatment.* New York: Columbia University Press.

Finkelhor, David. 1979. *Sexually Victimized Children.* New York: Free Press.

Fromuth, Mary and Barry Burkhart. 1987. "Childhood Sexual Victimization Among College Men: Definitional and Methodological Issues." *Victims and Violence* 2(4):241-53.

Jones, D.P.H. and E. M. McGraw. 1987. "Reliable and Fictitious Accounts of Sexual Abuse to Children." *Journal of Interpersonal Violence* 2(1):27-45.

Jones, D.P.H. and M. McQuiston. 1986. *Interviewing the Sexually Abused Child.* Denver: C. H. Kempe National Center for the Prevention and Treatment of Child Abuse and Neglect.

Risin, Leslie and Mary Koss. 1987. "The Sexual Abuse of Boys." *Journal of Interpersonal Violence* 2(3):309-23.

Russell, Diana. 1983. "The Incidence and Prevalence of Intrafamilial and Extrafamilial Sexual Abuse of Female Children." *Child Abuse and Neglect: The International Journal* 7:133-46.

Steinberg, M. and M. Westhoff. 1988. "Behavioral Characteristics and Physical Findings: A Medical Perspective." In *Child Sexual Abuse: An Interdisciplinary Manual for Diagnosis, Case Management, and Treatment,* by Kathleen Coulborn Faller. New York: Columbia University Press.

U.S. Department of Health and Human Services. 1981. *Executive Summary: National Study of the Incidence of Child Abuse and Neglect.* Washington, DC: Government Printing Office.

————. 1988. *Study Findings: Study of the National Incidence and Prevalence of Child Abuse and Neglect, 1988.* Washington, DC: Government Printing Office.

Weinberg, S. K. 1955. *Incest Behavior.* New York: Citadel.

Wyatt, Gail. 1985. "The Sexual Abuse of Afro-American and White American Women in Childhood." *Child Abuse and Neglect: The International Journal* 9:507-19.

Chapter 2

DEFINING AND UNDERSTANDING CHILD SEXUAL MALTREATMENT

Most mental health professionals think they know what sexual abuse is. However, there is, in fact, some disagreement about what professionals regard as sexual abuse, and certainly there are "gray area" cases. Moreover, the more knowledgeable the clinician becomes about sexual abuse, the more she or he must recognize what a wide variety of types of cases there are. In addition, mental health professionals may have many questions about why adults sexually abuse children and, in some respects, may be confused because there is confusion in the sexual abuse literature. These three issues—definition, types of cases, and causation—will be the foci of this chapter.

First, child sexual maltreatment will be defined. Types of sexual behavior, parameters that differentiate abusive from nonabusive encounters, and patterns of sexually maltreating encounters are the subcategories of the definition. Second, general differences in sexually abusive relationships based on the proximity of the relationship between victim and offender will be described. Third, a theory of why adults sexually abuse children will be presented. Causal factors will be divided into prerequisite and contributing ones, and the dynamics of their relationship will be discussed.

A DEFINITION

Three different components of a definition of sexual abuse will be discussed in this section: (1) the types of behavior, (2) the parameters of abusive versus nonabusive sexual encounters, and (3) patterns of sexual abuse.

Types of Sexual Behaviors

The types of behavior presented in Table 2.1 are usually included in a definition of sexual abuse. Each type is defined according to its subcategories and an example of the behavior involving children is given.

The list of types of sexual abuse provided in Table 2.1 consists of the most common ones but is not all-inclusive. For example, frottage, which involves the offender obtaining gratification from contact, usually of his genitals, with the child's skin or clothing, is not included. Acts in which the offender requires that the victim do something to her- or himself are not on the list. Examples might be the offender inducing the child to undress, to touch him- or herself, or to put a finger or object in his or her own vagina or anus. Interfemoral (dry or vulvar) intercourse is not designated. In this activity, the penis goes between the victim's upper thighs, and, in cases involving girl victims, there may be contact with the vulvar area. Sometimes the offender uses a lubricant to facilitate thrusting back and forth. Finally, attempted sexual acts are not included, although attempts to engage in sex with children are clearly abusive.

The types of sexual behavior are presented in roughly ascending order, from least serious to most serious. However, the rating of seriousness is from a professional perspective. The victim may experience a relatively nonserious sexual interaction as very traumatic. For example, a 12-year-old may be quite overwhelmed by her father telling her that she has nicer breasts than her mother and that he wants to suck them. No sexual contact takes place and, therefore, the behavior falls into the least serious category, but the child's relationship with her father is greatly damaged. Moreover, oral sex is conceptualized as less serious than penile penetration, but not only are some types of oral sex very intrusive, victims may be more disgusted by oral sex than by intercourse.

The mental health evaluator needs to know that the initial sexual abuse may be at the less serious end of the continuum, but, over time, the offender may engage in progressively more serious and intrusive types of abuse. However, in other instances of sexual abuse, the initial behavior is quite serious. A progression is not always found.

The Parameters of Sexually Abusive Relationships

The activities designated above are not abusive when the parties are consenting adults. To differentiate abusive from nonabusive sexual contact, three parameters must be defined: (1) who a perpetrator is, (2) what the age limits for a victim are, and (3) how to interpret apparently consensual sexual encounters between people at different developmental stages.

Table 2.1

Definitions of Types of Behavior

Type	Definition
1. Noncontact sexual abuse	a. Sexual comments to the child Example: The offender asks the child if she wants to have her pussy sucked; tells her girls really like this. b. Exposure of the intimate parts (genitals, anus, breasts) (flashing) Example: Offender shows the child his penis asking her if she has ever seen one; shows her how he can cause an erection by rubbing it. c. Voyeurism (peeping) Example: Mother's boyfriend removes the door from the bathroom so he can watch her 13- and 14-year-old daughters toileting. d. Fetishism—having an unusual sexual fixation on clothing or body parts (e.g., leather or rubber garments, underwear, feet, buttocks) Example: Grandfather takes his 12-year-old granddaughter's soiled underwear from the hamper and smells them while masturbating. e. Obscene phone calls Example: Adolescent offender calls his English teacher's wife and invites her to suck his dick. (He later masturbates while recollecting the phone call.)[a]
2. Fondling	a. Touching the child's intimate parts (breasts, genitals, buttocks) by the offender Example: Stepfather massages 7-year-old stepdaughter's vagina while wrestling with her. b. The offender inducing the child to touch his or her intimate parts Example: Mother persuades her 11-year-old daughter to caress her body and rub her vagina when they sleep in the same bed. c. Fondling can be on top of or beneath the clothing.
3. Digital or object penetration	a. Offender placing a finger or fingers in victim's vagina or anus Example: Day-care provider inserts his finger in the anus of a 3-year-old charge (while masturbating himself)[a]

Table 2.1

(*continued*)

Type	Definition
	b. Offender inducing the child to place a finger or fingers in the vagina or anus of the offender Example: Mother requiring her 6-year-old son to put four fingers in her vagina and move them in and out.
	c. Offender placing an object in the vagina or anus of the victim Example: Father putting crayons in daughter's vagina in the course of play (taking a photograph of this and later masturbating to the photograph)[a]
	d. Offender inducing child to place an object in the vagina or anus of the offender Example: Stepfather requiring his 6-year-old stepdaughter to put a vibrator up his anus (while he had intercourse with his 8-year-old stepdaughter)[a]
4. Oral sex	a. Tongue kissing Example: Five-year-old boy French kisses his grandmother. He tells her his mom does this to him.
	b. Kissing, licking, or biting other parts of the body Example: Ten-year-old describes how her uncle kisses her all over her body (and then on her vagina. He asks her to kiss his penis.)[a]
	c. Breast sucking, kissing, licking, biting Example: Eleven-year-old states her grandfather sucks on her breasts and bites her nipples. He has told her that this will make them grow.
	d. Cunnilingus—licking, kissing, biting, or sucking the vagina, or placing the tongue in the vaginal opening Example: Nine-year-old states her mom's boyfriend sucked her "wee-wee" and put his tongue inside. She says it felt weird.
	e. Fellatio—licking, kissing, sucking, or biting the penis Example: Four-year-old describes a child-care provider sucking his penis and calling this the baby game.
	f. Analingus—licking the anal opening Example: Brothers, ages 5 and 7, caught by foster mother engaging in analingus. They tell her their mom's friend taught them this. They say it's called "licking buttholes" and it tickles.

Table 2.1

(*continued*)

Type	Definition
	g. The offender may inflict these acts on the victim or require the victim to do them to him or her.
5. Penile penetration	a. Vaginal intercourse—penis in the vagina
	Example:
	Thirteen-year-old girl asserts her mother's boyfriend, over several months, gradually put his penis farther and farther in her vagina until he achieved complete penetration.
	b. Anal intercourse—penis in the anus
	Example:
	A 4-year-old girl bent over, pulled down her pants, and spread her buttocks, stating that's where her cousin poked her and that he put grease on her butt first.
	c. Penetration is usually of the victim by the offender.

a. Behaviors within parentheses are not illustrative of the sexual abuse being defined but nevertheless are part of the complete example.

(1) Who is a perpetrator? An act is only regarded as abusive when it involves people at different developmental stages. This usually means there is a significant age differential between the offender and the victim, five years being the commonly employed age gap, and the offender being, of course, the older party. Thus a situation in which a 16-year-old girl fondles a 5-year-old boy would be regarded as sexual abuse, but sexual fondling between a 5-year-old and a 6-year-old normally would not.

However, an age differential is not the only way an abusive act is differentiated from a nonabusive one. First, generally, the offender possesses superior knowledge about sex, and the victim is to some extent naive about the meaning of the sexual encounter. Second, the act is primarily for the sexual pleasure of the offender and does not represent mutual, consensual sexual exploration. Third, there is usually a power differential between victim and offender, the offender being in a position of superiority. Power may be exercised through manipulation, various threats, or the use of force.

Therefore, child-child sexual encounters where there is no age differential can be abusive, that is, ones where there is a predator child and a victim. In some cases, the victim may even be older than the predator child. For example, a 12-year-old boy might force sex on a 14-year-old girl, or an 11-year-old might trick or cajole a mentally retarded 16-year-old into sexual activity.

In many cases, predatory behavior signals the possibility of sexual abuse of the predator child by an adult. Children may learn about fondling through exploration of their own bodies and may observe sexual intercourse and try it, but knowledge about anal intercourse and oral copulation is more likely to be acquired through inappropriate exposure to sex, including sexual abuse.

(2) What is the maximum age for a victim? One of the difficulties in defining a sexually abusive relationship is making a decision about the upper age limit for a victim. In part, this is determined by the age cutoff for child protective services, which is usually 18. However, researchers have also had an influence upon maximum age. Some have used 18; others, 16. Moreover, the maximum age may vary according to sex, the upper age limit for boys being younger than that for girls. For example, some researchers have used 13 as the cutoff for boys (Risin and Koss, 1987). In addition, some have used a different maximum age depending upon the age differential between victim and offender; for example, the maximum age for the victim may be 16, if the offender is at least 10 years older (Finkelhor, 1979a). Finally, a retarded victim may be chronologically an adult but developmentally a child.

There is no definitive answer to the question of what an appropriate maximum age should be. Nevertheless, it is important for mental health professionals and others to consider this issue in cases where it is relevant, to assure that appropriate case management decisions are made.

(3) The issue of consent. An issue that is related to maximum age is consent. There is an assumption that the consent must be informed, that is, the child must have a full appreciation of the significance of the sexual encounter. Finkelhor (1979b) has argued that what makes sex between an adult and a child abusive and, therefore, wrong is that a child cannot give informed consent, both because he or she cannot really understand the meaning of the sex and because the child is not really free to say no. Therefore, situations where children agree to cooperate or actively participate are nevertheless abusive. So too are situations where previously victimized and/or disturbed children initiate sexual encounters with adults.

What about older children? Can an adolescent consent to a sexual encounter with an adult? This judgment is influenced by the age of consent, which varies from state to state, being as low as 14 in some states and as high as 18 in others (Crewdson, 1988). Therefore, it is difficult to arrive at a clear-cut answer. The following case example illustrates the dilemma posed by cases involving consenting adolescents.

Case example: Mrs. M had two daughters, Alma, 10, and Jeanette, 15. The girls had been sexually abused by their father. When Mrs. M found out about this, she threw Mr. M out of the house and refused him access to the children.

After the exit of Mr. M, she got a job working for a construction company, and she had a series of boyfriends. George, age 27, was one who moved in with the family. He was highly regarded by Mrs. M and the girls because he was a college graduate. However, after he had been living with the family for three months, Alma told her mother that George had come into her bed and fondled her vagina and rubbed his penis back and forth between her legs. Mrs. M discovered that he had been sexually abusing Jeanette as well.

Mrs. M threw him out as she had done with her husband. However, Jeanette went with him, informing her mother that she was in love with George. Further, Jeanette told her mother she was fat and drank too much. It was no wonder that George preferred her (Jeanette) to her mother. Jeanette moved in with George and began working as a waitress to support herself (and him).

There is no question that George's sexual encounter with Alma was abusive. She is 17 years his junior and she objected to what he did. From a legal standpoint, George is also sexually abusing Jeanette, but she does not perceive this relationship as abusive. She declares she is in love with him. Furthermore, if it weren't already known that George has a propensity to sexually abuse children (from his molestation of Alma), his relationship with Jeanette would not be so worrisome. The fact that Jeanette is supporting George, as her mother had done before her, adds to our concern. Should protective services or the juvenile court intervene and force Jeanette to return to her mother or, alternatively, place her in care? Or should she be allowed to remain with George and perhaps learn from this mistake?

Finally, just as gender affects maximum age, it also may have an impact on consent. Sexual socialization of boys differs from that of girls. In simplified and vernacular terms, boys are taught they should like sex and should seek it, that is, they should be the initiators. In contrast, girls are taught they shouldn't like it too much, and they should wait to be asked. When girls are asked, they should say "no". These normative differences, in part, reflect a concern about the risk of pregnancy for girls.

Gender differences in sexual socialization may affect perceptions of sexual invitations. For example, when a boy is asked to have sex with "an older woman," he may experience this as a compliment and an opportunity both to learn about sex and to experience pleasure. He may tacitly or overtly give his consent. Research on boy victims supports these clinical findings. Risin and Koss (1987) found that a substantial proportion of college-age males defined themselves as actively participating in sexual encounters with females, which, on the basis of age criteria, would be considered abusive. This was especially likely to be the case when the offenders were baby-sitters.

Patterns of Sexual Abuse

Sexual acts that are considered abusive may occur in a variety of patterns. Dyadic sex, group sex, sexual exploitation, sex rings, and ritualistic sexual abuse will be discussed.

(1) Dyadic sex. The most common pattern in which children are sexually abused is a dyadic one, that is, a situation where there is one perpetrator and one victim, and the perpetrator engages in sexual activity with a child. These encounters are characteristic of both intrafamilial and extrafamilial sexual maltreatment.

(2) Group sex. An increasing finding is sexual abuse that occurs in a group context. Group sex can take a variety of forms. A single offender may begin by initiating dyadic sex with more than one victim and then, by accident or design, have sexual encounters with two or more victims more or less simultaneously. This may happen in intrafamilial cases where, for example, a father is sexually involved with several of his children.

Another variation of group sex involves more than one offender and generally several victims. Polyincestuous families often practice this kind of group sex. In such families, sexual abuse is typically found intergenerationally and laterally in the extended family. Women as well as men are offenders, and often it is not possible to differentiate victims from offenders.

Group sex may also be the pattern in extrafamilial contexts, for example, in day-care situations, in institutions for children, in foster care, or in camps. In these instances, there usually is a single offender, but, in some cases, multiple offenders are involved. (See Chapter 8 for a discussion of sexual abuse in day care and Chapter 7 for a discussion of sexual abuse in foster care.)

(3) Sexual exploitation. Other patterns of victimization involve sexual exploitation of children. Children are used to produce pornography or are sold as prostitutes. Both of these activities violate federal statute when they result in interstate transport of goods or children and they violate state laws as well (Campagna and Poffenberger, 1988).

Child pornography may consist of children having sex with adults, with other children, or engaging in seductive or masturbatory activities solo. Photographs, videotapes, or films are then made of children engaging in these acts. Pornography may pander to persons with either heterosexual or homosexual tastes. In some cases, animals are involved or other perversions shown. This material is produced for the gratification of adults, although those producing child pornography are not necessarily sexually attracted to children. However, pedophiles[1] often make and collect pornographic pictures of their victims. These are later used for arousal; in trade (either the pictures or the children themselves) and, in some cases, to entice new victims into sexual activity (Burgess et al., 1984; Crewdson, 1988).

Child prostitutes are of all ages and of both sexes. Younger children will have a procurer. This may be someone who is a family member, an acquaintance of the child or family, or a pimp by profession. The circumstances in which adolescent girls prostitute are similar to those of adult women prostitutes. That is, they usually have a pimp, who at some level takes care of them, and they may be one of several girls in the pimp's stable. Adolescent male prostitutes, like adult male prostitutes, are likely to operate independently (Campagna and Poffenberger, 1988).

Many of the older children involved in sexual exploitation are no longer living with their families. Typically they are runaways. Children who are actually abducted for the purpose of sexual exploitation are few in number (Crewdson, 1988).

Another source of children for prostitution and pornography is the developing world, especially Southeast Asia and the Philippines, although some also come from Latin America (Campagna and Poffenberger, 1988; Sassoon, 1988). These children may be sold by their families, may be brought to the United States (or to Western Europe) under false pretenses, for example, allegedly to be adopted, or they may be abducted. Persons who are sexually attracted to children may also travel to developing countries on sex tours, where they have access to children who suit their tastes (Campagna and Poffenberger, 1988; Sassoon, 1988).

Finally, there appear to be increasing instances of parents making pornography involving their own children. In the past, when it was necessary to have a photographic laboratory to develop film and to make copies, family or amateur production of child pornography was limited. Further, the fact that professional photographic studios are required to report any person who asks to have such material developed or reproduced further inhibits persons without access to photographic equipment from producing child pornography. However, the current ready availability of video equipment, which is reasonably priced and does not require the services of a photographic laboratory, has greatly facilitated the production and copying of child pornography. It is also quite a lucrative enterprise, which further enhances its appeal.

(4) Sex rings. Children may also be sexually abused in sex rings. Boys are more likely to be victimized in sex rings than girls (Burgess et al., 1984). Sex rings are generally developed by pedophiles. In establishing sex rings, pedophiles develop for themselves, and sometimes for like-minded persons, a stable of children with whom they have sex. Pedophiles may choose

professions that allow them access to children, or they may merely put themselves in a situation where they can befriend and attract children (Crewdson, 1988; Faller, 1988a). Some boast special skills in selecting children who are vulnerable to sexual exploitation. These are typically children who are deprived and neglected. In addition, children from single parent, female headed families, may be targeted. Pedophiles assert that these children lack a male role model and therefore are likely to gravitate to the male pedophile.

Usually there is a seduction process involved, in which the children are initially plied with attention, friendship, and/or gifts and, as they become emotionally or materially dependent upon the perpetrator, sexual favors are demanded. In addition, current members of the ring may be used to recruit new members. These children serve as recruiters to enhance their relationship with the ring leader and to receive additional rewards. The recruiter may emphasize the material benefits of involvement and minimize the sexual activity. Some recruiters are children who are too old to be of sexual interest to the ring leader and engage in recruiting activities to maintain an emotional and/or material relationship with the ring leader.

In many cases, sexual activity in sex rings is group sex, that is, sexual activities involve several children simultaneously. Children may also be encouraged to engage in sexual activities with one another. However, in other instances, the leader of the ring has a series of dyadic encounters with ring members, although the members are likely to know of one another. In some cases, a ring involves more than one perpetrator (as well as several victims).

Leaders of sex rings may have very narrow tastes in children. They are likely to be particular regarding the sex of the child, as mentioned earlier, preferring boys; they may be restricted in terms of the age range they are attracted to; and they may prefer a particular physical type in their victims. In order to access desirable victims, the pedophile may become part of a network with other pedophiles and share children. Photographs of these children are often taken. These may be used to facilitate the selection of desirable children, or they may be sold or traded as pornography. In addition, if members of the network have proclivities toward children of different ages, one member may pass on to another a child who is too old to be of interest to him. (See Burgess et al., 1984, for a further discussion of sex rings.)

(5) Ritualistic sexual abuse. Yet another pattern in which children may be sexually abused is in a ritualistic context. Broadly defined, ritualistic abuse is maltreatment of children that occurs as part of some ritualistic practice. The abuse may be physical or sexual or both. Rituals may be private or involve a group of perpetrators.

(a) Private rituals. About 2.5% of my clinical sample (12 cases) consists of cases where there were private, idiosyncratic rituals. Sometimes it is difficult to distinguish offenders who have private rituals from offenders who have developed a standard pattern of sexual seduction and interaction because they have found that it works. Activities that involve cleansing, specific postures—often subservient ones—required statements, chants, or songs, or a particular kind of dress signal possible ritualistic abuse. Ritualistic offenders will not usually be gratified when the rituals are not fairly closely followed. They may become angry at their victims, or merely upset, if the rituals are violated. The following case example is illustrative:

Case example: Mr. L, the offender, insisted that Sally, the victim, wear a dress and no underpants, get down on her knees and call him master, wash his penis and then lick it. He would call her his little slave. He would take a switch and hit her lightly on her bare buttocks. He did not always ejaculate during these encounters, but later masturbated while recollecting them. He reported engaging in this ritual about 15 times with Sally, who was his 7-year-old niece, and having been involved in a similar ritual with his cousin when he was an adolescent.

In this case, there are a number of clues that the abuse contains ritual. First it has occurred in virtually the same manner about 15 times. Second, it requires the victim to be subservient to the offender. Third, she must use certain language, call the offender "master," and she is called "slave."

(b) Group ritualistic abuse. Other ritualistic abuse appears to involve more than two persons. It is also likely to include occult practices. These seem to be satanic in some cases, and there are reports of ritual torture and sacrifice of animals, children, and sometimes adults. I have evaluated several children who credibly describe rituals of this sort. For example, three children, who reported sexual abuse in their day-care center, described being taken to a graveyard and being required to drink the blood of a deer. That these kinds of activities may occur in sexual abuse in day care is corroborated by the work of Finkelhor, Williams, and Burns (1988). In a national study of sexual abuse in day care, they found that, in 13% of cases, ritualistic abuse was reported.

In another case I have seen, a 4-year-old boy and his 5-year-old sister described their father's involvement in activities that appeared to be satanic and, in the case of the boy, also to involve his sexual abuse as part of a satanic ritual. The sister reported being sexually abused by her father, but not as part of a ritual. Both children described observing children being killed. These appeared to be unrelated instances and occurred on two separate occasions, when each child was with the father. The mother stated that for a long time she was unaware that her husband was involved in satanism. She merely thought he had some strange ideas, that he was sent by God to perform a mission on earth, and that he had the right to abuse others, use drugs, and break the law in order to carry out this mission. When she concluded that he was involved in satanism, she left him, taking the children. After their departure, the children revealed sexual and other abuse and their observations of children being killed.

Other professionals who work with maltreated children have also heard accounts of ritualistic abuse, including human sacrifice. One of the bewildering features of children's descriptions of these practices is their marked similarity despite the fact that they involve different children in different geographic localities. For example, the same chants and ritualistic marriages have been reported in several contexts (Crewdson, 1988; Faller, 1988b). To date, however, there has been very little corroborating evidence; for example, no bodies of sacrificed children have been found. An exception to the general lack of corroborating evidence is the Country Walk case in Miami. A couple, Frank and Iliana Furster, ritualistically sexually abused preschoolers in their baby-sitting service. Children's stories of birds being tortured and killed and the Fursters dressing in costumes and engaging in sexual activities with one another and with the children seemed incredible. Nevertheless, Iliana Furster turned state's witness and testified against her husband, corroborating the children's statements (Hollingsworth, 1986). However, there was no child sacrifice alleged in this case.

In addition, Geraldo Rivera, a national talk show host, recently did a show on satanism in which he presented two women who stated that they were involved in satanic practices and had borne babies who were ritually sacrificed. And in a 1989 case in Matamoras, Mexico, the bodies of 12 adults who had been ritually sacrificed by a satanic cult were discovered. However, this case did not involve children, nor did it involve sexual abuse.

Therefore, the area of ritualistic abuse remains a controversial one for experts in child abuse. There are those who believe that occult ritualistic sexual abuse is widespread and others who doubt its existence. In my opinion, reality falls somewhere between these two positions.

A CONCEPTUAL FRAMEWORK BASED ON PROXIMITY OF VICTIM AND OFFENDER

There is considerable variability in the contexts in which children are sexually abused. One general way in which these contexts can be differentiated is based upon whether the abuser is someone within the family or outside. Intrafamilial sex offenders are typically fathers, stepfathers, grandfathers, uncles, mothers, grandmothers, aunts, or siblings of their victims. Extrafamilial abusers may be neighbors, friends of the family, or persons in a professional capacity, such as day-care providers, schoolteachers, school or camp counselors, mental health practitioners, pediatricians, or scout leaders. A small proportion of extrafamilial sex offenders are totally unknown to the victim prior to the abuse.

While intrafamilial versus extrafamilial sexual maltreatment is, in some respects, a useful way to conceptualize the contexts in which children are victimized, perhaps more instructive is viewing these relationships as being on a continuum from proximate to distant relationships. At the most proximate end of the continuum are sexual abuse by fathers and mothers of children for whom they have primary caretaking responsibility. At the most distant end of the continuum is abuse by strangers. Offenders with other role relationships fall at various points in between these two ends of the continuum.

This framework allows the mental health professional to better characterize relationships involving offenders such as mother's boyfriends, relationships in which the offender has major caretaking responsibility but is not a parent, for example, a day-care provider or a foster parent, and those in which the offender is in a mentor relationship to the child, for example, a priest, minister, or scout leader.

The degree of proximity in the relationship between offender and victim is likely to have an impact on many of the characteristics of the sexual maltreatment. First of all, proximity will influence the frequency and duration of the sexual abuse. Close relationships are likely to involve extended access to the victim by the perpetrator and, therefore, more frequent sexual encounters, extending over a longer time frame. In contrast, more distant relationships, such as those of family acquaintances or relatives who only see the child at family get-togethers, will involve few and intermittent sexual encounters. And, obviously, a sexual assault by a stranger will consist of a single episode.

Second, the strategies the offender uses to engage the child in sexual activities will vary according to the proximity of the relationship. Although to some extent these strategies depend upon the personalities of the offender and the victim, abusers in close relationships are more likely to rely on psychological manipulations of the child, such as appeals to the offender's need for affection or to the special relationship with the child. Persons with less close relationships are more likely to resort to threats or the use of force. The mental health professional, who has had experience with cases of sexual abuse, will recognize that this is a rough characterization. There are situations in which biological fathers induce their children's cooperation in very coercive ways, such as by threatening physical punishment or using physical restraint. Moreover, there are cases involving pedophiles, who progressively insinuate themselves into the child's psychological world, so that eventually they can rely on the child's psychological dependence upon them for gaining compliance in sexual activity. Nevertheless, as a general rule, related offenders rely on psychological means of persuasion and unrelated offenders, on physical means.

Third, the proximity of the perpetrator-victim relationship is likely to have an impact on whether the offender attempts to prevent the child from reporting the sexual abuse. An offender with a proximate relationship with his victim may be greatly concerned about the impact of disclosure. He may look forward to future sexual encounters with the child; he may value the relationship independent of its sexual content; and he may be fearful of the impact of disclosure on his relationship with the child's family. Therefore, such an offender is much more likely to attempt to inhibit the child from reporting than someone with a remote relationship to the child and/or the child's family. How the proximate abuser chooses to prevent disclosure can vary from appeals based upon the special relationship between himself and the victim to threats of bodily harm to the child or the family. (In Chapter 5, a continuum of methods offenders use to inhibit reporting of sexual abuse is provided.)

Fourth, it follows that children's reactions to sexual abuse are likely to vary depending upon the proximity of the relationship. In situations where children have close and dependent relationships upon the offender, they are likely to delay disclosure. In fact, we know from the reports of adult survivors that many heeded the admonitions of their abusers and never told. Moreover, as children in proximate relationships who do tell experience the consequences of disclosure, which may include pressure from or rejection by their family, placement in foster care, arrest of the perpetrator, testifying in court, and other traumas, they may recant. That is, they withdraw their accusation either because of pressure from the perpetrator or the family or because the intervention is experienced as worse than the sexual abuse.

In contrast, when the child is not close to the offender, the child is much more likely to disclose and adhere to the accusation. Nevertheless, there are many situations where victims are not dependent upon their victimizers, yet endure sexual abuse and fail to disclose for a significant period of time. The failure to report may relate to a sense of shame the child experiences or strategies used by the offender to discourage disclosure.

Fifth, the psychological impact of the abuse on the child is likely to vary depending upon the proximity of the relationship to the perpetrator. When the relationship is close, this implies that the person is one on whom the child has significant psychological dependence. For example, children are usually much more psychologically dependent upon their mothers than on their aunts. Therefore, abuse by a mother has a much more fundamental impact on the child's ability to trust women than abuse by an aunt. It is assumed that the psychological damage sustained from sexual abuse in a more distant relationship is less pervasive, because the child has other relationships with adults that are appropriate and nonexploitive. Although this is a general rule, it is important to appreciate that children may be seriously harmed if they are victimized by someone to whom the parent has entrusted them, such as a baby-sitter. The parent has usually implicitly or explicitly communicated to the child that she should trust and obey this person. When such a person exploits a child, the child may view this activity as being condoned by the parent.

Sixth, the intervention necessary to protect the child will vary depending upon the proximity of the relationship. When the person is a household member, in most cases, either the child must be removed or the perpetrator must leave. (In Chapter 6, various strategies for protection of the child are described.) In contrast, when there is a more distant relationship between victim and offender, the parent need merely be admonished not to allow the offender unsupervised access to the victim.

Seventh, the reaction of nonoffending caretakers will vary based on the proximity of the relationship between victim and perpetrator. Thus a mother will usually have greater difficulty believing sexual abuse by her husband than by a Boy Scout leader. However, this reaction is more directly governed by the nonoffending caretaker's relationship to the offender than the victim's. Thus a caretaker who is a paternal grandmother is likely to have significantly greater difficulty accepting sexual abuse by her son than might a maternal grandmother of her son-in-law.

Eighth, what is necessary in terms of treatment in large part will be determined by the proximity of the relationship. In intrafamilial cases, if the child is to return to the home, extended treatment involving the parents, the victim, and other family members is usually required. In contrast, when the abuser has a distant relationship with the victim, minimal treatment may be indicated. However, when making decisions about how much treatment is needed in the latter cases, the reaction to the sexual abuse, including the child's symptomatology and the family's coping ability, must be considered. Table 2.2 schematically presents where different perpetrator roles appear on a continuum based on the proximity of the perpetrator-victim relationship.

Table 2.2
Continuum Based on the Proximity of the Relationship Between Offender and Victim

Proximate 1. In House, Caretaker	2. In House, Related	3. In House, Unrelated	4. Out of House, Related	5. Out of House, Professional	6. Out of House, Unrelated	Distant 7. Stranger
a. Father Mother	a. Grandfather Grandmother	a. Mother's boyfriend Father's girlfriend	a. Grandfather Grandmother	a. Day-care provider	a. Baby-sitter	a. Person the child has seen before
b. Stepfather Stepmother	b. Sibling	b. Foster father Foster mother	b. Sibling	b. Camp counselor Teacher	b. Neighbor Family friend	b. Total stranger
Adoptive father Adoptive mother	c. Stepsibling	c. Institutional care provider Institutional pro- fessional (e.g., psychologist, social worker)	c. Stepsibling	c. School counselor Coach (recreation- al leader) Therapist Doctor	c. Family acquaint- ance Child acquaint- ance	
	d. Aunt Uncle Cousin	d. Roomer Unrelated adult Unrelated child	d. Aunt Uncle Cousin	d. Boy Scout leader Cub Scout leader Girl Scout leader Big Brother Big Sister	d. Person known of but not known personally	
	e. Other relative		e. Other relative			

WHY ADULTS SEXUALLY ABUSE CHILDREN

In order for mental health professionals to intervene in a planned and effective manner, they must have a clear understanding of why adults sexually abuse children. Most of the early efforts to understand sexual abuse focused on incest and consisted of clinical studies with usually no more than a half dozen cases. Clinicians, beginning in the 1930s (Bender and Blau, 1937; Bender and Grugett, 1952), placed considerable responsibility on the victim. Victims were regarded as engaging in seductive behavior or as being unusually attractive (and, therefore, irresistible). Later constructions (Justice and Justice, 1979; Lustig et al., 1966; Machotka et al., 1967; Sarles, 1975; Walters, 1975) blamed sexual abuse in incestuous families on the collusive mother, viewing her as the cornerstone of the incestuous triad.

Finally, theories placing responsibility on the victim and the mother have been elaborated into the theory of the incestuogenic family. In such families, the mother abdicates her maternal role responsibilities in the areas of child care, household management, and her sexual functioning. The oldest female child fills the vacuum left by the mother and may even be compelled into that position by the mother. This child is seen as not resisting the parental and sexual role (Mayer, 1983; Lustig et al., 1966; Weiner, 1964). Such theories present the offender as the victim, being seduced by the daughter, encouraged by the mother, or at the very least being at the mercy of family dynamics. Essentially, he bears no real responsibility for his sexual abuse of the child.

However, the notion of family factors being essential in creating incest has been refuted by recent research. First, the research of Becker and colleagues documented that incestuous abuse is not the first instance of sexual interest in children for most incestuous fathers. Half of incestuous fathers were found to have engaged in prior child sexual maltreatment as adolescent offenders. In addition, about one-third fantasized about sex with children prior to their marriages (Becker, cited by Sanford, 1988). Second, the assumption that incest offenders only target a single child (who is behaving in a seductive manner) is not supported by research. Multiple victims are the rule, not the exception, for all offenders, including incestuous ones (Faller, 1988a; Sanford, 1988). Third, the assumption that an incest offender is not a danger to children outside the home has also been refuted by recent research and clinical findings (Faller, forthcoming; Sanford, 1988). Such findings related to incest, as well as the research of professionals who work with a range of types of sex offenders, are responsible for more universally applicable theories, and ones that focus on offender functioning and characteristics, to explain why adults sexually abuse children (e.g., Abel et al., 1981; Abel et al., 1977; Avery-Clark and Laws, 1984; Barbaree et al., 1979; Quinsey et al., 1979).

The theory described in this section is based on experience as well as on current research findings. It posits that there are two types of factors that play a role in sexual abuse: prerequisite factors and contributing factors. The prerequisites will be discussed in some detail, and then the role of contributing factors will be considered.

Prerequisite Factors for Sexual Abuse

There are two prerequisites for sexual abuse: (1) sexual arousal to children and (2) the willingness to act upon the arousal. Together, they are both necessary and sufficient to cause sexual maltreatment. Each will be discussed separately.

(1) Sexual arousal to children. Sex offenders experience sexual feelings toward children (Abel et al., 1981; Abel et al., 1977; Avery-Clark and Laws, 1984; Gilgun and Connor, 1989; Quinsey et al., 1979). Perpetrators who are willing to discuss their activities describe how, for example, the smooth skin of a child, the victim's small stature, or the child's naïveté are exciting. Furthermore, sexual abusers experience the physiological signs of sexual arousal, for instance, erection and ejaculation.[2]

(a) The child is the primary sexual object. In some cases, the abuser experiences arousal only to children, as in the case of most pedophiles. Thus, for these offenders, their primary sexual orientation is toward children, and they will have little or no involvement with adult sexual partners. As noted earlier in this chapter, the sex and age of the desired object may vary depending upon the pedophile.

(b) The child is one of many sexual objects. Other abusers experience sexual arousal to many types of people, including children. A substantial proportion of their interactions with others are sexualized. Some of these offenders are aroused by children, adults, animals, and even inanimate objects. These are polymorphously perverse individuals. An example of a man who fits the polymorphous perverse category is the following case.

> *Case example:* Mr. G was 61 when he was referred for evaluation. His three daughters by his first marriage were charging him with sexual abuse. His son from that marriage reported having observed his father anally penetrate a cow and induce a heifer to suck his penis. His first wife died under suspicious circumstances, and he then married a woman with a 13-year-old daughter. He sexually abused this girl, and she had his child, a girl. He then divorced his

second wife and married her daughter. He beat and sexually abused his third
wife and sexually abused their daughter and a son, whom she subsequently
bore.

In this case, the offender was involved with adult women (at least two), male
and female children, including very young ones and adolescents, a cow, and
a heifer. He may have engaged in additional sexual activities that are not
known.

(c) The child is a circumstantial sexual object. Yet other abusers are
sexually aroused by children in specific situations. These may be situations
of stress, in which the offender regresses; they may be instances where other
sexual outlets are absent; or they may be contexts in which the physical
interaction between the offender and the victim precipitates arousal. Examples of the latter include the offender bathing with the child and becoming
excited by observing or having contact with the child's body, and the child
sitting on the offender's lap and moving in such a way as to result in sexual
arousal. In such instances, despite the fact that the original sexual arousal and
abuse may have occurred "accidentally," it is likely to be sufficiently gratifying as to result in subsequent "nonaccidental" sexual abuse.

Arousal to children is likely to vary in frequency and intensity. Some
offenders experience constant and compelling feelings of sexual desire for
children. These persons appear to be sexual addicts.[3] Other sex offenders
have mild or moderate arousal, and, as mentioned above, some only have
these feelings under particular circumstances.

(2) The willingness to act on sexual arousal to children. It is assumed
that a larger number of people have sexual responses to children than actually
act these out. A recent study of male college students by Briere and Runtz
(1989) supports this assumption: 21% of the respondents reported having
experienced sexual attraction to children. However, it is highly unlikely that
a fifth of the male population sexually maltreats children.

There are several reasons why an individual might act on his arousal.
These will be discussed below.

(a) Pervasive superego deficits. First, an offender may be deficient in
superego functioning; that is, he may lack a conscience. This condition may
be pervasive, in which case the person is likely to engage in a wide range of
antisocial activities. Thus the perpetrator may not only sexually abuse
children but sadistically physically abuse them, assault his wife, and be
involved in the sale of illegal drugs and firearms. Superego deficits may also
vary in degree, from no compunctions about violating norms whatsoever and

regarding those who adhere to social norms as stupid, to some qualms about antisocial behavior but nevertheless having times when social norms matter little.

(b) Lacunae in the superego. Second, the offender may not be inhibited from sexual abuse because he has specific deficits in the sexual area of superego functioning; that is, he may have holes or lacunae in his superego. These holes may relate to sexual activity in general or specifically to sex with children. Often such deficits are a consequence of early life experience, for example, socialization about sexuality or an experience of sexual abuse. Such offenders usually behave appropriately in other areas of their lives.

(c) Thinking errors. A third reason why an offender may be willing to act on sexual feelings is related to the two already mentioned. He may make thinking errors, that is, he persuades himself of the acceptability of the sexual activity. Thus he may rationalize that the child will enjoy the sex, that it is not really harmful, that his need for sex is greater than any harm to the child, that he is justified in having sex with the child because his wife is not sexually satisfying him, or that the absence of penetration means it is not abusive.

(d) Poor impulse control. Fourth, offenders may act on sexual arousal to children because they have poor impulse control. This condition can be differentiated from superego deficits in that the offender appreciates the inappropriateness of the sexual activity and may, indeed, not want to sexually abuse a child, but nevertheless does so because he cannot control his impulses.

(e) Diminished capacity. Fifth, an offender may act on sexual feelings toward children because of diminished capacity; that is, special circumstances inhibit his ability to control his behavior. A number of factors can diminish capacity. Probably the most common cause of diminished capacity is drug or alcohol use. In such instances, if the offender weren't drunk, he would be able to control himself. However, it is common to find that substance use is crucial to the initial victimization, but later encounters occur when the offender is not drunk or high. It is hypothesized that the sexual encounter is sufficiently gratifying to increase sexual arousal, so that the offender requires less to disinhibit him.

Another source of diminished capacity is psychosis. When the individual is psychotic, his ability to control libidinal feelings may be quite limited. In fact, he may have delusions that allow him to justify his sexual activity with a child. For example, one woman offender was convinced, when psychotic, of the absolute necessity of probing her son's anus with a lubricated finger to see if he had a stool in his bowel and of washing his genitals several times a day to get the urine off the end of his penis. When she was on psychotropic medication, she was quite bewildered that she had ever had these thoughts or engaged in the sexual behaviors.

Finally, a mentally retarded offender usually suffers from diminished capacity. Unlike the two other causes of diminished capacity, retardation is a permanent condition. A retarded person may have limited ability to appreciate the violation of norms implicit in sexual abuse and poor judgment as well as poor impulse control. These characteristics can lead to a willingness to act on sexual arousal to children.

Clinicians with experience working with sex offenders will appreciate that an individual's willingness to act may be a consequence of a combination of the factors described in this section. Thus a person may have superego deficits and poor impulse control, and he may get drunk before attempting molestation.

Factors That Contribute to the
Sexual Abuse of Children

A range of circumstances and factors can increase the probability of sexual abuse, but these factors by themselves cannot cause sexual maltreatment. The ones discussed here will be divided into the following categories: (1) characteristics related to the childhood experiences of the offender, (2) cultural factors, (3) the perpetrator's role relationship to the victim, (4) characteristics related to the offender's partner, (5) environmental factors, (6) child factors, and (7) fantasy. Additional factors can contribute to sexual abuse; however, the ones to be discussed here appear to be the most common.

(1) Childhood experiences of the offender. Three types of childhood experiences may contribute to the propensity to sexually abuse: having been sexually abused as a child, having been socialized to believe sexual use of others is appropriate, and the absence of appropriate nurturing as a child. Of course, in addition to these childhood factors, many others may directly or indirectly contribute to sexually abusive behavior.

Childhood sexual abuse can play a role in a variety of ways, but probably the most common is by leading to an identification with the aggressor. Thus the offender, in an effort to cope with a sense of vulnerability from the traumatic experience, takes on the abusive role. By victimizing others, he gains mastery over his own trauma. He is no longer a victim because he is a perpetrator.

Socialization to believe sexual use of others is appropriate can come about from being sexually victimized, but it can also be a consequence of what the abuser is taught or observes. For instance, witnessing a sibling being sexually abused by an adult or knowing such activity is happening in the family can result in the assimilation of such activity as acceptable.

Persons who are not adequately nurtured as children usually lack the skills to show love. It is assumed that affectionate behavior is learned experientially. As adolescents, such individuals learn of sex as a way of showing they care about someone. They may be at increased risk for sexually maltreating a child because they lack other ways of demonstrating affection.

(2) Cultural factors. Certain cultural norms may play a contributing role in child sexual abuse. These may be of four types. First, norms that sanction the right of adults to control and impose their will on children may be used to justify the imposition of the adult sexual desires on children. Second, norms that support male dominance can play a contributing role in sexual maltreatment. Third, similar cultural supports for paternal control over what occurs within the family may contribute to sexual victimization. And, fourth, male sexual socialization may be important. Norms related to male sexuality include the assumption that males should enjoy sex and seek it out and that they should prefer smaller and younger sexual objects (Finkelhor, 1984).

These cultural norms appear to be particularly salient in explaining the high proportion of male, as compared with female, perpetrators and the preponderance of female victims. However, it is also necessary to appreciate that there are competing norms. For example, there is an increasing belief in gender and sexual equality. Moreover, following the civil rights movement in the 1960s, women's rights, children's rights, and the rights of other disadvantaged and oppressed groups have become recognized.

Finally, when cultural supports for sexual abuse play a role, the sexual abuse usually represents an exaggerated and distorted version of these norms. Nevertheless, these factors can play an important role and help us understand gender differences in sexual abuse.

(3) Vulnerable role relationships. Research and clinical findings suggest that offenders in certain role relationships may be at greater risk for sexual abuse. The most consistent finding relates to stepfather vulnerability. Russell (1986) and Finkelhor et al. (1986) found that stepfathers were much more likely to sexually abuse their stepdaughters than biological fathers were to abuse their daughters—in Russell's research seven times more likely. It is hypothesized that the absence of the incest taboo as well as role confusion in a reconstituted family result in this increased vulnerability to sexually maltreat. It has also been found that other males not bound by the incest taboo, who have extended access to children and some caretaking responsibilities,

such as mother's boyfriends and foster fathers (see Chapter 11), may be at risk for sexual abuse.

Two other types of parents, noncustodial parents and single parents, may be vulnerable to sexual involvement with their children. In both cases, the parents may be experiencing considerable emotional upheaval because of the loss of a partner, and they are likely to have extended unsupervised access to the child. (See Chapter 10 for a discussion of sexual abuse allegations in divorce.)

In addition, certain professional roles, particularly those that place the adult in a mentor role, in a position of authority over children, and in a situation with extended periods of unsupervised contact with children, may be characterized by greater risk for sexual abuse. Some examples of these roles have already been discussed; they include teacher, counselor, day-care provider, recreational director, and Big Brother or Big Sister. Although these professional roles may increase risk, some persons who are sexually aroused by children will choose these positions with the conscious intent of sexually abusing children. Others are not consciously aware of their proclivities when they select a career or job, and think they are choosing to be with children for altruistic reasons.

(4) Partner characteristics. Although, as noted above, the role of the nonoffending partner has been overemphasized, it can play a contributing role in some cases. Rejection, ridicule, defiance, infidelity, the withholding of sex, as well as other partner behaviors, can trigger reactions in the offender that increase the propensity to sexually abuse. Moreover, as noted above, the desertion or absence of a partner and accompanying dynamics can enhance the risk for sexual maltreatment of children.

(5) Environmental factors. Some environmental factors appear to have the potential of playing a contributing part in sexual victimization. Two types will be discussed: those that make the child available to the potential offender and those that affect his self-esteem to create an emotional reaction that enhances his vulnerability to be sexual with a child. In a given case, additional environmental factors may play a role.

Factors that make the child readily available to the abuser include crowded living conditions, sleeping arrangements, such as the child and the offender sleeping in the same room or same bed, parents working different shifts, and the potential abuser left to supervise or baby-sit for potential victims on a regular basis.

Environmental factors that result in narcissistic insults to the perpetrator can set off reactions—such as regression, increased dependency, the need to exercise power, a sense of vulnerability, and anger—that can play a role in sexual abuse. These insults appear to be more important in sexual abuse by men than by women. They affect the potential offender's sense of self as a person capable of earning a living and his physical well-being. They include loss of a job, unemployment, and other financial setbacks as well as injuries, accidents, and illnesses. These environmental factors may not only affect the abuser's self-esteem, they may also afford him increased access to children.

(6) Child factors. Although victims are not to be blamed for their sexual abuse, some children have characteristics that may increase their vulnerability to victimization. However, it is also crucial to recognize that these may be much more in the eyes of the offender than in the behavior of the victim.

Children who have been sexually abused in the past may be at greater risk because they have been socialized by previous offenders to behave in ways that may be perceived as sexual invitations, and they have expectations that adults will be sexual with them. Sometimes developmentally normal behaviors, such as those of a little girl in the oedipal stage who evidences a preference for her father, or those of an early adolescent girl who practices flirtatious behavior on her father, are interpreted as sexual invitations by potential offenders. So too may sexual curiosity by a child, for example, a child observing an adult's genitalia and showing an interest because it is different from the child's.

In addition, as noted earlier in this chapter, children who appear to be neglected or deprived, as well as those from single-parent families, may be perceived by potential offenders as easy targets. Finally, a compliant child, a mentally retarded child, or one who has few friends may be singled out by a perpetrator because he or she is seen as a potential victim.

See Chapter 9 for a further discussion of child factors, particularly as they relate to sexual abuse of children in foster care.

(7) Fantasy. Mental health professionals working with sex offenders have become increasingly aware of the role that fantasy can play in sexually abusive behavior. Most adolescents and adults have sexual fantasies. These may be about past sexual experiences, desired sexual activity, or sexual acts the individual never intends to perform. These fantasies may be used to enhance arousal while masturbating or during sexual activity with a partner. In the latter case, the fantasies may or may not be about the partner.

Some sex offenders fantasize extensively about having sex with children. They may also use child pornography to stimulate their sexual interest in children and their fantasies. This type of activity can enhance arousal to children and increase the probability of sexual abuse.

Table 2.3

Explanatory Model: Why Adults Sexually Abuse Children

Prerequisite Causes	*Contributing Factors*

1. Sexual arousal to children
   a. child primary sex object
   b. child one of many sex objects
   c. child circumstantial object
2. Willingness to act on arousal
   a. pervasive superego deficits
   b. holes in superego
   c. thinking errors
   d. poor impulse control
   e. diminished capacity
	1. Childhood experiences
	2. Cultural factors
	3. Vulnerable role relationship
	4. Partner characteristics
	5. Environmental factors
	6. Child factors
	7. Fantasies

How Prerequisite and Contributing Factors Interact to Cause Sexual Abuse

See Table 2.3 for a visual representation of the role of prerequisite causes and contributing factors in sexual abuse.

(1) The interaction between arousal to children and the will to act on arousal. It is primarily the interaction between the offender's arousal level and willingness to act upon the arousal that determines whether or not he sexually abuses. There are a number of possible patterns. He may have frequent instances of and a high level of arousal and weak inhibitions against sexual activity with children. In such a case, he is likely to engage in numerous instances of sexual abuse. A pedophile may experience these dynamics.

Alternatively, he may have the same arousal pattern but greater inhibitions. In this instance, there may be bursts of sexual activity with children. Thus the offender resists the impulse on many occasions, but at some point can no longer do so and engages in sexual abuse, often several instances. Afterward, he experiences a lot of guilt and is able to avoid acting upon his sexual impulses for a period of time.

A third pattern is that of the offender who has less frequent and less intense arousal but no inhibitions against sexual abuse. Thus when he feels like having sex with a child, he does. This is often the type of offender who has pervasive superego deficits and, therefore, his behavior will be characterized by a range of antisocial acts, not merely by sexual abuse.

Finally, presumably there are individuals who experience mild or moderate and infrequent arousal to children, but have sufficient inhibitions against having sex with children that they do not victimize them.

(2) The role of contributing factors. It is theoretically possible to have sexual abuse without the presence of any contributing factors, although this is probably uncommon. Situations of sexual maltreatment by pedophiles are the most likely ones to be characterized by the absence of contributing factors. As already pointed out, contributing factors alone cannot cause sexual abuse. Thus a man does not sexually abuse his daughter because his wife refuses him sex. Most men choose other options: abstention, masturbation, or another adult partner. The offender must experience sexual arousal to a child for him to consider the option of sex with a child, and he must have an inadequate level of inhibitions so that he chooses to act.

Contributing factors can be conceived as operating in two ways: they may enhance either of the prerequisites or they may make an independent contribution to the propensity to sexually abuse. For example, desertion or divorce by a partner may lead to a sense of desolation and anger. Desolation may result in regression as well as more acute needs for acceptance. In addition, an adult sexual partner is not available. Together, these factors can play a role in sexual arousal on the part of the parent to his or her child. The emotional reaction to partner loss can also affect inhibitions against sexual activity with children. They can result in thinking errors and/or diminished capacity. Alternatively, desertion or divorce may not change either arousal to children or the willingness to act on the arousal. These remain constant and sufficient under certain circumstances to cause sexual abuse. However, loss of a partner may result in unsupervised access to the child and, therefore, the opportunity to sexually abuse.

The different contributing factors in Table 2.3 can enhance different subcategories of the prerequisites for sexual abuse. Thus childhood experiences are likely to contribute to the development of offenders whose primary sexual orientation is to children as well offenders who are polymorphous perverse. In addition, such childhood experiences may create persons with pervasive superego deficits and ones with lacunae in their superegos related to exploitive sexual activity.

Cultural factors may affect a person's responsiveness to many sexual objects and may play a role in the circumstantial choice of a child as a sexual object. Moreover, cultural norms may play a role in lacunae in the offender's superego and in thinking errors.

Being in a vulnerable role relationship with a child may lead to circumstantial sexual arousal to a child, although, as already noted, persons whose primary sexual orientation is to children may choose certain professional roles that provide access to children. In addition, persons in these vulnerable roles may engage in thinking errors in order to justify their sexual involvement with children.

Problems in relationships with a partner may enhance the risk for circumstantial attraction to children as well as increase the likelihood of thinking errors, poor impulse control, and diminished capacity. Environmental factors may result in circumstantial arousal to children, and, like partner problems, they may play a role in thinking errors, poor impulse control, and diminished capacity. Child factors may enhance circumstantial arousal to children and can encourage thinking errors.

For some offenders, fantasies play a central role, and they can contribute in a more complex way than the other factors discussed in this section. Fantasies about sex with children can increase any of the subcategories of arousal. An offender may masturbate to these fantasies or use them to achieve arousal or ejaculation in sexual encounters with appropriate partners. For some offenders, the association of fantasies with sexual gratification in these ways increases the desire for sex with children. In such a case, numerous instances of fantasizing about sex with children precede actual sexual abuse. Moreover, offenders may fantasize about the sexual activity with the child afterward, both during masturbation and during adult sexual encounters. This postincident fantasizing also enhances sexual responsiveness to children. In addition, these fantasies about sex with children can play a role in thinking errors.

(3) The reinforcing nature of sexual interaction with children. Finally, engaging in the sexually abusive act can be a very gratifying experience for the offender (Gilgun and Connor, 1989). Because of this, the sex itself, with or without accompanying fantasy, may affect the prerequisite factors, increasing the offender's arousal to children and decreasing inhibitions against sexual activity with them. Therefore, the more extensive the offender's sexual involvement with children has been, the more resistant to treatment his condition is likely to be.

Limitations of the Explanatory Model

The model described here represents my current thinking about why adults sexually abuse children. It is, therefore, in progress. Also, this is not a particularly tidy model. For example, contributing factors can affect prerequisites for sexual abuse as well as operating without changing prerequisites. In addition, the role of fantasy is more complicated than the role of other contributing factors. However, in defense of the untidiness of the model, the real world is not tidy either.

Because of this untidiness, the model is most useful to the clinician. It gives the clinician a clear focus for intervention by its emphasis on prerequisite factors. At the same time, it helps mental health professionals understand why sexual abuse might occur in a particular case and how causal factors might vary in different kinds of cases.

MAINTAINING A PERSPECTIVE ON SEXUALLY DEVIANT BEHAVIOR

While it is important to have a comprehensive theory, it is also necessary to appreciate that all acts do not represent the same degree of norm violation. For example, a person who engages in forcible intercourse with a 1-year-old is acting in a much more socially deviant manner than a person who seduces a 15-year-old. Similarly, a father who has intercourse with his daughter violates a stronger taboo than a cousin or a stepfather sexually abusing the same child.

CONCLUSION

If nothing else has been accomplished in this chapter, it should have made clear that defining and understanding child sexual maltreatment is complex. Although there is a fair amount of consensus about what types of behaviors are sexually abusive, issues of maximum age and consent complicate definitions. In addition, the more experience mental health professionals gain in child sexual abuse, the more varied its patterns and contexts turn out to be. It is important for professionals to appreciate these complexities and their implications. Specifically, the proximity of the relationship between victim and offender has a considerable impact on the characteristics of the sexual abuse, the child's reaction to it, the family's reaction to it, the effect of the victimization on the child, and what is necessary for intervention. Finally, the causes of sexual maltreatment are clearly quite complicated. Nevertheless, it is important to differentiate between prerequisite factors, that is, those that are necessary and sufficient to cause sexual abuse, and factors that can increase its probability. Such a conceptual framework for understanding sexual victimization should guide mental health intervention.

NOTES

1. The term "pedophile" is narrowly defined in this book and not used for sex offenders in general. These are persons whose primary sexual orientation is to children and who, during the course of their sexual careers, are likely to have scores and even hundreds of victims. Many had a sexual experience in their childhood that has led to their fixation on children. Often it is a sexual encounter that the pedophile does not define as abusive but as pleasurable. I have never encountered a female perpetrator who fit this definition of pedophile, nor are there any described in the sexual abuse literature.

2. Evidence of arousal is emphasized because some writers (Groth, 1979; Sgroi, 1982) have minimized the sexual component of sexual abuse and have described it as the abuse of power. It is an abuse of power, but what differentiates it from other abuses of power, for example, beating a child, is its sexual content, which is in part the outcome of sexual arousal. Thus sexual maltreatment cannot be adequately explained as an abuse of power.

3. There are sexual addicts who are addicted to sexual objects other than children, for example, adult women—acceptable sexual partners. However, what distinguishes the addict is the overriding preoccupation with sex.

REFERENCES

Abel, Gene, David Barlow, Edward Blanchard, and Donald Guild. 1977. "The Components of Rapists' Sexual Arousal." *Archives of General Psychiatry* 34:895-903.

Abel, Gene, Edward Blanchard, and David Barlow. 1981. "Measurement of Sexual Arousal in Several Paraphilias: The Effects of Stimulus Modality, Instructional Set and Stimulus Content on the Objective." *Behavior Research and Therapy* 19:25-33.

Avery-Clark, Constance and D. R. Laws. 1984. "Differential Erection Response Patterns of Sexual Child Abusers to Stimuli Describing Activities with Children." *Behavior Therapy* 15:71-83.

Barbaree, H. E., W. L. Marshall, and R. D. Lanthier. 1979. "Deviant Sexual Arousal in Rapists." *Behavior Research and Therapy* 17:215-22.

Bender, Loretta and A. Blau. 1937. "The Reaction of Children to Sexual Relations with Adults." *American Journal of Orthopsychiatry* 7:500-518.

Bender, Loretta and A. E. Grugett. 1952. "A Follow-Up Report on Children Who Had Atypical Sexual Experience." *American Journal of Orthopsychiatry* 22:825-37.

Briere, John and Marsha Runtz. 1989. "University Males' Sexual Interest in Children: Predicting Potential Indices of 'Pedophilia' in a Nonforensic Sample." *Child Abuse and Neglect: The International Journal* 13(1):65-76.

Burgess, Ann et al. 1984. *Child Pornography and Sex Rings.* Lexington, MA: Lexington.

Campagna, Daniel and Donald Poffenberger. 1988. *The Sexual Trafficking in Children.* Dover, MA: Auburn House.

Child Protection Report. 1989. Washington, DC: Independent News Service for Professionals Working with Children and Youth.

Crewdson, John. 1988. *By Silence Betrayed.* New York: Harper & Row.

Faller, Kathleen. 1988a. *Child Sexual Abuse: An Interdisciplinary Manual for Diagnosis, Case Management, and Treatment.* New York: Columbia University Press.

————. 1988b. "The Spectrum of Sexual Abuse in Daycare: An Exploratory Study." *Journal of Family Violence* 3(4):283-98.

————.1990 "Sexual Abuse by Paternal Caretakers: A Comparison of Abusers Who Are Biological Fathers in Intact Families, Stepfathers, and Non-Custodial Fathers." In *The Incest Perpetrator: The Family Member No One Wants to Treat*, edited by A. Horton. Newbury Park, CA: Sage.

Finkelhor, David. 1979a. *Sexually Victimized Children*. New York: Free Press.

————. 1979b. "What's Wrong with Sex Between Adults and Children?" *American Journal of Orthopsychiatry* 49(4):692-97.

————. 1984. *Child Sexual Abuse: New Theory and Research*. New York: Free Press.

Finkelhor, David, Linda Williams, and Nanci Burns. 1988. *Nursery Crimes: Sexual Abuse in Day Care*. Newbury Park, CA: Sage.

Finkelhor, David and associates. 1986. *A Sourcebook on Child Sexual Abuse*. Newbury Park, CA: Sage.

Gilgun, Jane and Teresa Connor. 1989. "How Perpetrators View Child Sexual Abuse." *Social Work* 34(3):249-51.

Groth, Nicholas. 1979. *Men Who Rape*. New York: Plenum.

Hollingsworth, Jan. 1986. *Unspeakable Acts*. New York: Congdon and Weed.

Justice, Blair and Rita Justice. 1979. *The Last Taboo*. New York: Human Sciences Press.

Lustig, Noel, John Dressler, Seth Spellman, and Thomas Murray. 1966. "Incest: A Family Group Survival Pattern." *Archives of General Psychiatry* 14:13-40.

Machotka, Pavel, Frank Pittman, and Kalman Flomenhaft. 1967. "Incest as a Family Affair." *Family Process* 6(1):98-116.

Mayer, Adele. 1983. *Incest*. Holmes Beach, FL: Learning Publications.

Quinsey, Vernon, Terry Chaplin, and Wayne Carrigan. 1979. "Sexual Preferences Among Incestuous and Nonincestuous Child Molesters." *Behavior Therapy* 10:562-65.

Risin, Leslie and Mary Koss. 1987. "The Sexual Abuse of Boys." *Journal of Interpersonal Violence* 2(3):309-23.

Russell, Diana. 1986. *The Secret Trauma*. New York: Basic Books.

Sanford, Linda. 1988. "Innovative Treatment Approaches to Child Victims" (Panel). National Symposium on Child Victimization, Anaheim, CA, April.

Sarles, Richard. 1975. "Incest." *Pediatric Clinics of North America* 22(3):637.

Sassoon, David. 1988. "The Sexual Trafficking of Children: Silence and Taboo Trigger Its Growth and Continuation." *Action for Children* 3(1):1, 10.

Sgroi, Suzanne. 1982. *Handbook of Clinical Intervention in Child Sexual Abuse*. Lexington, MA: Lexington.

Walters, David. 1975. *Physical and Sexual Abuse of Children*. Bloomington: Indiana University Press.

Weiner, Irving. 1964. "On Incest: A Survey." *Excerpta Criminologica* 4:37.

PART II

Collaborating With Institutions Having Mandatory and Legal Obligations

Chapter 3

WORKING WITH PROTECTIVE
SERVICES AND THE POLICE

Any mental health professional encountering child sexual abuse is confronted with the reality that the victim may be at risk for further sexual maltreatment and other harm and with the fact that the sexual encounter is a crime. Knowledge of the roles of child protective services and the police is crucial to effective case management and treatment. The mandates of these two institutions, the roles of their personnel, and how mental health professionals should interact with them will be addressed in this chapter. The first section of this chapter will deal with collaborating with protective services and the second with law enforcement.

COLLABORATING WITH PROTECTIVE SERVICES

Mental health professionals may be involved with protective services in sexual abuse cases in a variety of capacities. Most common is probably as a reporter of suspected sexual maltreatment, but additional roles are as an evaluator of a child and/or members of a child's family and as a therapist for individuals and families where sexual abuse has been diagnosed. Two issues that continue to present dilemmas to mental health professionals—when to

AUTHOR'S NOTE: I wish to thank Lisa D'Aunno, J.D., for her comments and suggestions for this chapter.

report and confidentiality—as well as the role of protective services will be covered in this section.

Reporting Requirements

In order to qualify for federal funding under the Child Abuse Prevention, Adoption, and Family Services Act of 1988 (P.L. 100-294), states must have a procedure for reporting child abuse and neglect. All states require that social workers (and usually other mental health professionals) must report when they suspect child maltreatment by a caretaker, except for seven states that have "everyone" report. In addition, 46 states specifically include sexual abuse among the reportable acts (Mayhall and Norgard, 1983). Statutes do not assume the reporter has absolutely determined that the maltreatment took place; often a phrase such as "reasonable cause" to suspect is used to designate the standard of certainty the reporter must have.

Making reports sounds fairly straightforward, but it may not be. The first issue is this: What is reasonable cause? A legal definition is what a reasonable person of the individual's profession would regard as reasonable cause. However, to some extent, this definition begs the question because the mental health professional must then decide what is reasonable for a person with his or her training. Moreover, the inclusion of material on the diagnosis of sexual abuse in mental health training is the exception rather than the rule. Nevertheless, it is clear that the professional need not have thoroughly investigated the case and proven sexual abuse before reporting. In fact, that is the role of protective services.

Another issue is that, despite the fact that protective services is mandated to investigate all reports of abuse and neglect, they may have their own standard for reporting abuse and neglect, and may set minimum criteria for accepting a referral for investigation. Moreover, these standards may vary from community to community. For example, some agencies will reject referrals based upon third- or fourth-hand information. A case in point is the following. If a social worker makes a report based upon information from a client who asserts her daughter has told her that a friend's father is sexually abusing the friend, in some cases, the social worker will be told to get more direct information, while, in others, the referral will be accepted and investigated.

A second question related to the obligation to report is how current the sexual maltreatment needs to be to require a report. Many professionals (Carnes, 1984; Faller, 1988; Groth, 1979; Knopp, 1984) regard the propensity to sexually abuse as a chronic condition. Moreover, a sex offender is more likely to victimize multiple children than a single child (Becker, 1985; Faller, 1988). Therefore, the fact that an incident occurred several years ago may not necessarily mean that the victim or others are not at risk. Illustrative is a case of a father who had sexually abused his daughter for about four years. The abuse stopped when the daughter told her mother, who took the children and left him. This man is now a grandfather and is frequently allowed to baby-sit for his grandchildren, both male and female. The daughter, the original victim, noted that these children, her nieces and nephews, had very advanced sexual knowledge and were engaging in oral sex with one another. She wanted her therapist to make a report to protective services, but the therapist did not think she had sufficient information.

A third question: Who is a caretaker? It is clear that a referral should be made when the alleged offender is a parent. Less clear is what to do about an uncle, a baby-sitter, or a neighbor. These persons may be reported to the police, but this action will not necessarily protect the child from them. A decision about a report to protective services should be based on the parental response to the alleged sexual abuse by such people. If the parent takes steps to prevent further contact, then a referral may not be legally necessary. Nevertheless, there may be other children who are at risk from this offender whom protective services could assist. Also, the involvement of protective services may be helpful to the victim and the parent in providing support, guidance, and access to therapy.

When caretakers are professionals who act in loco parentis, there may be a state agency separate from protective services that investigates reports. Examples of such caretakers are school personnel, day-care staff, camp counselors, and staff at child-care institutions such as residential treatment facilities, group homes, and psychiatric hospitals. Often responsibility for investigating reports about sexual abuse in these institutions is shared, because the institutions are subject to licensing, and sexual abuse in the facilities is a licensing violation. In addition, there will be different structures for investigating reports depending upon the institution involved, and the structures will not only vary from state to state but also by locality within a given state.

When a mental health professional has a question about any of these issues—what constitutes reasonable cause, how current the sexual victimization needs to be, and who investigates various caretakers—the best practice is to consult protective services for guidance. However, the protective services response may not always be pleasing to the potential reporter.

Confidentiality

The reporting provisions in most states provide for keeping the identity of the reporting person confidential. However, the intent of this provision is to facilitate reports by nonprofessionals whose well-being might be jeopardized should their identity become known. In general, it does not serve the therapeutic relationship well for a practitioner to make a report and not inform the client.

In most states, confidentiality between the reporting professional and involved parties (i.e., the victim, the offender, the nonoffending parent) is abrogated by statute.[1] Thus, despite the fact that a client entered a therapeutic relationship with the understanding that it would be confidential, if sexual abuse (or any other abuse) is disclosed to the therapist, privilege of information related to maltreatment of the child is abrogated. Because of this potentiality, some professionals, usually lawyers, are in favor of informing clients before they begin treatment that any child maltreatment must be reported to protective services. However, such a practice may seem irrelevant if the client comes to treatment for something entirely different and it may unnecessarily alarm the client. In contrast, if the client requests treatment for sexual abuse, the mental health professional should make it clear to the client that any situation where a child is at continued risk of sexual abuse must be reported to protective services and that the therapist may be compelled to testify in court regarding the safety of the child.

Once a report is made, that information as well as any other material in the protective services record of the reported family is confidential (P.L. 100-294). This provision has created problems in communication and understanding between protective services and reporters, as well as between protective services and other agencies involved with the family. States and communities have created procedures that do allow for the sharing of some information, but it is usually circumscribed.

The Role of Protective Services

Child protective services is the agency mandated by federal and state statute to investigate and intervene in cases of child maltreatment by caretakers. Service is delivered by a county-level agency, usually the county department of social services (variously called "human services," "children's services," "public welfare," and so on). Their goals are to protect children and ameliorate the home situation so that children will be safe. If the home situation does not improve as a consequence of intervention, then the agency is to find an alternate, safe living arrangement for the child. This requires court action.

(1) The process of investigation. In performing their investigative duty, protective services workers make home visits, interview family members, and contact other professionals who have been involved with the family. As a rule, protective services treats child maltreatment as a social or psychological problem rather than a crime. However, in recent years, this has become less the case with sexual abuse, and there is usually close collaboration between protective services and law enforcement in investigating child sexual abuse. Expertise in investigative interviewing in child sexual abuse has improved over the years so that specialized techniques are employed by protective services.

As a rule, in responding to a complaint of sexual abuse, the worker will first try to interview the child in a neutral setting, away from the influence of the alleged perpetrator and sometimes the rest of the family. The neutral setting is most frequently the child's school. Tapes, including videotapes, are often made of the investigative interviews.

The worker then typically interviews the child's mother. Assuming that the worker has concluded from the child interview that, indeed, the child has been sexually abused, the worker will share that information with the mother. The worker will be most interested in the mother's ability to protect, and thus will be assessing the mother's response to this information: Is she angry at the perpetrator? Is she angry at the victim? Does she believe that this could have taken place? What is her attitude toward the child? Maternal responses will help the worker assess the mother's relationship with the victim and her ability to perceive the child's needs, which may well be different from her own and the perpetrator's.

The alleged offender is the next person typically interviewed. Again, if the worker thinks this person has sexually abused the child, he or she will confront the alleged offender with that information. Sometimes a confession is obtained, but more frequently it is not. The police may be involved in this interview or may have responsibility for interrogating the offender, while the protective services worker takes responsibility for interviewing other family members.

Other children in the family should also be interviewed. Medical exams of the children may be sought and the alleged victim and other family members may be sent to a mental health professional for an evaluation. As a rule, the worker seeks the family's voluntary cooperation with all of these procedures. However, if they resist, the worker has the ability to go to court and seek a court order to force their compliance.

(2) The goals of protective services. The protective services worker's first
task is to determine whether or not sexual abuse has taken place. The second
is to determine whether the child is safe at home and, if not, to make
provisions for the child's protection. Finally, the worker intervenes to ameliorate harm to the child and to improve family functioning so as to reduce
the likelihood of subsequent sexual abuse. Each of these tasks will be
discussed below.

(a) Determining whether sexual abuse occurred. First, it is no easy task
deciding whether or not the child has been sexually abused. Unlike physical
abuse, there is usually no physical evidence. In a large percentage of cases,
it is the child's word against the alleged offender's and often the mother's as
well. In recent years, child protection workers and other mental health
professionals have come to realize that children have little or no investment
in making false allegations, and offenders have substantial investment in
persuading others that the child is lying, fantasizing, emotionally disturbed,
or mistaken (Faller, 1984, 1988; McCarty, 1981; Sgroi, 1982). Therefore,
professionals are increasingly likely to believe the child in the face of denials
by the alleged offender. In addition, a determination of sexual abuse may be
aided by medical findings and the child's behavior, either within the context
of a mental health evaluation or in other situations.

However, those cases in which the child is very young, the child is retarded
or mentally ill, the perpetrator is a prominent citizen or a person in a sensitive
profession (e.g., education, medicine, mental health, law enforcement, or
law) continue to be very troubling for protective services and other professionals as well. Frequently, these cases are not substantiated. Furthermore,
in many cases, there is insufficient evidence to make a determination about
whether sexual abuse occurred. The alleged victim may refuse to talk, may
recant an earlier disclosure, or may make inconsistent statements about the
abuse or who the perpetrator is. The family may refuse to cooperate and the
worker may be unable to obtain a court order. These clinical observations are
borne out by a recent study of sexual abuse cases referred to child protective
services in Denver, Colorado. The researchers found that 22% were denied
or not founded because there was insufficient information to make a determination (Jones and McGraw, 1987).

(b) Protecting the child. The worker will have three general strategies to
choose from as means for protecting the child: (1) leaving the child in the
family with some safeguards, (2) removal of the child, and (3) removal of
the alleged offender. The first strategy is used sparingly, not only because of
reservations about the potency of safeguards to prevent further sexual abuse

but also because of concerns that the child will be blamed for reporting, pressured to change her story, or otherwise punished for her disclosure.

Removal of the child is the strategy that has traditionally been used. The child may be placed with a relative, in foster care, or in a shelter. Although removal usually results in safety and may provide the child with a supportive and more appropriate living situation, it has some drawbacks. Often the child feels that she is the one being punished by separation from the family, her friends, and her school situation. In addition, the family may close ranks against the child, making her feel even more rejected and making it more difficult to treat the family.

Increasingly, removal of the alleged offender is becoming the strategy of choice for protecting the child. This can be accomplished by a voluntary agreement with the family and the offender, a court order, or arrest and incarceration of the offender. Its advantages are that it communicates to the victim, the offender, and the family that it is the alleged offender who has done something wrong, not the victim; it usually disrupts the family structure that facilitated the sexual abuse; and it allows the victim to stay within the family. Its potential disadvantages are that it may leave the victim vulnerable to family pressure and in an unhealthy living situation, and, unless the offender is in jail, he may violate the agreement or order. The decision about whether to remove the victim or the offender is based in large part on the mother's ability to be supportive to and protective of the victim, the compliance of the offender, and the level of family pathology.

(c) Intervention to ameliorate the family problems that led to the sexual abuse. Although protective services' first duty is to protect the child, its second is to preserve families. The general assumption is that children are better off with their own families. Therefore, protective services works toward the goal of family rehabilitation and reunification, unless there is a demonstrable indication that these are unachievable. In some instances, when the perpetrator refuses treatment, fails in treatment, is divorced by the mother, or is incarcerated, the unit for rehabilitation will be mother and children.

The protective services worker faces a number of problems in trying to provide appropriate treatment for the family. Foremost is finding adequate treatment resources. In ideal circumstances, the community will have a comprehensive treatment program for sexual abuse. Although an increasing number of communities do have specialized treatment for sexual abuse, this is not widespread and there may be a waiting list. In general, it is not advisable to send a sexually abusive family to a treatment provider who does not have experience with this client population.

Another problem is that little is known about what constitutes successful treatment. To date, there have been remarkably few evaluations of sexual abuse treatment (Daro and Cohen, 1984; Kroth, 1979; Sgroi, 1982). Better follow-up is found for treatment programs focusing on offenders than for those that provide family-oriented treatment for incest (Becker, 1985). Finally, there are some offenders and families that cannot be successfully treated with the technology currently available.

Limitations of Child Protective Services

In recent years, there has been considerable criticism of protective services (Besharov, 1986; Duquette et al., 1988; Faller, 1985; Heckler, 1987). Its workers have been accused of lacking necessary skills; it has been seen as both ineffectual and overly intrusive; and its ability to help families has been seriously questioned. These problems are real. They result from ever-increasing referrals; inadequate staffing to respond to emergencies, do careful and sensitive investigations, and provide appropriate intervention; and the inability to attract and retain qualified staff because of the stress of dealing with child maltreatment and the poor working conditions.

Moreover, because child protection workers often are not trained mental health practitioners and have a fairly narrow focus of concern (child maltreatment), mental health professionals experience a degree of dissonance in trying to communicate with them. Workers may be perceived as unable to appreciate the complexities of family and intrapsychic dynamics and unsophisticated in their approach. In addition, they may appear primarily concerned with the bureaucratic aspects of a case, such as whether protective services or another agency is required to provide service, or the need to close the case because the time limit for case activity has expired.

Because of the limitations of the child protection system, mental health professionals may fear for the plight of their clients if they report them and may be tempted not to report suspected sexual abuse. Failing to report is not an appropriate solution to the problems of the child protection system. First, there are legal penalties for failure to report. In most states, the practitioner opens him- or herself up to legal action. This may be for civil damages, based upon harm to the child because of professional negligence, or failure to report may be a misdemeanor, with conviction resulting in a fine and/or jail time (Mayhall and Norgard, 1983). Second, most mental health professionals who treat sexual abuse do not have the resources to remove a child from a dangerous situation and place him or her in a safe place. It is psychologically damaging to the victim, as well as ethically inexcusable, to act as if the sexual abuse is being alleviated by treatment when the abuse is ongoing. Third, the child protection system will not improve as long as professionals avoid it and do not confront its inadequacies. Mental health professionals have a duty to address the system's shortcomings, both on a case level by advocating for a particular client, and at the agency and community level by pressuring for improvements in service delivery.

COLLABORATING WITH LAW ENFORCEMENT

In this section, the avenues that lead to police-mental health collaboration, the role of law enforcement in sexual abuse cases, and issues related to the rights of suspects and confidentiality will be discussed.

How Mental Health Professionals Become Involved with Law Enforcement

In most states, the legal obligation mental health professionals have to report suspected child maltreatment does not require that a referral be made to the police.[2] Therefore, as a rule, collaboration with the police is undertaken when the mental health professional feels an ethical duty to contact the police. These situations are likely to be ones where the offender poses a danger to the victim(s), the victim(s)' family, the professional making the report, and/or the community. Examples of perpetrators who fall into these categories are violent sex offenders—offenders who make specific threats of bodily harm to the victim(s), the family, or the mental health professional, and pedophiles (persons with a history of sexually abusing many victims, who cannot control their behavior, and whose primary sexual orientation is to children). In addition, any case where criminal prosecution is in the victim's best interest and where no other agency has involved the police (i.e., protective services) warrants a police report. By and large, these will be situations where the perpetrator is not related to the victim. An example is the following case.

> *Case example:* Mr. and Mrs. I brought their 3-year-old son, Kevin, for an evaluation because they thought he had been sexually abused by his baby-sitter. They had fired her before seeking the evaluation. Kevin demonstrated and described how the baby-sitter had repeatedly pulled down his pants and fondled his penis and his anus. In addition, he showed how she had spanked him very hard. He also reported to his parents that he had been induced to bite her nipple.

> This woman was unlicensed. Before coming to work for the family, she baby-sat for another family for about four years, and prior to that she provided unlicensed day care out of her home. Mr. and Mrs. I knew that she was looking for another baby-sitting job because she asked them for a reference. They were also somewhat afraid of her because she had interacted with them in a rather bizarre fashion on a number of occasions. Kevin showed that he was quite frightened of her.
>
> The evaluator sent a copy of her findings to the relevant law enforcement agency. Included in the report was the name and address of the previous employer of the baby-sitter.

Because Mr. and Mrs. I reacted protectively to suspicions about the baby-sitter, it was not likely that protective services would pursue the case. In addition, because this baby-sitter is unlicensed, she does not come within the purview of social services or a licensing body. However, because this woman has committed a crime, law enforcement is the appropriate agency to involve. Although it was unlikely that Kevin would be able to testify against her in a criminal proceeding, both he and his family needed to know that someone was taking action. In addition, there are other children who may have been damaged by the sitter in the past, and she poses a threat to other children, should she continue providing child care. Moreover, the children for whom she previously sat may be judged competent witnesses for a trial. Finally, the parents have some fears that this woman might harm them, and police involvement offers some protection.

Mental health professionals may also collaborate with law enforcement when their assistance is sought in the investigation or prosecution of cases. For example, the police may ask for an assessment to determine whether an alleged victim has been sexually abused or is telling the truth. An additional area in which mental health expertise may be sought is regarding a victim's competence or ability to testify. Finally, the police may also ask a child's therapist to prepare a child to testify.[3]

The Role of Law Enforcement

The responsibility of the police is to catch criminals. Their role is to investigate alleged crime, obtain supportive evidence (or rule out criminal activity), arrest suspects, and see that they are criminally prosecuted and go to jail. While they may also be concerned with protecting victims and doing what is in their best interest, and with the well-being of their families, these concerns are secondary to their mission. Thus their goals differ markedly from those of protective services, and, while in many cases it is possible to reconcile these differences, in some it is not. Obviously, these divergent roles have significant implications because, in many communities, investigation of sexual abuse is done conjointly by protective services and law enforcement.

(1) Interrogating suspects. Although the police are often involved in interviewing the victim and nonoffending parent, their central role is interrogating the offender. Their goal is to obtain a confession. Other than informing the suspect of his rights (see the section below), there is no legal or ethical requirement that the police be honest with the alleged offender. It is quite acceptable to try to trick the perpetrator into confession. Alternatively, the interrogation may be quite coercive. However, many law enforcement personnel report greater success by appearing to care about the well-being of the offender and trying to appeal to the offender's concern for the welfare of the victim (Cage, 1988; Goldstein, 1987; Kleinheksel, 1988). Once a verbal confession is elicited, it is written and signed by the offender (Goldstein, 1987).

Because law enforcement's primary focus is on criminal prosecution, it is less concerned about such issues as the potential detrimental effect of having a child testify in court. Moreover, in cases where it is clear that the victim will not make a good witness, law enforcement often loses interest because there is no chance of a successful criminal prosecution.

(2) The polygraph. If an alleged offender protests his innocence during the police interrogation, he will often be offered a polygraph examination. The polygraph, or lie detector, is supposed to be able to determine whether or not the alleged offender is lying when he says that he did not sexually abuse the child.

It is important for mental health professionals to understand that the polygraph is not a litmus test; it cannot reliably differentiate liars from truth-sayers. In fact, in a critical evaluation of research on the polygraph, it was found to have a little better than chance probability of accurately distinguishing between subjects who were telling the truth and those who were lying (Lykken, 1987).

It is useful for mental health professionals to understand why the polygraph is flawed. First, what it measures are arousal responses as the interviewee answers questions. The responses most polygraph instruments measure are galvanic skin response (sweaty palms), pulse rate, blood pressure, and breathing rate. The assumption is that these will increase when a person is anxious, and that lying makes people anxious.

Taking the last assumption first, although lying does make some people anxious, clinical findings on sexual abusers suggest they are much less likely to become upset by their lying behavior than most people; that is, they lie habitually to conceal their sexually abusive behavior and may be character disordered (some being at the extreme end of the continuum and psychopaths) and, therefore, have no compunctions about lying. Moreover, Reid and Inbau (1977), two advocates for the polygraph, state that it is not useful with neurotics or psychopaths. This qualifier rules out its utility with most sex offenders.

It is also important to recognize that anxiety is not the only emotion that can lead to arousal. For example, anger or sexual excitation might also lead to increased rates of pulse, heart beat, and breathing. Moreover, when anxiety is the cause of arousal, it may not be related to lying but merely to the situation of being questioned about sexually abusive behavior. It is also important to appreciate that arousal responses can be controlled, both voluntarily and by the use of drugs and medication.

Finally, who administers the polygraph is a predictor of its utility. Like a mental health evaluation, the polygraph is dependent upon the skill of the examiner. The training and experience of polygraphists is highly variable (Saxe et al., 1987). In addition, a distinction needs to be made between the results of a polygraph administered by a police agency and a private polygraphist. One strategy some offenders use (usually following the advice of their attorneys) is to initially refuse the police polygraph but go to a private polygraphist. If they are successful at passing a private polygraph (and they may take a number until they are desensitized enough to pass one), they then produce the results and sometimes offer to take a police polygraph.

Because of the limitations of the polygraph, it is not admissible in court in most states.[4] Arguments for its use, despite its problems, are that a refusal to take the polygraph is suggestive of guilt, and a failure to pass may result in a confession. Nevertheless, it is important for mental health professionals (and others) to realize that the fact that an alleged offender passes a polygraph does not mean that he is innocent and the victim is lying.

(3) Collecting physical evidence. In addition to interrogation responsibilities and administration of the polygraph, law enforcement is responsible for gathering physical evidence in sexual abuse cases. In some cases, there will be evidence from the scene of the crime. Examples of such evidence are bed or other clothing that might contain minute pieces of physical evidence, for instance, body hairs, clothing fibers, or dirt. Clothing might also have traces of seminal fluid, blood, saliva, or other secretions. In addition, any instru-

ment, for example, a vibrator or a weapon, that might have been employed in the abuse, and evidence supportive of any physical activity, for instance, signs of a scuffle, would be obtained and/or documented by the police. Both the victim's and the perpetrator's clothing might be confiscated. Other types of physical evidence that might be collected by the police are letters written by the alleged offender to the victim, other written records or correspondence, suggestive or pornographic pictures taken of the victim or offender, other pornography, and equipment for producing pornography (Cage, 1988; Moreau, 1987a, 1987b).

The police are also responsible for seeing that a forensic medical exam is completed and that the evidence collected is conveyed to the police crime laboratory. The exam will be conducted on the victim by a physician. Specimens collected include smears that might contain evidence of sexual activity, samples of pubic and scalp hair, combings from the victim's pubic hair and hair on her head, and any other evidence of the sexual activity (Moreau 1987a, 1987b; Steinberg and Westhoff, 1988). Physical evidence is more likely to be sought and found in situations of child rape or recent sexual assault and in cases where the alleged offender is thought to be a pedophile who has a lengthy history of sexual involvement with children.

Law enforcement has the capability of preserving the chain of evidence, that is, they have official procedures for seizing, labeling, and storing in a secure place any evidence that is obtained. Child protection workers and others who might be involved in an investigation of sexual abuse do not have this capability. Being able to establish a chain of custody for any physical evidence is a prerequisite for its admission in a court proceeding (Moreau, 1987a, 1987b).

Legal Protections and Confidentiality

Police may interview an alleged offender without advising him of his rights if they have not taken him into custody. However, because of judicial concerns about coerced confessions, if the police arrest someone, before they question the suspect, they must inform him of his *Miranda* rights (*Miranda v. Ariz*, 384 US 436 [1966]). These are the right to remain silent (that any statement may be used as evidence against him in a court of law) and the right to the presence of an attorney, should he choose to be interviewed. Neither protective services workers nor others involved in the investigation of alleged sexual abuse take people into custody or are required to give such warnings, and clearly these practices are likely to result in a very different interview than one conducted under less frightening circumstances.

Police files are not necessarily confidential. The Freedom of Information Act (e.g., *Michigan Compiled Laws Annotated,* 15.321) makes such records potentially available to the public. Law enforcement has discretionary power not to disclose information in investigative records under certain conditions,[5] but it is wise not to expect confidentiality.

Therefore, any information in police records may be available not only to the parties involved in the case but also to the public, including the press. It is important for mental health professionals and others involved to be aware of this. In writing reports, responding to questions by the police, and turning over written material to the police, it is necessary to bear in mind that this material could eventually be quoted in the newspaper.

CONCLUSION

Protective services and the police both play vital roles in the appropriate management of sexual abuse cases. To be effective, mental health professionals must appreciate that they cannot act alone but must, in many instances, collaborate with these two key players. Nevertheless, it is important to understand that both their training and their responsibilities for a sexual abuse case differ from those of a mental health professional. Therefore, working together presents a challenge. However, this challenge must be met in order to assist victims of sexual abuse and their families.

NOTES

1. States vary in their provisions for waiver of confidentiality: 20 states waive confidentiality for all persons except attorneys; 22 limit the waiver to physicians (Mayhall and Norgard, 1983).

2. Fifty states (and Washington, DC) designate the social services department either as the exclusive agency to which a person must report or as one of two or more agencies. Nineteen states allow professionals to report either to protective services or the police. Two (Idaho and Nebraska) require the report go to law enforcement (Mayhall and Norgard, 1983).

3. Sometimes others, for example, the protective services worker or the prosecutor, will ask the mental health professional to perform these services.

4. However, in 20 states, results of the polygraph are admissible if both parties agree to their admission, and, in Massachusetts and New Mexico, they are admissible even if one party objects (Wrightsman et al., 1987).

5. Investigative records are exempt from disclosure if their release would (1) interfere with a law enforcement proceeding, (2) deprive a person of a fair trial, (3) constitute unwarranted invasion of privacy, (4) disclose law enforcement techniques, or (5) endanger the life or physical safety of a law enforcement officer (M.C.L.A. 15.321).

REFERENCES

Becker, Judith. 1985. "Evaluating and Treating Adolescent Sexual Offenders." Paper presented at the Seventh National Conference on Child Abuse and Neglect, Chicago, November.

Besharov, Douglas. 1986. " 'Doing Something' About Child Abuse: The Need to Narrow the Grounds for State Intervention." *Harvard Journal of Law and Public Policy* 8:459-566.

Cage, John. 1988. "Criminal Investigation of Child Sexual Abuse Cases." In *Vulnerable Populations: Evaluation and Treatment of Sexually Abused Children and Adult Survivors.* Vol. 1, edited by S. Sgroi. Lexington, MA: Lexington.

Carnes, Patrick. 1984. *The Sexual Addiction.* Minneapolis: CompCare.

Daro, Deborah and Anne Cohen. 1984. "A Decade of Child Maltreatment and Evaluation Efforts: What We Have Learned." Paper given at the Second National Conference of Family Violence Researchers, Durham, NH.

Duquette, D., K. C. Faller, and L. D'Aunno. 1988. "Putting Protective Services in Its Place." In *Child Protective Services in Michigan: Recommendations for Policy and Practice,* edited by D. Duquette, K. C. Faller, and L. D'Aunno. Ann Arbor: University of Michigan, Interdisciplinary Project on Child Abuse and Neglect.

Faller, Kathleen Coulborn. 1984. "Is the Child Victim of Sexual Abuse Telling the Truth?" *Child Abuse and Neglect: The International Journal* 8:473-81.

———. 1985. "Unanticipated Problems in the United States Child Protection System." *Child Abuse and Neglect: The International Journal* 9.

———. 1988. *Child Sexual Abuse: An Interdisciplinary Manual for Diagnosis, Case Management, and Treatment.* New York: Columbia University Press.

Goldstein, Seth. 1987. *Sexual Exploitation of Children.* New York: Elsevier.

Groth, Nicholas. 1979. *Men Who Rape.* New York: Plenum.

Heckler, David. 1987. *The Battle and the Backlash.* Lexington, MA: Lexington.

Jones, David and E. Melbourne McGraw. 1987. "Reliable and Fictitious Accounts of Sexual Abuse to Children." *Journal of Interpersonal Violence* 2(1):27-46.

Kleinheksel, Kenneth. 1988. "The Role of Law Enforcement in Investigating Child Sexual Abuse." Workshop delivered at "A Community Approach to Child Sexual Abuse," Ann Arbor, MI, June.

Knopp, Faye Honey. 1984. *Retraining Adult Sex Offenders: Methods and Models.* Syracuse, NY: Safer Society Press.

Kroth, Jerome. 1979. *Child Sexual Abuse.* Springfield, IL: Charles C Thomas.

Lykken, David. 1987. "The Detection of Deception." Chap. 2 in *On the Witness Stand,* edited by L. Wrightsman, C. Willis, and S. Kassin. Newbury Park, CA: Sage.

Mayhall, Pamela and Katherine Norgard. 1983. *Child Abuse and Neglect: Sharing Responsibility.* New York: John Wiley.

McCarty, Loretta. 1981. "Investigation of Incest: An Opportunity to Motivate Families to Seek Help." *Child Welfare* 60(10):679-89.

Michigan Compiled Laws Annotated (M.C.L.A.). 15.321. "Freedom of Information Act."

Michigan Compiled Laws Annotated (M.C.L.A.). 15.243. "Items Exempt from Disclosure."

Moreau, Dale. 1987a. "Concepts of Physical Evidence in Sexual Assault Investigations." In *Practical Aspects of Rape Investigation,* edited by R. Hazelwood and A. Burgess. New York: Elsevier.

———. 1987b. "Major Physical Evidence in Sexual Assault Investigation." In *Practical Aspects of Rape Investigation,* edited by R. Hazelwood and A. Burgess. New York: Elsevier.

Public Law (P.L.) 100-294. 1988. Child Abuse Prevention, Adoption, and Family Services Act.

Reid, J. E. and F. E. Inbau. 1977. *Truth and Deception: The Polygraph Technique*. 2nd. ed. Baltimore: Williams and Wilkins.

Saxe, Leonard, Denise Dougherty, and Theodore Cross. 1987. "The Validity of Polygraph Testing: Scientific Analysis and Public Controversy." In *On the Witness Stand*, edited by L. Wrightsman, C. Willis, and S. Kassin. Newbury Park, CA: Sage.

Sgroi, Suzanne. 1982. *Handbook of Clinical Intervention in Child Sexual Abuse*. Lexington, MA: Lexington.

Steinberg, Mary and Mary Westhoff. 1988. "Behavioral Characteristics and Physical Findings: A Medical Perspective." In K. C. Faller *Child Sexual Abuse: An Interdisciplinary Manual for Diagnosis, Case Management, and Treatment*, edited by K. C. Faller. New York: Columbia University Press.

Wrightsman, L., C. Willis, and S. Kassin. 1987. "Section I Summary." In *On the Witness Stand*, edited by L. Wrightsman, C. Willis, and S. Kassin. Newbury Park, CA: Sage.

Chapter 4

COLLABORATING WITH ATTORNEYS

Most helping professionals are not very well trained in the legal aspects of mental health work and are not very comfortable with how lawyers may operate in the mental health field. Because child sexual abuse is a crime as well as a mental health problem, it is important to be knowledgeable about the way lawyers and courts operate. The following topics will be discussed in this chapter: (1) mental health roles that require collaboration with lawyers, (2) the courts involved in sexual maltreatment litigation, (3) the roles lawyers take in sexual abuse cases, and (4) testifying in court.

COLLABORATION BETWEEN MENTAL HEALTH PROFESSIONALS AND ATTORNEYS

Mental health professionals working on sexual abuse cases may encounter lawyers in a variety of ways: as a reporter of suspected sexual abuse, as a therapist for one or more of the parties, or as an evaluator of one or more of the parties. Regardless of the role, encounters with the legal system present challenges.

Reporter

A mental health professional who has reported a case of sexual abuse may later be called to testify concerning the suspicions that led to the report. As

AUTHOR'S NOTE: I wish to express appreciation to Lisa D'Aunno, J.D., for reading of and suggestions for this chapter.

noted above, when a person, including a professional, makes a report of suspected sexual abuse, the reporter's name can be held confidential. However, this is only so if the case does not result in litigation. If the child protection agency initiates court action, the reporter may be subpoenaed to provide testimony. This possibility is another argument for letting the family know when making a report. An additional problematic aspect of providing this testimony is that usually the case comes to trial months and sometimes years after the referral was made. Initial observations and concerns may seem moot by then, and the reporter's memory may have faded. Professionals should take good notes at the time of the referral in anticipation of the eventuality of the case going to court.

Therapist

Probably more frequently, mental health professionals testify as therapists. This role presents varying problems depending upon whose therapist the practitioner is.

As the victim's therapist, the professional will have a number of concerns. The first is the impact of the testimony upon the victim. A second is what the victim wants the therapist to say. Yet a third is what is in the victim's best interest for the therapist to say. Children may feel supported when there will be someone else there who is on their side. Yet they may also be upset that the therapist is going to tell everything about the sexual abuse to a room full of people. The victim may also have said something against the parents or the perpetrator in treatment that she or he does not want revealed to others. The child may also be fearful that the therapist's testimony will result in an undesired outcome, for example, a criminal charge, conviction of the offender, or termination of parental rights. The therapist cannot refuse to answer any questions related to the safety of the child and should not say anything that is untrue (that is, perjury) but should nevertheless take into account the child's feelings. One way of moderating the potentially negative impact of testimony on the child is for the witness to talk to the child ahead of time and explain what she or he is likely to say and the reasons for saying it.

More troubling are situations where the clinician is working with the offender, the victim's mother, or the family and is called to testify. The mental health expert may be required to make statements that the client perceives as very negative. This does not mean that the therapist is being dishonest with the client in treatment. Rather, therapy is a process of helping people change, and issues are dealt with one at a time and in an order that maximizes the likelihood for change. Testimony occurs at a particular point in time and requires the clinician to telescope either forward or backward. In addition, the clinician may have to address issues that have not yet been dealt with in treatment because the client is not yet able to handle them. Therefore, testimony may interfere with the therapeutic process. The example below illustrates how this can happen.

Case example: Ms. G was providing therapy to the S family, where Mr. S had sexually abused his two daughters, Angela, 10, and Sally, 8. Both children were in the care of an aunt and Mr. and Mrs. S remained together. Ms. G was seeing the girls as a dyad and the mother and father separately. At the point Ms. G was asked to provide testimony, Mr. S was saying that he might have done something inappropriate but he was drunk and did not remember. Mrs. S still could not acknowledge that her husband could have sexually abused their children. She said that he knew how much her sexual abuse as a child had affected her, and, therefore, he would not do such a thing. The girls had described fondling and fellatio by their father and his admonition that, if they told, their mother would have a nervous breakdown. Sally disclosed that she had tried to tell her mother, but her mother told her that her father was just disciplining her. Both children were saying they never wanted to go home.

Ms. G was working with Mr. S to get him to admit to the sexual abuse. With Mrs. S., she was focusing on Mrs. S's own victimization, believing that the mother needed to work through that before she could accept her daughters' sexual abuse.

In her testimony, although Ms. G had some positive things to say, she also revealed that she thought the father was lying to her, that Sally had told her mother about the sexual abuse, and that both children were saying that they never wanted to go home. Mrs. S did not hear the positive things and was incensed by the testimony that Sally had told her (she probably had repressed Sally's disclosure). Her husband encouraged her to believe that Ms. G was generally untrustworthy, for, in addition to stating Mrs. S knew about the sexual abuse, she was also wrongly accusing him of sexual abuse and had turned their children against them. In subsequent therapy sessions, the parents focused on the therapist's testimony rather than the sexual abuse. They also demanded to see another therapist, one of their own choosing. Eventually, this request was granted by the Department of Social Services.

In the S case, it is clear that treatment was at a very delicate stage when Ms. G had to testify. Hearing the therapist's testimony alienated the mother, and the father manipulated the situation to derail the treatment.

Evaluator

Mental health professionals are often involved in the legal process as persons who evaluate cases of alleged sexual abuse and offer an opinion. The opinion may be about whether sexual abuse occurred, the dynamics that led to the victimization, what sorts of treatment are necessary, or what the treatment prognosis is for various parties. In addition, the evaluator may be asked whether it is safe to leave the child in the home, whether the child can return home if she has been removed, or whether it is appropriate to terminate parental rights. The party requesting the evaluation may be the protective services worker, the guardian ad litem (in a protection case), one or both parents or their lawyer, the prosecutor, or the court.

It is important ethically to carefully consider the conditions of involvement. The central issue here is that the court arena fosters an adversarial process, that is, persons involved must take sides. Not only will many mental health professionals have questions about whether an adversarial confrontation is the best way to address a problem of sexual abuse, but it is unusual for a mental health professional to find that one side is all right and the other all wrong.

Generally, as the expert for protective services, the guardian ad litem, or the court, the mental health professional will not encounter serious difficulties, because each of these entities is primarily concerned with the child's best interest, albeit from different perspectives. Difficulties arise when the mental health professional is asked to act as an expert for the parents in a protection proceeding, for one parent against the other in a divorce matter, or for either the prosecutor or the defendant in a criminal trial.

A mental health professional may do an evaluation, arrive at conclusions not supportive of the client, and then simply not be called to testify. The lawyer is not under any obligation to disclose the findings of the evaluation to any other parties in the proceeding. Or more subtle problems may occur. Most mental health professionals want to help; therefore, if they are asked by a client to be involved, they will want to be supportive. This pressure may, without the evaluator intending it to, influence the findings. A related problem is that the attorney will, of course, be advocating for his or her client and, therefore, will describe the situation of the case from that viewpoint. The attorney may even selectively furnish written information and not supply material detrimental to his or her client. A final issue is money. The mental health professional usually expects to be paid by the side who retains him or her. Most mental health professionals cannot be bought, but nevertheless the financial arrangement may subtly influence the evaluation results.

There are several ways of handling these problems, none of which successfully addresses all of the issues mentioned above, but sometimes these strategies can be used in combination. One is to make a prior agreement with the client that the report of the evaluation will be made available to all parties. That is, regardless of the findings, all sides will receive the results. This allows the possibility of other parties calling the expert to testify should the original client be dissatisfied with the findings and not call the evaluator as a witness.

A second strategy is to demand to see documents, such as protective services reports, police investigations, and other evaluations, in order to make a preliminary determination of the efficacy of the case before agreeing to do the evaluation. For example, if an attorney describes his client as wrongly accused of rape by a lying, conniving, 14-year-old vixen, but the records show that the client has already served time for sex offenses against minors, has an alcohol problem, and was found in possession of an extensive collection of child pornography, the evaluator can turn the case down. Less obvious cases will be more problematic.

A third strategy is to require, as a condition for doing the evaluation, permission to contact and, if necessary, interview all parties and to obtain documents from all sides. One problem that often occurs with this strategy is refusal to cooperate by persons on the other side. Sometimes a court order can be obtained to compel their involvement. However, the evaluator must then appreciate the effect being coerced in this manner is likely to have on the interviewees. Even more than in other evaluations, they are likely to perceive the evaluator as a hostile party and may be quite guarded or hostile themselves.

A fourth strategy is to require that all sides agree that the mental health professional be the evaluator for the case. This approach is most relevant to divorce situations but may also work in child protection proceedings. In addition to assisting the evaluator in being impartial, this strategy may have the added advantage of avoiding multiple assessments, which can be quite stressful on all parties but especially on the victim.

THE ROLE OF THE COURTS

The courts that might have jurisdiction in a sexual abuse case and the stages of the court process will be described in this section.

Courts That May Have Jurisdiction

Several different courts might have jurisdiction in a sexual abuse case. First, the juvenile or family court, which hears child protection matters, may be involved. Second, there may be a criminal case against the offender, which would be heard in a state district or circuit court. Third, if the sexual abuse was revealed at the time of parental divorce or if it started after a divorce, the case may be heard in whatever court, family or circuit, that handles divorces. Fourth, sometimes victims or their guardians file civil suits against sex offenders or institutions in which children were sexually abused. To further complicate matters, frequently there is more than one court involved.

Not only will the goal of court action vary, so will the "standard of proof" or amount of evidence necessary to prove the case, depending upon the court context. In a protection case, the child welfare agency will be seeking to prove the parents have been abusive or neglectful so that the court will take jurisdiction over the child. The standard of proof necessary for the child protection agency to get the court to take temporary jurisdiction over the child varies from state to state, with some requiring a "preponderance of the evidence" (about 51% probability that the child has been sexually abused or allowed to be sexually abused by the parents) and others requiring "clear and convincing evidence" (about a 75% probability level). If the court is to take permanent jurisdiction, that is, terminate parents' rights, in all states the agency must prove the case with "clear and convincing evidence" (Duquette, 1981; Long, 1988).[1]

In a criminal case, the goal is to get the court to decide that the defendant sexually abused the child and impose a sentence that will limit his liberty (e.g., place him on probation, put him in jail, send him to prison). The standard of proof is higher, beyond a reasonable doubt (about 95% probability that the defendant sexually abused the child).

In a divorce case, relevant issues are custody of and visitation with the child. It is not always necessary to prove that sexual abuse occurred. The court is interested in what is in the "child's best interest," which must meet the standard of "preponderance of the evidence," unless the child's best interest requires a change of custody, in which case the standard of proof is "clear and convincing evidence" (Duquette et al., 1988). Finally, in a damages suit, the goal is to prove that the person or institution charged is responsible for harm resulting from sexual abuse. The standard of proof for a damages suit is "preponderance of the evidence."

Stages in Court Proceedings

A further confusion for those unfamiliar with courts is that there are several stages of court proceedings. The names of these will vary depending upon the court and the jurisdiction. However, there are generally three main stages: a preliminary hearing of some sort, a trial or adjudication, and a disposition or sentencing. The purpose of the preliminary hearing is for the court to determine if there is sufficient evidence (or some credible evidence) to try the case. The trial is the hearing where the case is either proven or not (e.g., the court finds the offender guilty of sexual abuse or the parents negligent resulting in their child being sexually abused). The dispositional hearing is where the court decides what to do about it (e.g., send the offender to prison, take the children away from the parents). There may also be review hearings, and termination of parental rights in protection cases is usually a separate hearing. Mental health professionals are more likely to be called to testify at the adjudication or the disposition.

ATTORNEY ROLES

In each type of court proceeding, there will be several attorneys, each having a distinct role. The roles of attorneys in protection, criminal, divorce, and damages cases will be described.

Lawyer Roles in Child Protection Proceedings

Protective services goes to court on behalf of sexually abused children when a parent is the offender or a parent fails to protect a child from sexual abuse and the coercive arm of the court is deemed necessary to assure the safety of the child. Usually this entails the child's removal from the parental home. There are three different attorney roles: the attorney for protective services, the attorney for the child, and the attorney for the parents.

(1) Attorney for protective services. This attorney brings the case to court on behalf of protective services. Protective services' lawyer is usually the initiator of the court proceedings, although other attorneys may request hearings later on in the court process.

In most communities, protective services will be represented by an attorney from the prosecutor's office. Although there may be a consistent prosecutor who handles child protection cases, in many jurisdictions, a variety of different attorneys may be assigned. The problem with this procedure is that the prosecutor may not gain sufficient expertise and may not have an opportunity to develop a good working relationship with child protection staff. Furthermore, in some jurisdictions, the most inexperienced attorneys are assigned to juvenile work and, as they gain experience, they are promoted to more prestigious work. (Juvenile cases are not regarded as high status.)

In addition, some prosecutors feel that they are to represent "the people" in child protection proceedings, as they do, for example, in a criminal case. The problem that can arise in this circumstance is that the prosecutor may decide that the remedies child protective services wishes to seek are not in "the people's" interest and refuse to pursue them in court.

For these reasons, some child protection agencies have their own attorneys. This is more likely to be the case in communities with large child protection caseloads.

The attorney and the child protection worker should work closely in preparing a case for court. The attorney ascertains whether legal grounds exist for intervening as the worker wishes. The worker suggests who might be appropriate witnesses for proving the case. The attorney usually contacts and prepares the witnesses and/or subpoenas them. Usually the worker will sit with the attorney during the court proceedings to advise him or her.

(2) Attorney for the child. The term "guardian ad litem" is often used for the child's attorney. The federal Child Abuse Prevention and Treatment Act requires that all state child protection laws provide for a guardian ad litem in child protection legal proceedings, if the states are to qualify for certain federal funds. That attorney is supposed to represent the child's best interest. Sometimes conflicts arise between what the child says she or he wants and what the lawyer deems is in the child's best interest. For example, the child may want to go home, but the attorney believes this is not in the victim's best interest because the perpetrator is there and has persuaded the mother that he did not sexually abuse the child.

This conflict is sometimes resolved by the attorney communicating to the court what the child's wishes are as well as his or her opinion about the child's best interest. In other instances, separate attorneys or one attorney and a guardian ad litem, who is not an attorney but acts in the child's best interest, may be appointed, one to represent the child's wishes and the other the child's best interest.

The guardian ad litem is supposed to conduct an independent investigation in order to determine the child's best interest. Few guidelines exist on how to do this, and many attorneys are poorly prepared for such an undertaking. Moreover, in some instances, guardians are appointed for the hearing and paid only for their appearance in court, rather than being the child's counsel for the entire time the child is under court jurisdiction. Such a structure does not encourage any considered investigation. Frequently, the guardian merely discusses the case with the child protection worker or reads the record in order to arrive at an opinion. He or she may not ever see or talk to his or her client!

In recent years, there have been some efforts to define the child's attorney's role as well as some creative experiments in representation. For example, a team of a mental health professional and an attorney or a volunteer who works with an attorney may act as guardian (Duquette and Ramsey, 1987).

(3) Parents' attorney. The parents' attorney represents the parents' wishes and seeks the outcome they want in court, regardless of his or her belief about their guilt or innocence. Outside of the hearing, the parents' attorney can attempt to persuade or counsel them toward a different position. However, if unsuccessful, the attorney must vigorously pursue the parents' goals.

In many cases of sexual abuse, the mother and father have different interests, because the father is the abuser and the mother reacted protectively when she discovered the sexual abuse. In most instances, this situation requires separate attorneys for mother and father. Thus, when the mental health professional testifies in court, she or he will face examination by two attorneys representing the parents rather than one.

Although legal representation for parents is not a federal requirement as it is for the child, in many jurisdictions, parents receive court-appointed attorneys when they are indigent. Frequently, there is roster of attorneys from which the judge appoints parents' attorneys. This arrangement assures an attorney for the parents but not necessarily one who will vigorously pursue their interests. The reasons for this problem are two—the attorney may not want to be too difficult because he may not receive subsequent appointments and, like the child's attorney, he may be paid for the hearing rather than for how much time he spends on the case, a situation that may discourage investment of time.

Lawyer Roles in Criminal Proceedings

There are just two attorneys involved in a criminal case, the prosecutor and the defense attorney. The victim has no counsel, except in very rare cases where a guardian ad litem is appointed (Toth and Whalen, 1987). Sometimes, however, there is a support person who assists in the preparation of the child for court. This person may be employed by a victim-witness assistance program.

(1) The prosecutor. As noted earlier, in a criminal case, the prosecutor represents "the people." As the police are completing their investigation, they bring their findings to the prosecutor. He or she then makes a decision whether or not to pursue criminal prosecution. He or she may also ask the police to do further investigation. The decision about whether or not to prosecute may turn on a variety of factors. However, probably foremost is whether or not there is a good case, that is, the likelihood that the prosecution will be able to persuade the fact finder (judge or jury) that the child has been sexually abused. This usually depends upon the persuasiveness of the victim as a witness. Because many children who are sexually abused are young, hesitant in describing their maltreatment, and easily intimidated, criminal prosecution only occurs in a small percentage of cases.

(2) The defense attorney. The role of the defense attorney is to gain acquittal for his or her client. If the attorney feels that he or she is going to be unsuccessful in doing that, he or she may negotiate an outcome that is less onerous than the anticipated outcome of the trial. Thus the attorney may have the client plead to a lesser charge, which has a lesser penalty. For example, a sexual act that does not involve penetration will usually carry a mild sentence, sometimes merely probation.

Anyone accused of a crime such as sexual abuse has a legal right to representation. If the defendant cannot afford counsel, the court will appoint one.

Attorney Roles in Divorce Proceedings

Issues that are related to child sexual abuse in a divorce court are custody and visitation. An attorney for a parent might seek change of custody, change of visitation so that it is less frequent or of shorter duration, supervision of visitation, or no visits. Typically, these solutions will be sought against the parent who is alleged to have sexually abused the child, but sometimes they will be sought against the parent who is stating the other sexually abused the child. The latter may be part of a strategy by an attorney who is asserting that his or her client has been wrongfully and maliciously accused.

In a divorce case, each parent will usually be represented, and in some hotly disputed custody/visitation cases, the child will have a guardian ad litem. (See also Chapter 6.)

(1) Parents' attorneys. In most instances, each of the parents will have legal representation. However, unlike child protection and criminal proceedings, there are no legal guarantees of representation. Parents may have to rely

upon legal aid, they may bankrupt themselves to pay attorney's fees, or they may act on their own behalf.

More so than in the legal proceedings described so far, a settlement that is acceptable to both parties is likely to be sought by divorce lawyers. In fact, many divorce courts have mediation services to facilitate settlements. Because of the emphasis on mutually agreed-upon settlements, matters often are resolved without there ever being a formal hearing and without evidence regarding the sexual abuse being heard by the judge (Duquette et al., 1988).

(2) Guardian ad litem. In unusual cases, where the judge feels the child needs someone other than her or his parents to represent her or his best interest, he may appoint a guardian ad litem (Duquette et al., 1988). The role of the guardian ad litem in a divorce proceeding is even less well defined than in a protection proceeding.

Attorney Roles in Damages Cases

Increasingly, adult survivors and guardians on behalf of child victims are suing sexual abusers, institutions where they abused, and insurance companies who provide coverage for these individuals or institutions for money damages. This money is frequently sought to pay for treatment for the victims.

Sometimes the parents of victims will independently decide to take such actions. However, such clients are often sought out by personal injury lawyers. The attorneys involved are those for the complainant, for individuals being sued, and for institutions and their insurance companies.

(1) Attorney for the victim of sexual abuse. Usually lawyers who handle personal injury cases, including those involving sexual abuse, do not request a retainer (money up front) from the client. Their pay will be a proportion of the damages money from the other side, usually one-third. Any expenses, such as payment for expert witnesses, are subtracted before the compensation is divided. The attorney for the victim will argue that she or he has been harmed by the abuse and deserves compensation. Issues that must be proved are that the sexual abuse took place, that the person being charged is responsible, and that current problems are a result of the sexual abuse. A mental health professional might be called to testify on any of these issues.

(2) Attorneys for defendants in damages cases. As noted, these attorneys may represent individuals who are the alleged offenders, individuals in authority positions in a facility where the offense took place, the facility or the facility's board of directors, or the insurance company for the individual

or facility. Often there are several defense attorneys with different clients in such a case. In situations where there have been several victims and the potential costs to the defense are very high, they may spend a lot of money hiring witnesses to support their side, undertaking extensive investigation of the complainant and her or his witnesses, and resorting to procedural maneuvers to prevent resolution and, for them, a negative outcome in the case.

TESTIFYING IN COURT

The most stressful aspect of a mental health professional's involvement with lawyers is testifying in court. This is because the norms for behavior are very different from those that mental health professionals ordinarily adhere to. First, the process is an adversarial one, and, second, the courtroom is a stage, and it is the performance that counts. Each of these issues will be discussed below and suggestions will be offered for maximizing effectiveness and maintaining professional integrity.

The Adversarial Nature of the Court Process

A court of law is supposed to be an arena in which equal parties compete, presenting their various perspectives to be examined by an impartial arbiter, judge or jury, who then makes findings of fact and ultimately decides what the remedy should be.[2] It is assumed that a process in which parties can, by question and answer, develop their own case and challenge that of their adversaries maximizes the presentation of the facts. Although many mental health professionals may question whether a court of law is the optimal arena for getting at the truth and resolving problems, the issue of concern here is how mental health experts should conduct themselves as witnesses. The issues of impartiality, communicating in court, and dealing with hostile questions will be addressed.

(1) Should the mental health expert try to be impartial? A fundamental dilemma for the mental health witness is that she or he may feel caught in the middle of the adversarial process. That is, each party has a particular theory of the case, or viewpoint, and the mental health professional may not entirely agree with any of these. Exacerbating this problem is the fact that usually the witness has been called to testify by one of the sides and that side will expect the witness's testimony to support its case.

To counter this pressure and maintain some degree of impartiality, some mental health professionals take a passive stance. They leave it to the attorney to discover what they might have to say, both favorable and unfavorable, for the attorney's client's case. They avoid having contact with the attorneys outside of the courtroom. They may even avoid forming an opinion about the case or the various actors. One problem about this stance is that very important information related to the case and the well-being of the parties involved may never be heard in court.

I favor a different and partisan stance, but not necessarily one supporting any side in the dispute. Regardless of the mental health professional's role in the case, she or he will have gathered some information (from the case records, the victim, the offender, or others) and usually will have arrived at a diagnosis, formed an opinion, and/or developed some recommendations for intervention. These findings are usually relevant to the questions being considered by the court, and it is these findings that the mental health witness wants to support with testimony in court.

Approaching the court process with this stance is very liberating. It allows the witness to feel fairly comfortable revealing any information that has been considered in coming to an opinion about the case. Typically, the professional will have examined material that is both supportive and damaging to the various parties concerned and, having weighed the material, formed certain conclusions. Thus sharing information that might appear damaging to one side will not damage the professional's credibility because, in fact, it is part of the basis for the conclusions toward which she or he is partisan.

For example, suppose the witness has concluded that an adolescent has been sexually abused by her stepfather, but also that the child is sexually active with her boyfriend. The witness should not hesitate to reveal the sexual activity with the boyfriend because it is a matter already considered and judged not to be a basis for invalidating the assertion of sexual abuse by the stepfather.

An additional advantage of this approach to testifying is that it probably adds to the credibility of the testimony and the witness. Astute fact finders realize that it is the rare situation that is either all black or all white and the unusual individual who is all good or all bad. To provide such one-sided testimony is to damage one's credibility.

In the example that follows, the evaluator for protective services provided testimony that was balanced.

Case example: Dr. X was asked to evaluate the T family, where two children, Betina, 7, and Kathy, 3, were saying Mr. T had sexually abused them. Mr. T was the father of Kathy and the stepfather of Betina.

Mr. and Mrs. T had separate attorneys, the children had an attorney, and the prosecutor represented protective services. Mr. T's attorney wanted testimony supportive of his client's strengths, Mrs. T's weaknesses, the children's emotional disturbance, and his client's innocence. Mrs. T's attorney intended to elicit confirmation of Mr. T's guilt, Mrs. T's protective reaction to discovery of the sexual abuse, and her ability to parent the children with the assistance of her new partner. The children's attorney wanted recommendations for termination of parental rights and no visits with either parent. The prosecutor wanted to elicit information that would substantiate sexual abuse by Mr. T and neglect by Mrs. T, but also a recommendation for intervention that would keep the children with Mrs. T and work toward improving her functioning.

A summary of Dr. X's testimony is as follows: Mr. T had sexually abused the girls, but appeared to feel quite guilty about what he had done. One of the precipitators was the fact that his wife bossed him around and refused to have sex with him. She appeared to be an alcoholic, to have neglected the children before she married Mr. T, and to be neglecting them again now he was out of the home. Mr. T seemed to be the more nurturing and appropriate parent, despite his sexually abusive behavior. Both children reported that they had repeatedly told their mother about the sexual abuse, but she did not do anything until she got a boyfriend and wanted Mr. T out of the house. The children missed their father and wanted him to come back home so their mom wouldn't be so mean to them. They said she hit them with a belt and left them alone while she went to Happy Joe's, a neighborhood bar, with Ronnie, her boyfriend. They did not like Ronnie because he also hit with a belt, but not just on the butt, sometimes on the head.

Dr. X's recommendations to the court were for removal of the children from Mrs. T's care to potentially long-term placement. If an appropriate relative could be found, such a placement would be the first choice. Treatment should be provided to the children with the involvement of their caretakers. There should be supervised visits with both parents. Both Mr. and Mrs. T should receive a six-month trial of treatment to assess their potential for change. Further intervention plans should be made after the six months.

In the T case, the viewpoints of the various parties are more divergent than they are in most, and frequently one or more parties will alter their positions to comply with that of the mental health expert before the case gets to court. Nevertheless, the case illustrates how a mental health expert can take a look at the total picture and arrive at a position that does not entirely support that of any of the parties in the adversarial process.

(2) How to state one's viewpoint in court. Testifying for a viewpoint that does not support one of the parties in an adversarial process is easier said

than done. In fact, probably none of the parties will be interested in having the mental health expert testify regarding the whole picture. Rather, each will be interested in eliciting findings, opinions, and recommendations supportive of his or her side. Three possible strategies may be helpful.

First, it may be advisable for the witness to seek out the attorney whose position is closest to the mental health expert's and persuade that party to ask questions that will allow a full presentation of the expert's findings. Often the argument presented above, that a position that is not too one-sided is more credible, can be used.

Second, the expert should go over the case materials before testifying and decide exactly what points she or he wants to be sure to make. Some experts put these on an index card and refer to them during testimony;[3] others memorize these points. The witness then looks for opportunities when questions are asked to expound the important points. Sometimes this requires creativity and improvisation and occasionally a violation of courtroom etiquette.

For example, taking the T case above, the mother's attorney asked Dr. X, if "on Oct. 22, 1988, when Betina told Mrs. T that her daddy stuck his finger in her wee-wee, didn't Mrs. T throw him out of the house?" Dr. X might merely have answered, "Yes, she did." However, what Dr. X did was to add "but the children informed their mother on at least three previous occasions of the sexual abuse, and she appears to have ignored this. It was only after she took up with Ronnie that she seemed willing to protect the children from Mr. T." Similarly, when the children's attorney asked Dr. X, "Didn't Mr. T repeatedly fondle and penetrate his daughter and stepdaughter over a three-year period?" Dr. X replied, "That is what the children report. Nevertheless, they miss him and appear more attached to him than to their mother."

Attorneys will sometimes object to this more balanced testimony or will ask the expert to merely answer the question posed and not elaborate. The expert should not be surprised that the attorney is displeased. However, the bottom line is the impact on the fact finder, which will be either the judge or the jury. The expert should use their reaction to determine whether to continue to testify emphasizing essential points or to revert to giving the kinds of answers the attorneys want.

Another issue to be sensitive to is whether these essential points, even though they have been made, are becoming obscured. If the testimony goes on for several hours or days, or if other testimony is emphasized, the essential points may not have their impact.

An example of the latter can be taken from the T case. Dr. X stated on direct examination by the prosecutor that, in her opinion, the two girls had been sexually abused, but the father had some strengths and the mother was very dysfunctional. Mr. T's attorney asked numerous questions about Mr. T's strengths: "Didn't he support the family, even though not all the children were his?" "Didn't he keep Mrs. T from being a neglectful parent?" "Didn't the kids miss him?" "Didn't they want him to come home?" "Wasn't he the more nurturant parent?" "Didn't he love the kids?" "Hadn't he made lots of sacrifices for the children?" "Hadn't he endured lots of verbal abuse from Mrs. T to stay with the children?" The attorney also asked comparable questions about Mrs. T's dysfunction. Dr. X responded affirmatively to the attorney's questions, but from time to time added that "it was important to remember that Mr. T also seems to have sexually abused these girls."

A third strategy for making essential points is to use the opportunity at the end of all the direct and cross-examination, when the judge asks questions, as an occasion for getting those points across. The judge's questions may provide the opening or the expert may merely add, "Your honor, there is one more point I want to make." The advantage of waiting till the end of testimony is that it will be a "parting shot." The potential disadvantage is that the judge may not choose to ask any questions or may not be amenable to allowing the expert to make one or more last points.

(3) The adversarial process. One of the most difficult aspects of court testimony for mental health professionals is how one is treated by the adversaries. This treatment violates expectations mental health practitioners have for professional courtesy. Frequently, this goes well beyond distorting the findings or testing the profession's techniques, the expert's assumptions, and the conclusions drawn. Very likely, it includes challenging the expert's competence, suggesting practitioner bias, implying the mental health professional has been bought, alluding to malpractice that is totally fictitious, and asserting that the professional's personal life disqualifies her or his competence. Moreover, both the tone of voice and the way questions are asked may be quite offensive.

To illustrate, an attorney for an alleged offender demeaned the therapist witness because she only had a master's degree in social work, she believed the victim, who was a slut, and she was unmarried and had no children. He punctuated his remarks by throwing his pencil at her and declaring he wouldn't trust her to give him the right time of day.

There are no simple rules of thumb for dealing with these various insults and challenges. However, here are a few suggestions. If there are likely to be challenges to expertise, experience, or bias, it is important to anticipate them and have a considered response.

To give a very simple example, when the attorney asks whether the witness's professional education included material on sexual abuse, the witness can simply point out that most degree programs give scant or no coverage to sexual abuse and note the continuing education workshops attended or books on sexual abuse read. Similarly, if the expert can reasonably anticipate being challenged for always finding sexual abuse or never finding sexual abuse, it is important to have relevant statistics in mind and to point out any biases in the referral process that might cause findings in a particular direction. For example, if the expert only deals with allegations involving very young children, the substantiation rate might be lower than that of persons dealing with older children.

It is also probably a good strategy not to show anger, although there are times when righteous indignation is an appropriate response. Nevertheless, becoming angry may make the witness appear defensive and may give the impression that the expert has stooped to the attorney's level.

Sometimes the attorney who has subpoenaed the expert will object and interrupt an inappropriate or abusive line of questioning. However, the witness should not rely on that possibility. Sometimes an appropriate response to a question is this: "How is that relevant to the issue before the court?" when the attorney begins to inquire about the expert's personal life.

Another possible strategy is appealing to the judge, stating that the line of questioning seems abusive or irrelevant. However, because most judges are also lawyers and they are probably desensitized to these attacks by extensive exposure, they may not be sympathetic.

Finally, a helpful perspective can be to recognize that harassing a witness may ultimately damage an attorney's case. Particularly if a jury is the fact finder, an overall impression that the attorney is "a bad guy" may obscure any points he has scored in his cross-examination. Additional ideas about how to deal with cross-examination will be discussed in the next section.

The Courtroom as a Stage

Mental health witnesses must appreciate the importance of their performance in court. Although the judge and/or jury may also receive the professional's written report and curriculum vitae and refer to these while making decisions, testimony is an opportunity to infuse the written word with the professional's competence, conviction, and integrity. Preparation, dress and demeanor, knowing the fact finder, and responding to questions on direct and cross-examination will be discussed in this section.

(1) Preparation. Like any performance, court testimony requires a great deal of preparation. Depending on the complexity of the case, the expert should expect to spend three to five times as much time in preparation as on the witness stand. The expert should review her or his written report (assuming there is one) so that the material in it is thoroughly familiar. Case characteristics need to be memorized, for example, names, ages, and educational levels of family members, marriage and divorce dates, number of and reasons for protective services referrals, length of time the children have been in placement and names of substitute caretakers, interventions tried with the family, and other professionals involved. If the witness has read other reports or records in coming to conclusions about the case, these need to be reviewed. Notes other than the expert's report should also be reread. If there are audio- or videotapes, it is advisable to go over these. Finally, because time may have passed and family circumstances changed, it is important to ascertain the current status of the family.

The importance of this final point is illustrated by a case in which a mental health expert was subpoenaed to provide testimony about a child whom she had seen a year earlier and determined to have been sexually abused by her stepfather. The mother had divorced the man and left the state with the victim and her younger sister, the offender's biological child. The expert assumed she was to testify about the man's fitness to have supervised access to the children. It was not until she was on the stand that she learned that the mother had abandoned both children and the court was deciding about their custody. The expert's testimony about the fitness of the mother and her appropriate reaction to the discovery of the sexual abuse was irrelevant to the case.

Having reviewed all the documents cited above, the witness decides on the essential points she or he wants to make during testimony, and, as noted above, either commits them to memory or makes notes. Moreover, thorough review of the material will enhance the expert's capability to respond accurately to questions and to critically evaluate questions and the attorney's theory of the case before responding. Committing case characteristics to memory will avoid factual mistakes that can damage the witness's performance. It will also eliminate shuffling through records in a way that interrupts the pace of the testimony and makes the witness appear unprepared, indecisive, or lacking knowledge.

A preparatory interview with the attorney who has issued the subpoena before the court date can be extremely useful, and, if the attorney fails to contact the expert, she or he should seek him out. Sometimes this interview does not occur until just before the hearing and it may be conducted in the hallway at the courthouse. Regardless of when the meeting occurs, it is important to have decided upon the essential points of testimony beforehand. These can then be communicated to the attorney and some negotiation can take place so appropriate questions are asked. Sometimes it is wise to prepare a list of questions for the attorney. Tact needs to be used in conveying these to the attorney, for he or she may regard this as the witness telling him or her how to do his job.

(2) Dress and demeanor. The mental health professional should dress in a manner that shows respect for the court and reflects her or his professional status. A good rule of thumb is dress as the attorneys do. This usually means wearing a suit.

Sit up straight, speak up, and try to portray conviction about the points you are making. One of the somewhat awkward aspects of the court process is that the person who asks the questions is not the person to whom the answers are directed. Attorneys ask the questions but it is the judge and/or jury the witness wants to persuade. To further complicate matters, usually the expert must also speak into a microphone. The expert may look to the attorney as the question is being asked but then turn to the fact finder to respond. The witness does well to keep in mind that testimony is not a contest in which she or he is trying to beat the attorney but an opportunity to persuade the judge and/or jury of her or his viewpoint about the case.

(3) Know the fact finder. Judges are individuals each with his or her unique view of a judge's role, with more or less substantive knowledge about sexual abuse, with varying levels of experience, and with personal opinions that may affect how they perform their role. Examples of the latter follow: Some judges may be skeptical about the performance of protective services workers; others may not believe in rehabilitation for sex offenders; still others may regard children as incompetent witnesses; and some may have no use for mental health testimony. Whenever possible, the mental health witness should try to find out about the judge's background and tailor testimony accordingly. For instance, if the witness discovers that this is the judge's first sexual abuse case, she or he should try to assume an educative role, providing background information about the dynamics of sexual abuse, its treatability, and so forth. Similarly, if the judge thinks children are incompetent, the expert should be prepared to cite the research that supports their competence as witnesses. When the mental health professional meets with the lawyer who has called her or him, questions to elicit appropriate testimony can be arranged.

Juries are more of an unknown quantity than judges. However, in general, they will have much less knowledge about sexual abuse and less mental health expertise than the judge. Therefore, the educative role of the witness will be much more prominent in the testimony. Some jurors may have very little education. Consequently, if the trial is by jury, the expert should give careful consideration about what concepts are absolutely necessary for the jury to understand and then develop an explanation of them in layman's language using concrete illustrations.

For example, suppose the witness needs to explain the "child sexual abuse accommodation syndrome" (Summit, 1983)—that is, the delay in telling about the sexual abuse and recantation—to a jury. The mental health professional might cite Summit's article for the judge's benefit, but then go on to state that children may love and/or fear someone who sexually abuses them, causing them to wait a very long time before telling anyone. The expert would then describe how mom may tell the child to say it didn't happen, dad may also, and the child may feel sorry for dad sitting in jail. Family members may also threaten the child and make her feel bad about all the trouble the family is in.

Moreover, a jury's emotional reactions are likely to play a more prominent role in their decision making than a judge's. In sexual abuse, this may be disbelief: "How could anyone do such a thing to a little child or his own daughter, especially a man who looks so respectable?" Alternatively, jurors may be incensed that someone could harm a child in this way and take a vengeful attitude. In the first instance, the mental health professional needs to focus testimony on the prevalence of sexual abuse and the fact that people who are normal in other respects may, under certain circumstances, sexually abuse a child. In the latter case, it may be important to emphasize the potential for rehabilitation the offender has and the fact that the victim wants him to get help.

There has been research related to jurors' reactions to sexual abuse cases. This does not focus on expert testimony but on jurors' propensity to believe victims (Aman and Goodman, 1987; Goyette and Rosenberg, 1986). This research suggests that, as a rule, jurors are likely to be skeptical about child testimony; however, women are significantly more likely to believe victims than men are. The implication for the mental health professional is that, if the jury is mostly men, more emphasis needs to be placed on the credibility of children's statements about their sexual abuse.

(4) Admissible evidence. It is important for mental health professionals to appreciate that some of the kinds of information they rely on heavily may not be admissible in court. Hearsay, which is any secondhand information or "an out of court statement offered to prove the truth of the matter asserted" (Federal Court Rules, 192-278) may not be admissible. Common examples of the kind of hearsay mental health professionals rely on heavily in sexual

abuse cases are what the child told the professional regarding the sexual abuse or sexual behavior the mother observed and related to the mental health professional. The reason hearsay may not be admissible is because it does not allow the opponent to confront and cross-examine the real witness and expose weaknesses in his testimony (Lilly, 1978, p. 157).

The admissibility of hearsay will depend on the stage of the court process, the state's court rules, the court that is involved, and whether the mental health professional has been qualified as an expert witness or is merely a material witness. Probably the best advice that can be given to the potential witness is to consult with the attorney who has issued the subpoena. However, some general guidelines will be offered.

As a general practice, the court rules, or rules making hearsay inadmissible, will be more closely observed at the trial or adjudication stage of a court proceeding. As noted earlier, other types of hearings are the preliminary, dispositional, review, and termination of parental rights hearings. At any hearing other than a trial, a mental health professional may merely be asked to submit a written report or an affidavit and not be required to testify. The written word is hearsay because the professional is not there to be cross-examined by the accused. Alternatively, if the practitioner does appear, the rules of evidence will usually be relaxed and the witness will be able to include hearsay or rely on hearsay in testimony. However, a termination of parental rights hearing may be considered a new trial, and, if that is the case, rules regarding hearsay will be more strictly applied.

In all state and in federal court rules, there are exceptions to the hearsay rule; that is, information that is hearsay but is acquired in select and clearly defined circumstances will be admissible because it is regarded as inherently reliable. Hearsay exceptions vary from state to state. However, some common exceptions that are used in sexual abuse cases are statements made to the witness by one of the parties to the court proceeding (e.g., the alleged sex offender in a criminal case or the mother of the victim in a protection proceeding), statements made during the course of medical diagnosis and treatment (e.g., the child's assertions about sexual abuse to a medical or mental health professional), and excited utterance (e.g., the child's distressed, spontaneous account of the sexual victimization to a parent or other adult, usually occurring soon after the abuse). Business records (agency records) are allowed as exhibits and can also be relied on in testimony. In addition, the opinion of an expert witness, which may be based in part or wholly on hearsay, will usually be admissible. However, the general admonition made above also applies here: Mental health professionals need to consult with the appropriate attorney regarding what hearsay will be admissible.

Admissibility of hearsay will vary depending upon whether the case is a criminal or a civil one. Testimony will be most circumscribed in a criminal case. In fact, there is very little a mental health professional will be able to attest to in a criminal trial.

If the offender has confessed to the mental health professional, the confession is admissible if the professional has told the offender their relationship is not confidential or if the legal proceeding is one of child protection. However, if the witness is basing her or his opinion that the defendant is the abuser merely on the observation that he has characteristics commonly found among sex offenders, that will not be admissible (Melton, 1987). The expert will not be able to assert the opinion that the child is telling the truth when the child states she or he was sexually abused but may be able to testify that the child's statements are consistent with a true allegation of sexual abuse or that the child's statements and behavior are consistent with the "sexually abused child syndrome" (Lloyd, 1981) or the "child sexual abuse accommodation syndrome" (Summit, 1983). Finally, the expert may be able to testify as a rebuttal witness, that is, to refute assertions made by the defense about the child or other witnesses who are claiming that the offender is guilty of sexual abuse.

Civil proceedings include those related to child protection, divorce, and civil damages. There will be greater flexibility and leeway regarding what a mental health professional can say in hearings in these types of cases and, in general, hearsay is more likely to be admissible. Some states have recently passed legislation that broadens the scope of mental health testimony in these proceedings so as to protect child victims from having to testify.

CONCLUSION

Collaboration with attorneys is perhaps the most challenging task for mental health professionals working with sexually abused children and their families. The purpose of this chapter is to assist the practitioner in understanding the various courts that may be involved, the court process, the orientations of the range of attorneys who may be encountered, court rules, and how to be both effective and ethical in an environment that is antithetical to many mental health values.

NOTES

1. Standards for intervention to protect Native American children are higher. Under the Indian Child Welfare Act (1978), the standard for temporary placement of an Indian child (as

defined by the statute) is clear and convincing evidence, and the standard for permanent custody or termination of parental rights is beyond a reasonable doubt (U.S.C.A. 25, sec. 1912 [e] and [f]).

2. When there is a jury, it will typically be charged with making findings of fact (e.g., in a protection proceeding, whether the parent has neglected the child; in a criminal proceeding, whether the offender is guilty of criminal sexual conduct), but the judge will decide what should be done (e.g., in a protection proceeding, to remove the child from the home; in a criminal case, that the offender should serve 5-15 years in prison). When there is no jury, but only a judge, he or she will decide both questions of fact and disposition.

3. These notes are discoverable, that is, any of the parties may ask to see them and they may be admitted into evidence. However, this will not harm the case or the testimony.

REFERENCES

Aman, Christine and Gail Goodman. 1987. "Children's Use of Anatomically Detailed Dolls: An Experimental Study." Unpublished manuscript (available from Dr. Gail Goodman, Department of Psychology, State University of New York at Buffalo).

Duquette, Donald. 1981. "Legal Aspects of Child Abuse and Neglect." In *Social Work with Abused and Neglected Children*, edited by K. C. Faller. New York: Free Press.

Duquette, Donald, K. C. Faller, and L. D'Aunno. 1988. *Child Protective Services in Michigan: Recommendations for Policy and Practice.* Ann Arbor: University of Michigan, Interdisciplinary Project on Child Abuse and Neglect.

Duquette, Donald and Sarah Ramsey. 1987. "Representation of Children in Child Abuse and Neglect Cases: An Empirical Look at What Constitutes Effective Representation." *Journal of Law Reform* 20(2):341-407.

Goodman, Gail. 1988. "Research on the Credibility of Children as Witnesses." Paper presented at the National Conference on the Victimization of Children, Anaheim, CA, April.

Goyette, Michele and Mindy Rosenberg. 1986. "Adult's Beliefs About Children's Eyewitness Testimony: Perceptions of the Child and Verdict in a Case of Child Sexual Assault." Paper given at the National Conference of Family Violence Researchers, Durham, NH, July.

Indian Child Welfare Act Public Law 95-608. 1978. U.S.C.A. 25 Sec. 1912 (e) & (f).

Lilly, Graham. 1978. *An Introduction to the Law of Evidence.* St. Paul: West.

Lloyd, David. 1981. "The Corroboration of Sexual Victimization of Children." In *Child Sexual Abuse and the Law*, edited by J. Bulkley. Washington, DC: American Bar Association, National Legal Resource Center on Child Advocacy and Protection.

Long, Gregory. 1988. "Legal Issues in Child Sexual Abuse: Criminal Cases and Neglect and Dependency Cases." In *Handbook on Sexual Abuse of Children*, edited by L. A. Walker. New York: Springer.

Melton, Gary. 1987. "Overview of Legal Research." Paper presented at the Family Violence Research Conference for Practitioners and Policymakers, Durham, NH, July.

Summit, Roland. 1983. "The Child Sexual Abuse Accommodation Syndrome." *Child Abuse and Neglect: The International Journal* 7:177-93.

Toth, Patricia and Michael Whalen. 1987. *Investigation and Prosecution of Child Abuse.* Alexandria, VA: National Center for the Prosecution of Child Abuse.

PART III

Assessment and
Case Management

Chapter 5

DECIDING WHETHER OR NOT
SEXUAL ABUSE HAS OCCURRED

The goal of this chapter is to give the mental health professional essential tools for deciding whether or not children have been sexually abused. First, how the diagnostic role of a mental health professional on sexual abuse cases differs from other diagnostic roles will be clarified. Second, a framework and techniques for the mental health professional to use in assessing an allegation of sexual abuse will be provided. Third, a protocol for assessing the veracity of an accusation of sexual abuse, with illustrative material, will be presented. Fourth, the controversy related to the reliability of children's statements and relevant research will be discussed. And, fifth, the issue of deciding what is credible evidence of sexual abuse, and pertinent research, will be covered.

THE ROLE OF THE
MENTAL HEALTH PROFESSIONAL

Being required to determine whether or not a child has been sexually abused is a new responsibility for mental health professionals. Traditionally, they have not been asked this kind of question. In order to appreciate how this role diverges from typical roles, it is useful to briefly characterize the diagnostic questions ordinarily posed for mental health professionals. They are asked what individuals, couples, or families are like and why they are the way they are. Mental health professionals answer these questions by administering psychological tests, taking social histories, observing behavior, interviewing clients, talking to others involved with the clients, and reading past records. The diagnosis may be expressed in the form of a specific disorder (e.g., schizophrenia, borderline personality, or adjustment reaction) or in a descriptive statement about the client's problems. In addition, mental health professionals have traditionally been asked: What should be done about the findings? Is therapy necessary? If so, what sort of therapy? Is hospitalization required? Should the client be removed from the family? Will medication help?

The role of mental health professionals in cases of physical abuse and neglect is generally quite close to their traditional role. For, even in cases of physical abuse and neglect, mental health professionals are not usually the ones who determine whether maltreatment has occurred. Physical abuse is likely to result in bodily injury, which is generally diagnosed by a physician. Neglect is evidenced in the child's physical condition (e.g., the child is dirty, poorly clothed, or hungry) or the conditions of the home (e.g., there is no food in the house, there is no heat, the plumbing is not working, or the home is dangerous to children).

Typically, in cases of physical maltreatment, the questions asked of mental health professionals are of the following sort: Why did the parents do it? What psychological harm has the child experienced? Are the parents amenable to treatment? If so, what sort of treatment? Does the child need treatment?

Sexual abuse is somewhat different from other types of maltreatment because physical evidence of the abuse is unlikely. Therefore, the expertise of physicians and observers of physical conditions are much less useful. However, mental health professionals are not the only ones asked to address the question: "Did the sexual abuse happen?" In most cases, the first persons who try to answer this question are child protection workers and the police. Nevertheless, because of the constraints of their roles, as well as, in some cases, their lack of expertise, mental health professionals may also be asked to be involved. In fact, it is quite common, after a police or protection investigator has concluded his or her inquiry, for him or her to refer the case to a mental health professional for a second opinion. This may be deemed appropriate because the investigator is not sure about the abuse, because other questions aside from the likelihood of sexual maltreatment must be addressed, or because an "expert" is needed to buttress the conclusions of the investigator.

Mental health professionals must adapt their traditional skills and take on a few new ones if they are to address the question: "Did sexual abuse occur?"

GUIDELINES FOR ASSESSMENT

In order to conduct an assessment of sexual abuse that will be of value in elucidating what happened, the evaluator must have a thorough understanding of the typical dynamics of sexual abuse disclosure and a clear view of the criteria to be employed in validating or invalidating an allegation.

Focus on the Child's Statements and Behavior

There appears to be a fair amount of consensus among mental health professionals about both the strategy and the criteria for deciding whether a child has been sexually victimized (Conte et al., 1988; Corwin, 1988; Faller, 1984, 1988; Jones and McQuiston, 1986; McCarty, 1981; Sgroi, 1982; Walker, 1988).[1] The main indices for determining the truth of an allegation of sexual abuse are the child's statements and behavior. Therefore, the interview with and/or evaluation of the child is the most important part of the investigation of an allegation of sexual abuse. An interview and assessment of the alleged offender almost always results in a denial, and, therefore, its primary value is for understanding the dynamics of the sexual abuse; what treatment, if any, might be successful; and the treatment prognosis. This general assertion does not rule out the need to interview the offender and other significant people in the child's life. The evaluator will always consider other explanations for the child's statements and behavior, and an interview with the alleged offender or others may well assist in either ruling these out or coming to a conclusion that something other than sexual abuse better explains the evidence. The example below is illustrative.

> *Case example:* Lucy, 5, and Jane, 6, were sisters who reported having been digitally penetrated by their mother's boyfriend. When they were interviewed by protective services, they stated they had told their mother several times about this abuse. Because the mother had difficulty believing her boyfriend would do such a thing, the children were removed and placed with their paternal grandmother. The girls, their mother, and the grandmother were referred to a sexual abuse treatment program.
>
> The grandmother was highly suspicious of the mother. While the girls were with the grandmother, she questioned them extensively about their mother's habits. The grandmother informed the therapist that Lucy and Jane had told her that their mother also "put fingers in their pussies."

The therapist interviewed the girls and they indeed reported that their "momma touched and rubbed our pussies." This happened in the bathroom. She used her hand and a wash cloth.

The mother was confronted with their statements. She said that Jane did not wash her vaginal area and that, on more than one occasion, the mother had to spread Jane's legs and forcibly clean her. She asserted she used a cloth, not her hand.

The therapist concluded that probably no sexual abuse took place involving the mother; that she had been cleaning the girls, but that they perceived the incidents as comparable to the sexual abuse by the mother's boyfriend.

In this case, the mother did not deny the behavior and there is a great deal of similarity in what the children describe and what their mother admitted to. It was assumed that the discrepancy resulted from distortions caused by the grandmother's rather pointed questioning, a failure to recall or report some use of the hand by the mother, or a mistaken perception of the children. However, there still is the question of intent on the part of the mother. Was the behavior a sexual act disguised as child care or was it merely child care? The therapist concluded that it was the latter. However, in her treatment, she emphasized the importance of letting the girls wash themselves and was alert for any other indications that the mother might be a sexual abuser. None was found.

There will also be cases where the child interview is inconclusive, and interviews with the offender and others will assist the evaluator in understanding the situation. For instance, the child may be quite vague but she suggests perhaps that something sexual has happened.

Illustrative is the case of an 11-year-old girl who stated that she and her dad had secrets. At one point, she said she could not remember what these were; at another, she stated they were about bad touching; and at yet another point, she indicated they were about her mom's birthday party. When the father was interviewed, he noted how attractive his daughter's body was, particularly now that she is developing. He also commented that it is unfortunate that, when his daughter grows older, her mother will persuade her to wear a bra. Finally, he stated that he does not regard fondling as particularly harmful to children, but he would never engage in intercourse with a child. In this case, the father's statements were very worrisome, and the evaluator concluded that either there had been sexual abuse or there was a potential for sexual abuse, and the daughter and both parents required treatment. The daughter was removed from the home, however, for educational neglect rather than probable sexual abuse.

Motivations of the Victim, the Offender, and the Nonoffending Parent to Lie at the Time of Disclosure

A mental health evaluator must appreciate that the assessment process is not a contest between the child and the offender to see whose story is the most persuasive and convincing. Children have very little to gain by making a false allegation of sexual abuse. In fact, they may think they have little to gain by disclosing an actual situation of sexual abuse, often because the offender has continually admonished them not to tell and has threatened dire consequences that will result. The child may have been threatened with loss of love of the offender or a nonoffending caretaker, loss of family because of placement in an institution or a foster home, loss of friends and playmates, or loss of life. In addition, the offender may warn her that she will be held responsible for all sorts of negative outcomes, such as marital breakup, imprisonment of the offender, family financial hardship, the nonoffending parent's mental anguish, and coercive intervention into the family.

In addition, the victim may be highly intimidated by the prospect of talking about the sexual abuse because of what others might think of her and her family as well as because of specific threats the offender may have made. Moreover, if she tells, she is, in fact, very likely to suffer greatly as the threats, such as removal from the home, rejection by the family, and arrest of the offender, begin to come true.

In contrast, the offender will be most unlikely to admit to his sexually abusive behavior because the consequences of discovery are potentially devastating. They include loss of custody of the child, loss of spouse or family, in some cases, loss of employment, and loss of liberty (the offender may end up in jail or prison). In addition, for him as well there may be social stigma and personal shame attached to disclosure.

Although the nonoffending parent is more likely than the abuser to acknowledge or accept the victimization and to respond appropriately to the victim, this caretaker may also deny, disbelieve, or discount the allegation, especially in intrafamilial sexual abuse cases. A great deal is at stake if the sexual abuse is validated. The nonoffending parent must acknowledge shortcomings as a parent and often as a spouse. In addition, she must decide whether to remain with or leave the offender and must deal with the practical consequences of that decision. Finally, the nonabusive caretaker must cope with professionals, who, at least for a period of time, will play an intrusive role in the family.

The dynamics related to disclosure discussed here are likely to result in a reluctance on the part of a victim to describe sexual abuse and sometimes retraction as the child experiences the consequences of telling, despite the veracity of the accusation (Summit, 1983). Moreover, these dynamics usually result in adamant denial by the offender and a reluctance to believe by the nonoffending parent.

Techniques for Eliciting Information About Sexual Abuse from Children

Over the past five years, there has been increasing attention focused on how to interview children regarding possible sexual abuse. To a considerable extent, this interest has been in response to criticisms of the interview techniques of those evaluating sexual abuse cases. Criticisms have been based primarily on a view that interviewers might be eliciting false positives rather than false negatives. In response to these concerns, some professionals (Boat and Everson, 1988; White et al., 1986; Yuille, 1988) have advocated the use of a protocol when interviewing children. However, the danger of having a protocol is that it might too rigidly dictate the activities of the evaluator, who must be flexible to the particulars of the case and the needs of the child. Instead, I favor general guidelines for evaluators and the capability of addressing the allegations in a variety of ways. I also recommend exploring the possibility of sexual abuse using more than one approach before concluding that the child has or has not been sexually abused.

The discussion in this section will be in two parts, the use of media in interviewing children and techniques for asking questions. However, the reader must appreciate that this division is artificial, for, in an actual evaluation, media are used in combination with questions.

(1) Media that are useful in interviewing children. A variety of media have been successfully employed in interviewing children alleged to have been sexually abused. The choice of medium will vary depending upon the child's age, the child's response to various media, and the circumstances of the alleged sexual abuse. In addition, evaluators may be more familiar or feel more comfortable with particular assessment techniques and, therefore, have preferences.

In a recently completed survey of 212 professionals who evaluate sexual abuse cases in 40 states, Conte and colleagues (1988) report the following findings regarding techniques for interviewing children: 92% report using anatomically explicit dolls, 50% use other dolls, 66% use anatomically correct drawings, 88% employ free drawings, 47% use puppets, 28% employ psychological tests, and 4% use the polygraph.

Although this study indicates that use of anatomically explicit dolls is the most widely employed technique, certainly it is not the only technique, nor should it be. However, anatomically explicit dolls have the distinct advantage of having sexual parts, which can markedly improve and facilitate communication between the evaluator and the child. Thus the evaluator knows for sure what a "dinky" is because the child points to the "dinky" on the doll. Similarly, the interviewer clearly understands what "doing the wingding" (fellatio) is because the child demonstrates this activity with the dolls. There are a variety of ways to use the dolls, but probably the least leading is by having the child show with the dolls what happened and asking questions about what the child demonstrates.

However, there are a variety of dolls that are not anatomical that have considerable utility in these evaluations. Doll house people have the advantage of coming in sets representing families as well as being in a house; both circumstances that may be found in the victim's experience of abuse. Other types of dolls are also useful. Because dolls without private parts are much cheaper than those with parts, the clinician can afford to have dolls of both sexes representing different aged children and children of different races. Having dolls similar in these characteristics to the interviewees may facilitate the children's ability to identify with the doll and use the doll to represent themselves in talking to the evaluator. Barbie and Ken dolls (and their variants) have been found useful in sexual abuse interviews. Their rather sexual bodies may facilitate expression of sexual material. In addition, a Barbie variant, the Sunshine family, which includes young children, may trigger interactions between adults and children, including sexual interactions. Even paper dolls can be employed in sexual abuse evaluations. The clothing usually comes off paper dolls, which may facilitate discussions of what happens when clothing is removed.

Free drawings are appropriate for somewhat older children. Standardized projective drawings such as the house, tree, person, or the "draw a person" may be less instructive than asking the child to draw a picture of the alleged offender, the sexual abuse, or where the abuse happened. However, other fairly standard drawing tasks, such as asking the child to draw a picture of him- or herself and respond to questions about the picture, or doing the Kinetic Family Drawing (a picture of the child's family doing something) may be quite enlightening.

In using puppets, the evaluator may employ a puppet to ask the child questions or both the evaluator and the child can use puppets, so that, for example, Mr. Fox (employed by the evaluator) asks Mr. Bear (employed by the victim) what happened to Sally (the victim). There are even anatomically explicit puppets that can be used in these assessments.

It should be noted that a rather small proportion of respondents to Conte and colleagues (1988) use psychological tests. This is because most psychological tests are not structured to elicit material that is conclusive of sexual abuse. They are more helpful in evaluating the child's overall functioning, eliciting findings that might be consistent with having been sexually abused, and assessing characteristics courts often consider to be related to the reliability of the child's statements.

Another, as yet unvalidated but very promising, instrument for eliciting statements from children is Projective Story Telling Cards (Caruso, 1987). These cards depict scenes that could represent sexual abuse, physical abuse, neglect, and family conflict. They can be used in a manner similar to the TAT in that the child is asked to tell the evaluator what is happening in the picture.

In general, the media just discussed enhance a child's ability to communicate in two ways. Some media, such as anatomical and other dolls and anatomically explicit drawings, allow the child to demonstrate what has happened. The purpose of using them is, therefore, to have the children both show and tell, although some children will primarily show. Because young children are likely to be less skilled at communicating verbally than behaviorally, techniques that allow them to demonstrate what happened are likely to elicit a clearer picture of the abuse than mere language. In addition, children are likely to be more adept at communicating behaviorally because their experience with play is akin to these modes of expression.

Nevertheless, it is inappropriate to conclude, based solely on a child's demonstration of sexual activities with dolls or other media, that a child has been sexually abused. If the child shows sexual acts with the dolls, the evaluator must ask, "Who does that?" or "Where did you learn about that?" or "What does that feel like?"

The second advantage of media is that they allow children to share difficult material in an indirect way. For example, with puppets, the child can have the puppet describe the abuse. With Projective Story Telling Cards, the child tells what is happening in the picture, rather than what happened to her. And, even with dolls, the evaluator can give the doll a name other than the child's, and then query if there is something that is worrying the doll or if the doll has some secrets. Because young children may feel more comfortable describing a traumatic event once removed, so to speak, they may be more forthcoming.

If the evaluator elicits material indirectly that supports sexual abuse, it is necessary to ask the child directly if these things also happened to the child. This additional exploration is especially important when the child's statements or behavior include general themes rather than explicit descriptions. The case that follows is illustrative.

Case example: Nadine, 9, came from a multiproblem family, which had been involved with child protective services for physical abuse and neglect for a number of years. Finally, she and her four siblings were removed from the home and placed in foster care. While in care, the children were noted to engage in sexually aggressive behavior, and their worker became concerned about possible sexual abuse.

Nadine was evaluated using the Projective Story Telling Cards, anatomically explicit dolls, and direct questions. Her story in response to card A24, which shows a man lying on his back on a bed and a female child of about 4 on top of him in an intercourse position, both of them clothed, was concerning. She said that the father was thinking about raping the little girl. When asked what rape meant, Nadine said that the father would take all his daughter's clothes off. As to what would happen next, she replied she did not know. She appeared quite distraught and would say nothing further about the card. She denied ever knowing anyone who was raped, ever knowing someone who had raped another person, and anyone wanting or trying to rape her.

She was shown two other cards involving men and children in circumstances that might suggest sexual abuse. To the second card, she again described the people as a father and daughter. However, when recounting what was happening in the card, she hesitated and said, "No, he's just going to hurt her." She said she didn't know how he was going to hurt her. Her response to the third card was similar to that of the second.

Because of these worrisome responses, the evaluator introduced the anatomically explicit dolls. Nadine was questioned using the dolls but denied knowledge of the names for the body parts, anyone ever doing anything to her private parts, ever seeing anyone else's private parts, ever being asked to do anything to someone else's private parts, or any observation of sexual activity. She was also asked questions related to sexual activity involving her siblings and whether her uncle or father had ever done anything to her private parts. All of these questions elicited negative replies.

The evaluator concluded that some of Nadine's responses to projective techniques were suggestive of possible sexual abuse but that no conclusion could be drawn on the basis of the evaluation. Therapy was recommended, with one issue being further exploration of possible sexual victimization.

Some mental health professionals might find the information given by Nadine sufficient to conclude that sexual abuse occurred. That is, not only does she provide one very suggestive story but she appears to avoid disclosing material elicited by subsequent cards. Moreover, her assertion that she has no names for the private parts and has never seen private parts (when she has three brothers) suggests significant discomfort with sexual matters. However, there are other possible explanations for her reactions. For example, given her family's functioning and considering her age, she may well have been exposed to sexual material in ways other than by having been sexually abused. Her avoidance and discomfort may be related to attitudes in her family about sex and nakedness and not to sexual victimization.

(2) Techniques for questioning children. Questions may be employed to elicit information independent of the use of media such as those described above, or they can be used in conjunction with media.

Although the evidence suggests that children are not led by inappropriate questioning techniques (Goodman, 1988), it nevertheless is prudent to ask about sexual abuse in such a way as to facilitate the child's disclosure rather than using questions that suggest the response (i.e., leading questions). The evaluator must nevertheless live with the reality that some children will require leading questions in order to disclose their sexual abuse. Thus the evaluator should begin with open-ended questions but should resort to more close-ended questions if the former do not facilitate description of sexual abuse. However, the evaluator should be more tentative in concluding that sexual abuse has occurred based upon responses to leading questions.

Even though the interviewer will use open-ended questions, these cannot be as open-ended as they might be with some adults. For example, in assessing an adult rape victim, a mental health professional might ask the person general questions, such as how they have been feeling or why they are here today, and elicit an account of the rape. General questions are much less likely to lead to a discussion of sexual abuse by a child. Moreover, children will need more prompting and probing questions than adults.

(a) Focused questions. The term "focused question" refers to questions that are directed toward the possible context of the sexual abuse but are open-ended. There are several types of focused questions that evaluators of sexually abused children typically employ. Some focus on the possible

offender, others on body parts, and still others on the circumstances of the sexual abuse.

(i) Person-focused questions. One of the most useful types of focused questions is directed toward significant persons in the child's life, including the alleged offender. The evaluator asks these sorts of questions about most of the important people in the child's life, usually beginning with persons who have positive relationships with the child and delaying discussion of the possible offender until close to the end of this line of questioning. If there is more than one possible offender, or if one of the involved parties is likely to suggest that the perpetrator is someone else (e.g., an older brother rather than the father or the stepfather rather than the biological father), the evaluator should try to ask about all possible perpetrators. The child is asked questions such as the following:

Does your mom/dad have another name in addition to mom or dad?
(If so) What is it?
Where does your mom/dad live?
How do you get along with your mom/dad?
What sorts of things do you do with your mom/dad that you like?
Is there anything she/he does that you don't like?
(If so) What don't you like?
If the child gives a response unrelated to sexual abuse, the evaluator will ask if there is anything else the parent does that the child doesn't like.
Is there anything your mom/dad does to your body that you don't like?
Do you have any worries about things your mom/dad does?
(If so) What?

As the reader can see, the initial questions are neutral. Additional neutral questions, such as "Do you know where your dad works?" can be asked before focused questions about possible abuse are asked. If the evaluator elicits material indicative of sexual abuse, he or she will pursue the allegation further using additional focused questions as well as other types of questions described below.

(ii) Questions focusing on the body parts. Another type of focused question relates to the child's experience with or knowledge about body parts. Such questions flow most naturally from the child's identification and naming of body parts using anatomically explicit dolls or pictures. The following are examples of focused questions that might elicit relevant information:

Questions related to the penis (assuming the offender is a male)

Who has one of those?

If the child responds my brother, ask if anyone else has one.

What is it for?

If the child answers that it's for going pee, ask if it does anything else.

Did you ever see one?

If the child responds yes, the evaluator asks whose.

(Then) When did you see it?

What do daddies (men) do with it?

Does it ever do things you don't like?

(If so) What?

Did you ever touch one?

(If so) Whose?

Did anyone ever want you to or make you touch theirs?

(If so) Who?

Does anything ever come out of it?

(If yes) What? What color stuff?

Did you ever have to put one in your mouth?

(If so) Whose?

What was penis in the mouth like?

Questions related to the vagina (assuming the victim is a female)

Who has one of these?

What do you do with yours?

Do you know how yours got hurt?

Has anyone ever touched yours?

Has anyone ever done anything to yours?

If the child responds affirmatively to either of the two previous questions, the child should be asked who did this and what they did it with.

Has anyone ever tried to touch yours?

Has anyone ever wanted to put something in yours?

(If so) What?

Questions about body parts should, of course, be varied according to the sex of the alleged perpetrator and victim. However, it is a good idea to ask the child questions about both male and female private parts. Often the contrast between the child's responses related to the alleged offender's genitalia and a nonoffending parent can be enlightening. In addition, a substantial percentage of children are sexually abused by more than one person (Faller, forth-coming) and sometimes adults of both sexes (Faller, 1987). Thus it is prudent to ask about all private parts in order to assess whether there are other potential offenders.

(iii) Questions focused on the circumstances of the sexual abuse. Focused questions about the circumstances of the sexual abuse can relate to environmental circumstances, how the offender characterizes the abuse, or how the offender induces the child not to tell. Possible questions are as follows:

Is there a reason why you don't like to stay with your mom's boyfriend?

What do you do when you stay up late at night?

What do you do when you go over to grandpa's?

Do you ever play games with your dad?

(If so) What kind of games?

Do you have any secrets in your family?

(If so) What secrets?

What does your mom get mad at your dad about?

Does anyone help you take a bath?

(If so) Who and how do they help you?

Where do you sleep at your house?

If the child responds she or he sleeps with someone, the evaluator should ask if anything happens when she or he sleeps with that person.

Do you go to the bathroom by yourself?

(If no) Who helps you and what do they do to help?

What does your dad do when he drinks?

Does your dad have parties?

(If yes) Can you tell me about the parties?

The evaluator will usually have some idea of the circumstances of the alleged sexual abuse that will guide the kind of focused questions to be asked.

Often the possible context of the sexual abuse must be asked about in several different ways before relevant information is elicited. A large percentage of children will be reluctant to reveal the negative things that happen, for example, at grandpa's or at night, and will say "I don't know," "I don't remember," or will relate neutral or positive events. Children may need to become convinced that the interviewer really does want to know or that the advantages of telling outweigh the disadvantages.

(b) Multiple-choice questions. Multiple-choice questions should be considered if the child does not respond to focused questions. Multiple-choice

questions are more likely to be asked about the context of the victimization rather than the sexual behavior. In addition, when asking multiple-choice questions, the interviewer tries to anticipate all the possible choices and pose them for the child, to avoid putting the child in the position of having to choose between two or more wrong answers. Thus if the child responds that she has touched a penis, but does not answer when asked whose, the evaluator should ask whether it was her dad's, her uncle's, or someone else's, not merely whether it was the father's or the uncle's. The following are some examples of multiple-choice questions:

> Did it happen before you went to bed or after you went to bed, or both?
>
> If the child does not respond to the question, "What were you wearing?" the interviewer might ask if the child was wearing her day clothes or night clothes.
>
> Similarly, the victim could be asked whether her clothes were on, off, or some on and some off.
>
> If the child says "I don't know" when asked how many times the abuse happened, the evaluator could ask if it happened one time, two times, or lots of times.
>
> If the child says she can't remember what the offender said, the evaluator might ask if the offender said anything about telling or not telling.

It is preferable to elicit responses to focused questions rather than to multiple-choice ones. However, some children have a great deal of difficulty describing their sexual abuse and need more directed questions. A good indicator that the child is describing a genuine experience is when he or she puts the response into his or her own words rather than using one of the response choices. An example would be a child who is asked if she was wearing her day clothes or night clothes and replies she had on her pink nightie with the blue bow.

(c) Questions requiring a yes or no answer. Somewhat less preferable are questions that require the child to answer yes or no. They should be used when other more open-ended questions do not elicit responses. Some critics have argued that yes-no questions suggest their answers, that is, affirmative ones. However, this need not be the case. The evaluator can just as easily ask questions that expect a negative response as ones where the reply is anticipated to be positive.

Nevertheless, if yes-no questions are used, the evaluator should be alert to a pattern of answers that is either all positive or all negative. The former may signal social desirability responses, and the latter may indicate the child does not want to answer or is being oppositional. At times, it is a good strategy to interject a question that should elicit a reply the opposite of the child's pattern of responses, for example, ask a question whose response is yes (did you come here with your mom today?) when the child is providing only no answers. The child's answer to the question then provides a context for discussing why the child is persistently giving negative responses.

Sometimes an evaluator has the experience of a child contradicting earlier statements, usually by denying earlier assertions of sexual abuse. It is appropriate to raise this issue with the child. For example, the evaluator may say, "Is that what you told your mother?" when, for example, the child denies that grandfather did anything. Many children will respond by saying no, and then the evaluator asks what the child told her or his mother. Then the evaluator asks which statement is true.

Examples of yes-no questions are as follows:

Was your mother there? An evaluator might ask this question when "Where was your mother?" did not elicit sufficient information.

Did your father do something to your pee-pee? If the child answers affirmatively, the interviewer can revert to a more open-ended question, "What did he do?"

Did he use his penis? This question can be asked if the child has stated that her dad has hurt her pee-pee but did not respond to a focused or multiple-choice question about what he hurt her with.

Did he touch your sister's privates, too?

Did he tell you not to tell?

(d) Leading questions. Leading questions are not appropriate when an evaluator is trying to find out what happened from a child. However, such questions are used in interrogation or cross-examination when the questioner is trying to get the interviewee to affirm what he or she already believes to be the facts. Much more than yes-no questions, leading questions indicate the desired answer.

The following are examples of leading questions:

He put his finger inside your pee-pee, didn't he?

She told you to say it was your brother, not your father, who did it. Isn't that right?

Didn't he want you to suck his dick?

Haven't you lied to your parents before?

(3) A final admonition. Even when the interviewer has an array of possible techniques and a clear sense of how to go about questioning a child, the task is not an easy one. Although there are some children who will readily describe their sexual victimization, they are the exception rather than the rule. Most

children will have a great deal of trouble indicating what they have experienced. Many fears and inhibitions must be overcome, and the child may only say a few words about her victimization to an evaluator. A great deal of patience is required, and often several interviews are necessary. Moreover, many children do not tell despite efforts of interviewers to facilitate their disclosure. Therefore, the outcome of some evaluations is a failure to substantiate because of insufficient information from the child. It may be important for the evaluator to emphasize that failure to substantiate does not mean that sexual abuse did not occur.

INDICES FOR DETERMINATION

As noted above, the statements and behavior of the child are the primary sources of documentation of sexual abuse. Even though false allegations by children are quite rare, it is essential for the careful investigator to systematically examine the child's responses, verbal and nonverbal, for characteristics that are considered indicative of a true allegation. There are three aspects of the child's statement and behavior that should be explored: (1) the child's ability to describe or demonstrate specific sexual acts, (2) the child's ability to indicate the context of the sexual abuse, and (3) the child's emotional reaction when describing the sexual abuse. Findings will not be expected in all three areas, but, without some characteristics indicative of a true allegation, the investigator will not be able to validate the case. (As already noted, the absence of validation does not necessarily mean that sexual abuse did not occur. It merely means that the investigator could not make a positive finding that sexual abuse occurred.)

The protocol that follows is to be used by persons undertaking investigations of sexual abuse.

PROTOCOL FOR DETERMINING THE
LIKELIHOOD SEXUAL ABUSE OCCURRED

I. *The child's ability to describe (either verbally or behaviorally) the sexual behavior*—the statement or behavior preferably will be made in the presence of the investigator but could be provided to (1) another professional or (2) a nonprofessional

   A. Sexual knowledge beyond what would be expected for the child's developmental stage
      Examples:
      A prepubescent child knows what penetration feels like.

A prepubescent child knows what semen tastes like.

A prepubescent child knows that "white stuff" comes out of the penis.

B. Sexual behavior described from a child's viewpoint

Examples:

A 7-year-old child states that "snot came out of my dad's dinky."

A 4-year-old child asserts the offender "tried to suck pee out of my wiener."

A 9-year-old child says "he put his ding-dong in my mouth and I choked."

C. Explicit accounts of sex acts

Examples:

A 5-year-old child says "he put his pecker between my legs and rubbed back and forth."

A 7-year-old child says "his dick went squirt, squirt and the white yucky stuff drooled on the floor."

II. *The child's ability to describe the context of the sexual abuse*—it is expected that the child will be able to provide three or more details about the context of the victimization; these might include information about the following:

A. Where it happened

1. The address
2. Whose house
3. Which room in the house

B. When it happened (the child's location of the event in time will be in terms of events and times significant to the child)

Examples:

"When Daddy was on a trip."

"On the day I don't go to day care."

"When Mom was at the store."

"After I went to bed."

C. What the offender said to obtain the child's involvement

Examples:

The child tells the interviewer that "Mom's boyfriend gave me candy for sucking his dick."

The child says her stepdad told her he wouldn't love her anymore if she didn't let him "touch my peepee."

D. Where other family members were

Example:

When the worker asks where her mom would be, the victim replies "at the store" or "doing the laundry."

E. What the victim was wearing

Example:

The victim says she was "wearing my pink and white party dress" and the offender told her they were "going to have a party."

    F. What clothing was removed

       Example:

       In response to a question about whether any clothing was taken off, the victim replies "my panties and my shorts."

    G. What the offender was wearing

       Example:

       The child tells the worker the offender was wearing "his green shorts and he took them off."

    H. What clothing of his was removed

    I. The child's description of her or his emotional state during the abuse (children might describe being scared, feeling bad, or being confused)

    J. Whether the offender said anything about telling or not telling

       Examples:

       The victim says the offender told her he would "kill my mom" if she told.

       The victim states the offender told her that he would say it was her idea and she would be blamed.

    K. Whether the child told anyone

       Example:

       The child said she told her mom and her mom said "don't tell anyone."

    L. Reactions of persons the child has told

       Example:

       Grandmother, in whom the victim has confided, tells her her daddy must be sick.

III. *The child's affect when recounting sexual abuse*—showing an emotional reaction while describing the sexual abuse is less common with boys and very young children (i.e., 2- and 3-year-olds); the following are common emotional reactions to disclosure:

    A. Reluctance to disclose

       Example:

       The child was quite talkative and bubbly until the worker mentions the secrets she told the teacher. She then hangs her head and says "I don't remember."

    B. Embarrassment (common with younger children)

       Example:

       The child covers her face as she describes how she had to "touch the boy's dick."

    C. Anger (more common with boy victims than girls)

       Example:

       The child throws the anatomical male doll across the room and says "he's a bad man."

    D. Anxiety (more common with adolescent girls)

Example:
The victim begins to cry and has difficulty speaking when asked to describe the sexual acts.

E. Disgust (more common when describing oral sex)

Example:
When asked to describe what happened, the child says "yuck, it makes me want to puke!"

F. Sexual arousal (more common with younger and emotionally disturbed children)

Example:
The little boy begins to play with his penis as he responds to questions about the sexual abuse.

G. Fear (common if the offender has threatened the victim with dire consequences of disclosure)

Example:
The child begs the worker "don't tell daddy I told."

IV. *Medical evidence*—only found in about 10%-20% of cases; the probability of medical findings is greater with younger children, acute abuse, and the availability of a skilled medical examiner (most medical evidence will be described as consistent with or suggestive of sexual abuse rather than as conclusive)

V. *Confession of the offender*—full confession during evaluation and investigation occurs in only about 10% of cases

A. Complete confession

Example:
The offender admits to all the sexual abuse described by the victim.

B. Partial confession

Example:
The offender admits to some but not all sexual abuse described by the victim. Typically, the admission is to lesser acts (e.g., nonpenetration).

C. Indirect admission

Example:
The offender indicates without directly stating so that he sexually abused the child (e.g., he says the child wouldn't lie; that he accidentally mistook the child for his wife).

VI. *Other witnesses*

A. Children
   1. Victims
   2. Nonvictims
B. Adults
   1. Nonoffending parent
   2. Other adult

The Appendix, which appears at the end of this chapter, is a checklist for coding findings from this protocol.

THE RELIABILITY OF CHILDREN'S STATEMENTS

Several related issues have been raised regarding the reliability of children's assertions that they have been sexually abused. First is the possibility that they are confusing reality with fantasy. The second is that children are suggestible and, therefore, are at risk for being duped by adults (or possibly other children) into making false allegations. Third, the adequacy of children's memories has been questioned. Finally, a concern is that children feel less of an obligation to tell the truth than adults because they do not adequately appreciate the impact of their false allegations.

Allegations of Sexual Abuse as Fantasy

The origin of the concern that children are fantasizing when they allege sexual abuse has been attributed to Freud (Goodwin, 1988; Lerman, 1988; Masson, 1984). Freud initially regarded the source of the mental disorder, hysteria, to be sexual victimization during childhood, but, later, as he encountered scores of women with a reported history of sexual abuse and as he experienced rejection of his theory by colleagues, he concluded that the problem could not be so prevalent. He then decided that these accounts were fantasy rather than reality. An interesting twist to this transformation of allegations into fantasy is that not only were they then seen as having their origins in the victim, rather than the offender, but they were also viewed as positive for the victim. That is, she wished to have sex with her father and, therefore, developed a fantasy that this had happened.

Probably the most important factor in changing this interpretation of children's allegations has been the prevalence rates of sexual abuse documented in research conducted on adult populations (e.g., Finkelhor, 1979, 1984; Russell, 1983, 1984, 1986; Wyatt, 1985). When between one-fifth and two-thirds of the adult female population and a tenth to a sixth of the adult male population are reporting sexual abuse during childhood, children's statements cannot be passed off as merely the wish on the part of the child to have sex with an adult. Moreover, developmental psychologists have asserted that children really cannot fantasize about something that is out of their realm of experience. When children describe intimate and realistic details about sexual activity, the logic of attributing these assertions to the child's imagination is hard to support.

Children's Suggestibility

Some critics (e.g., Wakefield and Underwager, 1988) have argued that children are very suggestible and more likely to be influenced into making false assertions than adults. They contend that parents and professionals are guilty of subtly or not so subtly influencing children to make false allegations of sexual abuse when these adults are convinced that the children have been sexually abused and communicate this belief in their mode of questioning. Because children are vulnerable to being influenced by people in authority, they respond in the manner these parents and professionals wish them to.

The research studies Wakefield and Underwager cite to support these assertions are of two kinds. The first is a variety of social psychological studies, primarily of college students, in which intentional deception on the part of the experimenter is involved. Although the findings—such as that subjects can be deceived and that interviewer bias may affect results—give additional support for the kind of interviewing and systematic exploration of an allegation described earlier in this chapter, the circumstances of this particular type of research only remotely resemble an interview of a sexually abused child.

The second type of research cited is a series of studies of children as witnesses, most of which demonstrate that children are fairly reliable witnesses, although Wakefield and Underwager emphasize the negative aspects of the findings. The most important of these studies will be briefly reviewed (Aman and Goodman, 1987; Goodman, 1988; Goodman and Reed, 1986; Yates, 1987).

The work of Goodman and her colleagues is the most relevant to clinicians trying to understand children's vulnerabilities and strengths as witnesses. These researchers create simulations that are as close as possible to situations in which children experience sexual abuse. That is, there is an attempt to make the research ecologically valid. Goodman notes that previous studies of children's memories and suggestibility were often done in situations that were alien to children and not representative of the contexts in which they might have to recall sexually abusive experiences.

In the Goodman research, after the child has participated in the experiment, she or he is asked a series of questions about it. Children are provided both objective (factual) questions and suggestive (misleading) questions. The latter include leading questions as defined earlier in this chapter, and trick questions, which suggest an event that did not take place. An example of a trick question is asking the child, "How many times did he spank you?" when no spanking occurred. Suggestive questions can refer to either abusive or nonabusive acts. The researchers were interested in the child's ability to recall (memory) and their susceptibility to suggestion. Errors of omission and commission were of concern. However, of overriding concern were positive responses to suggestive questions, which, in real-life circumstances, could lead to a false alarm of abuse.

Goodman and colleagues varied the age of the child, the sex of the child, whether the child was an active participant or a bystander, whether the experience was traumatic or not, the use of props (anatomically explicit dolls) in questioning, and the length of time between the experience and questioning about it.

Three of their studies will be briefly described and then findings will be summarized. One of these studies involved 48 children (3- to 4-year-olds and 5- to 6-year-olds) who went to a local clinic to receive inoculations (a stressful experience). These visits were videotaped so that the researchers would have an accurate record of what took place. Children were interviewed between three and nine days afterward and 22 of them were reinterviewed a year later (Goodman et al., 1987).

A second experiment consisted of having children enter a trailer with a strange man (a confederate). The children, 4- and 7-year-olds, were involved in pairs, one participant and one bystander. The man played games with the participant children for 10 minutes, for example, putting on costumes (over their clothing), having their pictures taken, and engaging in a game in which the children touched the man's nose and hand. After 11 or 12 days, they were asked about this experience, with some interviews involving no props, some involving anatomically explicit dolls, and some involving regular dolls (Aman and Goodman, 1987; Goodman et al., 1987).

A third study was of 66 girls, 5- and 7-year-olds, who received a routine physical required for school, except that the physicals of 31 children included a genital and rectal exam, while the exams of the other 35 included an exam for scoliosis. After a week or a month, the girls were questioned about their physicals (Goodman, 1988).

The findings from these studies are fairly consistent. They indicate that children do have adequate recall of past events. Stress does not appear to negatively affect their ability to recall. Children remember situations in which they are actively participating more accurately than those in which they are bystanders. Older children recall more than younger children. In general, children are resistant to leading questions, but older children are more accurate than younger ones. When children do make errors, these are usually errors of omission rather than errors of commission. Older children almost never made errors of commission, and only one child could provide any detail suggestive of an actual abusive experience (Goodman, 1988). Children continued to have good recall a year after the simulation; however, it was not as good as shortly after the simulation. There was also a slight increase in suggestibility over time (Aman and Goodman, 1987; Goodman, 1988; Goodman et al., 1987).

Children's Memories

The question of how accurate children's memories are has been raised because in part we do not know what children can recall before they are able to communicate it, that is, when they are preverbal. A second concern is how good the memory is when the cognitive capacity to organize experiences is still undeveloped. The implication of the latter concern is that everyday experiences would make more sense to a young child and, therefore, be easier to recall.

The findings from the research of Goodman and her colleagues cited above, that children do have adequate recall, address these concerns. The younger they are, the fewer details they will remember (Goodman et al., 1987; Yates, 1987). However, a traumatic event, such as sexual victimization, is remembered as well by children as by adults (Marin et al., 1979; Yates, 1987).

Moreover, Yates (1987) points out that children can remember as long as adults. It is just that, over time, they may become more reluctant to talk about material that is difficult for them. In sexual abuse cases, a question that often arises is whether a child of 6 can remember something that happened at 3 years of age. Children do have memories of events occurring as early as 3, and younger, but they often cannot encode these recollections so that adults can understand them. Furthermore, if an incident of abuse is considered by the child and perhaps discussed with someone else from time to time, this process will enhance the child's recall. The implication of this point is that a good approach to preparing a child for court testimony is periodic review of the sexual abuse with the victim. Often this takes place naturally during treatment. In doing this review, it is best that the material come from the child rather than from the person discussing abuse with the child. An audio- or videotape of a child's earlier description of the victimization is a good way to facilitate such a discussion.

The Child's Sense of Obligation to Tell the Truth

A final concern is that children may not feel the same sense of obligation to tell the truth that adults do. This problem could result in a false allegation of sexual abuse, failure to disclose, or recantation. The argument is that children have primitive or immature superegos and, therefore, are guided by the consequences of their behavior to themselves rather than by the moral obligation to tell the truth.

Perhaps the mistaken assumption here is that adult behavior is primarily determined by moral obligation rather than consequences. Children's actions are not any more likely to be determined by consequences than adults. What differs is their understanding of consequences. Children will comprehend that mommy will be mad or the perpetrator will be pleased, but they may not understand what it means to lose a job, go to jail, or allow someone to be free to molest others. A requirement of those who are concerned about the child's sense of obligation to tell the truth is to explain to her or him the consequences, beyond pleasing or displeasing someone, so that the child fully comprehends these.

This educational activity needs to take place long before the child gets to court and is assessed for competency by the judge or takes an oath to tell the truth. In fact, neither of these processes is likely to affect, very much, whether or not the child tells the truth.

THE VALIDITY OF THE CRITERIA FOR SUBSTANTIATING THE ALLEGATION

One of the dilemmas related to determining the credibility of children's statements about their sexual abuse is that there is not entire agreement about the characteristics of true and false allegations. For example, Green (1986), Schetky and Green (1988), and Yates and Musty (1988) have all described what they consider to be characteristics of false allegations. Their assertions have been disputed (e.g., Berliner, 1988; Corwin, 1988; Corwin et al., 1987; Hanson, 1988).

An important research question is how to determine the characteristics of true and false allegations. One type of research that has been conducted is to survey professionals in the field and ascertain the criteria they use. Thus Jones and McQuiston (1986) reviewed the literature related to characteristics of true assertions of sexual abuse.

More recently, Conte and colleagues (1988) canvassed 212 sexual abuse experts to determine what criteria they use and the importance attributed to them. They found seven criteria that 90% or more of the respondents used. These were (1) child has age-inappropriate sexual knowledge, (2) child's report of abuse is consistent over time, (3) child exhibits sexualized play during interview, (4) physical evidence, (5) child's description of the abuse relates elements of pressure or coercion, (6) child exhibits precocious or apparently seductive behavior, and (7) excessive masturbation. Of these characteristics, physical evidence was regarded as the most important, and age-inappropriate sexual knowledge was the second most important. Such research is very useful because it offers guidelines to professionals regarding current consensus. However, there can be consensus that is wrong.

What is needed to validate criteria that are used is an independent measure of whether the child has been sexually abused. Of course, one of the dilemmas inherent in sexual abuse diagnosis is that frequently the only evidence is the child's statement. Nevertheless, several possibilities for independent measures that could be considered are the following: (1) physical evidence, (2) eye witnesses, and (3) offender confession.

Physical evidence may hold considerable promise in the future because medical diagnosis of sexual abuse is becoming increasingly sophisticated (David Chadwick, personal communication, Washington, DC, 1989; Durfee et al., 1986; Emans et al., 1987; Woodling, 1985, 1986). However, at this point, medical evidence is only found in 10% to 20% of cases.

Because of the secrecy surrounding sexual abuse, there are rarely eye witnesses. Moreover, when witnesses do exist, they are likely to be either other children or accomplices of the offender. The credibility of child witnesses is just as likely to be questioned as that of child victims. Accomplices, because of the role they play, are not likely to come forward and reveal what they know.

This leaves offender confession as a possible independent measure of whether or not the child has been sexually abused. Although most offenders do not admit to abusing, especially during the assessment process, I have accumulated 103 cases in which the offender made some level of admission to sexual abuse, and there was an interview with the child focused on assessing whether or not the child had been sexually abused (Faller, 1988b).

Offender confession was at three levels: (1) full confession ($n = 62$), the offender admitted to all the acts the child alleged; (2) partial confession ($n = 23$), the offender admitted to some but not all of the acts the child described; and (3) indirect admission ($n = 18$), the offender indicated, without saying so, that he had sexually abused the child.

The following are examples of indirect admissions. The offender might say the child would not lie about such a thing. Or he could assert that he

Table 5.1

Relationship of Number of Characteristics in Victim's Statements to
Level of Perpetrator Confession

	None		One		Two		Three		Total	
	No.*	R %**	No.	R %	No.	R %	No.	R %	No.	R %
Full confession	4	6.5	7	11.3	10	16.1	41	66.1	62	60.2
Partial admission	2	8.7	3	13.0	4	17.4	14	60.9	23	22.3
Indirect admission	0	0	1	5.6	2	11.1	15	83.3	18	17.5
Total	6	5.8	11	10.7	16	15.5	70	68.0	103	100.0

SOURCE: Reprinted from "Criteria for Judging the Credibility of Children's Statements About their Sexual Abuse," *Child Welfare* (1988).
*Number of cases; **row percent.

doesn't remember what he does when he is drunk. Another example might be admitting that he fondled his daughter in the night but saying he thought she was his wife. Finally, he might say it happened, but the intent wasn't sexual. To illustrate, a father of a 3-year-old girl admitted that his fingers slipped and went up his daughter's vagina while he was bathing her. He also admitted that this had happened on three separate occasions.

To test the utility of children's statements as a way of validating sexual abuse, the first three criteria listed in the protocol (above) were used as indicators that sexual abuse had occurred: (1) the child's ability to describe the sexual behavior (found in 84% of cases), (2) the child's ability to describe the context of the sexual abuse (found in 81% of cases), and (3) an appropriate affective or emotional response (found in 84% of cases).

Table 5.1 shows the relationship between the level of admission and the presence of one, two, or three of the characteristics in the child's statement. As can be seen from the table, in almost two-thirds of the cases in which there was a full confession, the child's statement contained all three characteristics deemed to be indicative of a true allegation, supporting the validity of these criteria. The fact that these characteristics were missing in about a third of cases where there was a full confession is a reminder that many children are sexually abused and do not tell a credible story.[2]

It is also important to note that, in cases with the least evidence from the perpetrator, the indirect admission category, the proportion of cases with all three characteristics of a true allegation is the highest (83.3%). What this finding indicates is that, in the absence of a confession, cases are not validated without the presence of a persuasive statement by the child. This point is reinforced by data from 302 cases in my sample where the offender did not give some level of confession. In these cases, 75.5% ($n = 228$) of children's statements had all three characteristics of a true allegation (chi square = 13.3; $p = .004$).

This piece of research and the consensus research conducted by Conte and colleagues (1988) indicate that characteristics of a child's statements about sexual abuse are not only agreed-upon criteria for substantiating an allegation but seem to be valid ones.

CONCLUSION

Making the decision about whether or not sexual abuse has occurred is not only central in cases of sexual abuse but it often becomes the responsibility of mental health professionals. In order to make this decision, the mental health evaluator must conduct an assessment that differs from traditional ones because the practitioner must decide about the facts of the situation rather than merely focus upon the functioning of the individuals involved. In doing so, the statements and behavior of the child related to the allegations of sexual abuse are the crucial factors in decision making. The evaluator should anticipate that the alleged offender will deny the sexual abuse and that the victim's mother may be disinclined to believe the child.

The hallmarks of a true accusation of sexual abuse are the victim's ability, either through words or behavior, to describe the sexual behavior and the context of the sexual abuse, and an emotional reaction consistent with the sexual abuse being described. These criteria have been demonstrated to be valid through research, which determined their presence in cases where there was offender confession.

A variety of media are acceptable for use in interviewing children, including anatomically explicit dolls. Children can also be questioned in a variety of ways; however, most professionals advise the use of open-ended rather than close-ended questions. There is an assumption that the more close-ended a question, the less reliable the child's response.

Historically, there has been a reluctance to rely on a child's word in making a decision that the child has been sexually abused. However, research that attempts to create situations comparable to those in which children have been sexually abused, and to assess their memories and suggestibility, indicates that they are reliable historians.

NOTES

1. There is some disagreement regarding strategies in custody disputes, which are discussed in Chapter 6. In addition, there are a few persons who make a living out of attacking mental health professionals and other individuals who believe children when they state they have been sexually abused.

2. The reader will note in Table 5.1 that there are four cases where the offender gave a full confession but the child's data had no characteristics of a true allegation. These cases were classified as full confession even though the child gave no evidence supporting sexual abuse because they seemed to fit better in this category than in other categories of admission. In one instance, the child was 11 months old and, in another, under 2 years. The other two cases involved boys who denied sexual abuse despite perpetrator admission and statements made by other victims of the offenders.

REFERENCES

Aman, Christine and Gail Goodman. 1987. "Children's Use of Anatomically Detailed Dolls: An Experimental Study." Unpublished manuscript (available from Dr. Gail Goodman, Department of Psychology, State University of New York at Buffalo).

Berliner, Lucy. 1988. "Deciding When a Child Has Been Sexually Abused." In *Sexual Abuse Allegations in Custody and Visitation Cases*, edited by B. Nicholson and J. Bulkley. Washington, DC: American Bar Association.

Boat, Barbara and Mark Everson. 1988. "Interviewing Young Children with Anatomical Dolls." *Child Welfare* 67(4):336-52.

Caruso, R. 1987. *Projective Story Telling Cards.* Redding, CA: Northwest Psychological.

Conte, Jon, Erin Sorenson, Linda Fogarty, and Julie Dalla Rosa. 1988. *Evaluating Children's Reports of Sexual Abuse: Results from a Survey of Professionals.* Chicago: University of Chicago, School of Social Service Administration.

Corwin, David. 1988. "Early Diagnosis of Child Sexual Abuse: Diminishing the Lasting Effects." Pp. 251-269 in *The Lasting Effects of Child Sexual Abuse*, edited by G. Wyatt and G. Powell. Newbury Park, CA: Sage.

Corwin, David, Lucy Berliner, G. Goodman, J. Goodwin, and S. White. 1987. "Child Sexual Abuse Allegations and Custody Disputes: No Easy Answers." *Journal of Interpersonal Violence* 2(1):91-105.

Durfee, Michael, Astrid Heger, and Bruce Woodling. 1986. "Medical Evaluation." In *Sexual Abuse of Young Children*, edited by K. Macfarlane et al. New York: Guilford.

Emans, S. J., E. R. Woods, N. T. Flagg, and A. Freeman. 1987. "Genital Findings in Sexually Abused, Symptomatic, and Asymptomatic Girls." *Pediatrics* 79(5):63-70.

Faller, Kathleen Coulborn. 1984. "Is the Child Victim of Sexual Abuse Telling the Truth?" *Child Abuse and Neglect: The International Journal* 8:473-81.

————. 1987. "Women Who Sexually Abuse Children." *Victims and Violence* 2(4):263-76.

————. 1988a. *Child Sexual Abuse: An Interdisciplinary Manual for Diagnosis, Case Management, and Treatment.* New York: Columbia University Press.

————. 1988b. "Criteria for Judging the Credibility of Children's Statements About Their Sexual Abuse." *Child Welfare* 67(5):389-401.

————. Forthcoming. "Children Sexually Abused by More than One Person." *Victimology.*

Finkelhor, David. 1979. *Sexually Victimized Children.* New York: Free Press.

————. 1984. *Child Sexual Abuse: New Theory and Research.* New York: Free Press.

Goodman, Gail. 1988. "Research Forum." Presented at the National Symposium on Child Victimization, Anaheim, CA, April.

Goodman, Gail, Jodi Hirschman, and Leslie Rudy. 1987. "Children's Testimony: Research and Policy Implications." Paper presented at the Symposium for Research in Child Development, Baltimore, April.

Goodman, Gail and Rebecca Reed. 1986. "Age Differences in Eyewitness Testimony." *Law and Human Behavior* 10(4):317-32.

Goodwin, Jean. 1988. "Obstacles to Policymaking About Incest: Some Cautionary Folktales." In *The Lasting Effects of Child Sexual Abuse,* edited by G. Wyatt and G. Powell. Newbury Park, CA: Sage.

Green, Arthur. 1986. "True and False Allegations of Child Sexual Abuse in Custody Disputes." *Journal of the American Academy of Child Psychiatry* 25:449-56.

Hanson, Graeme. 1988. "The Sex Abuse Controversy." Letter to the editor. *Journal of the American Academy of Child and Adolescent Psychiatry* 27(2):258.

Jones, David and Mary McQuiston. 1986. *Interviewing the Sexually Abused Child.* Denver: C. H. Kempe Center for the Prevention and Treatment of Child Abuse and Neglect.

Lerman, Hannah. 1988. "The Psychoanalytic Legacy: From Whence We Come." In *Handbook on Sexual Abuse of Children,* edited by L. Walker. New York: Springer.

Marin, B., B. Holmes, M. Guth et al. 1979. "The Potential of Children as Eyewitnesses." *Law and Human Behavior* 3:195-305.

Masson, Jeffrey. 1984. *Assault on the Truth: Freud's Suppression of the Seduction Theory.* New York: Farrar, Straus, and Giroux.

McCarty, Loretta. 1981. "Investigation of Incest: An Opportunity to Motivate Families to Seek Help." *Child Welfare* 60(10):679-89.

Russell, Diana. 1983. "The Incidence and Prevalence of Intrafamilial and Extrafamilial Sexual Abuse of Female Children." *Child Abuse and Neglect: The International Journal* 7(2):133-46.

————. 1984. "The Prevalence and Seriousness of Incestuous Abuse: Stepfathers Versus Fathers." *Child Abuse and Neglect: The International Journal* 8(1):15-22.

————. 1986. *The Secret Trauma: Incest in the Lives of Girls and Women.* New York: Basic Books.

Schetky, Diane and Arthur Green. 1988. *Child Sexual Abuse: A Handbook for Health Care and Legal Professionals.* New York: Brunner/Mazel.

Sgroi, Suzanne. 1982. *Handbook of Clinical Intervention in Child Sexual Abuse.* Lexington, MA: Lexington.

Summit, Roland. 1983. "The Child Sexual Abuse Accommodation Syndrome." *Child Abuse and Neglect: The International Journal* 7:177-93.

Wakefield, Hollinda and Ralph Underwager. 1988. *Accusations of Child Sexual Abuse.* Springfield, IL: Charles C Thomas.

Walker, Lenore, ed. 1988. *Handbook on Sexual Abuse of Children.* New York: Springer.

White, Sue, Gerald Strom, Gail Santilli, and Bruce Halpin. 1986. "Interviewing Young Sexual Abuse Victims with Anatomically Correct Dolls." *Child Abuse and Neglect: The International Journal* 10(4):519-30.

Woodling, Bruce. 1985. "The Sexually Abused Child." Presentation given at the Seventh National Conference on Child Abuse and Neglect, Chicago, November.

————. 1986. "Clinical Signs of Acute and Chronic Sodomy in Male and Female Children." Presentation given at the Fourth National Conference on the Sexual Victimization of Children, New Orleans.

Wyatt, Gail. 1985. "The Sexual Abuse of Afro-American and White Women During Childhood." *Child Abuse and Neglect: The International Journal* 9:507-19.

Wyatt, Gail and Gloria Powell. 1988. *The Lasting Effects of Child Sexual Abuse.* Newbury Park, CA: Sage.

Yates, Alayne. 1987. "Should Young Children Testify in Cases of Sexual Abuse?" *American Journal of Psychiatry* 144(4):476-79.

Yates, Alayne and Tim Musty. 1988. "Preschool Children's Erroneous Allegations of Sexual Molestation." *American Journal of Psychiatry* 145(8):989-92.

Yuille, John. 1988. "The Systematic Assessment of Children's Testimony." *Canadian Psychology* 29(3):247-59.

Appendix

Checklist for Determining the Likelihood Sexual Abuse Occurred

---

Child's name _____   Case number _____

Child's address _____   Date _____

I. The child's ability to describe (either verbally or behaviorally) the sexual behavior.

    A. Sexual knowledge beyond what would be expected for the child's developmental stage   Y   N
       Comments: _____

    B. Sexual behavior described from a child's viewpoint   Y   N
       Comments: _____

    C. Explicit accounts of sexual acts   Y   N
       Comments: _____

II. The child's ability to describe the context of the sexual abuse.

    A. Where it happened   Y   N
       Comments: _____

    B. When it happened   Y   N
       Comments: _____

    C. What the offender said to obtain the child's involvement   Y   N
       Comments: _____

    D. Where other family members were   Y   N
       Comments: _____

    E. What the victim was wearing   Y   N
       Comments: _____

    F. What clothing of victim was removed   Y   N
       Comments: _____

(continued)

G. What the offender was wearing   Y   N
   Comments: _____

H. What clothing of offender was removed   Y   N
   Comments: _____

I. Whether the offender said anything about telling or not telling   Y   N
   Comments: _____

J. Whether the child told anyone   Y   N
   Comments: _____

K. Reactions of persons child has told   Y   N
   Comments: _____

III. The child's affect when recounting the sexual abuse.   Y   N
    Comments: _____

A. Reluctance to disclose   Y   N
   Comments: _____

B. Embarrassment   Y   N
   Comments: _____

C. Anger   Y   N
   Comments: _____

D. Anxiety   Y   N
   Comments: _____

E. Disgust   Y   N
   Comments: _____

F. Sexual arousal   Y   N
   Comments: _____

G. Fear   Y   N
   Comments: _____

IV. Medical evidence   Y   N
     Comments: _____

V. Confession of the offender

    A. Complete confession   Y   N
    B. Partial confession   Y   N
    C. Indirect admission   Y   N
      Comments: _____

VI. Other witnesses

    A. Children   Y   N
      Comments: _____

    B. Adults   Y   N
      Comments: _____

Chapter 6

RISK ASSESSMENT IN
CHILD SEXUAL MALTREATMENT

Risk assessment is a concept with a great deal of currency in the child welfare field. Child protection experts and others are greatly concerned about which family situations render children in danger of maltreatment. Efforts are currently under way to develop risk assessment measures in many states (e.g., Baird and Neuenfeldt, 1988; Johnson and L'Esperance, 1984; Martinez, 1987; Pecora et al., 1986-87; Schene, 1987; Tatara, 1987). Moreover, a number of national organizations concerned about the welfare of children (Child Welfare League of America, American Public Welfare Association, and American Humane Association) and the federal government have supported efforts to develop procedures and instruments for risk assessment. However, little work has been undertaken to develop risk assessment measures for sexual abuse. A major reason for the failure to address risk issues in sexual abuse is because they differ markedly from those in other types of child maltreatment.

In this chapter, how issues of risk differ for sexual abuse cases and other kinds of maltreatment will be discussed first. Second, a range of types of risk will be differentiated. Third, a protocol for risk assessment will be presented.

AUTHOR'S NOTE: Preliminary work on the material in this chapter was undertaken as part of a project funded under DHHS contract #05CT3552, "Child Welfare Services Collaborative Training Model," and involving Wayne State University School of Social Work and Wayne County, Michigan, Office of Children and Youth Services.

Finally, guidelines for using the protocol to assess different types of risk will be described.

The material in this chapter will be most instructive for assessing risk in intrafamilial sexual abuse cases. However, the protocol itself allows for the consideration of a range of possible role relationships between offender and victim. As is the case elsewhere in this book, this discussion refers to the offender as male, the nonoffending parent as female, and the victim as female, because this is the most common pattern. However, the protocol takes into account other gender configurations.

DIFFERENCES BETWEEN SEXUAL ABUSE AND OTHER TYPES OF MALTREATMENT

It is useful for mental health professionals to appreciate differences, both real and attitudinal, between sexual victimization and other types of child maltreatment. These unique characteristics affect case management decisions.

One factor that differentiates sexual abuse from other kinds of maltreatment is the attitude of professionals toward reincidence. Whereas some additional instances of neglect and physical abuse may be tolerated while intervention is being provided, reincidence of sexual abuse is not. Consequently, the threshold of risk for removal for sexual abuse is lower than for other types of maltreatment.

In addition, in part prompted by the negative effects of placement on successful treatment and on the victim, the alternative of removal of the offender has become favored. Offender removal is rarely used in other types of maltreatment, and, therefore, it is another distinguishing characteristic of sexual abuse cases. Removal of the offender has its own set of consequences. Certainly it is much more disruptive than removal of the victim and is likely to anger the family more than victim removal. However, this disruption may be important in motivating change during treatment, and it may make the victim feel less responsible for the abuse.

In cases of sexual abuse, there are two risks that can result from leaving the victim at home. The first is *reincidence of sexual abuse* and the second is *emotional abuse*. In the latter instance, the child is pressured to change her statement that she has been sexually abused, is blamed for the sexual abuse, or is blamed for the consequences of disclosure of the sexual abuse. The consequences may be the arrest of the offender, involvement of the family in protective services, requirements that the family participate in and profit from treatment, the necessity of going to court, and lawyer's fees. This kind of emotional abuse is more common in sexual abuse than in other types of maltreatment because discovery of abuse by professionals and consequent intervention is more likely to be based primarily on the victim's disclosure. (As noted in Chapter 5, in cases of physical abuse and neglect, the diagnosis is more likely to be made on the basis of physical evidence.)

Consequently, offender removal is not always the intervention of choice. The decision of how best to protect the victim is based in large part on the functioning of the nonoffending parent and to a lesser extent on the functioning of the perpetrator. Factors to assess in determining the functioning of these people are covered in the risk assessment protocol and will be discussed at the end of this chapter.

The risk of harm to the child from sexual abuse is also regarded by professionals as greater than that from other types of maltreatment. Therefore, treatment is more likely to be provided for victims of sexual abuse than for victims of other types of maltreatment.

TYPES OF RISK

Before guidelines for risk assessment in sexual abuse are provided, it is important to discuss what is meant by "risk." In fact, a sexually abusive situation might pose a variety of different kinds of risk to children. These are listed below and will be discussed.

(1) risk of potential sexual abuse
(2) risk that sexual abuse has occurred
(3) severity of sexual abuse
(4) risk of harm from sexual abuse
(5) risk for recurrence of sexual abuse
(6) risk of harm from recurrent sexual abuse
(7) risk of placement because of sexual abuse

Very little attention has been given to identifying situations that are high risk for sexual abuse but where no victimization has actually occurred. Risk of potential sexual abuse implies that characteristics of the potential offender, the victim, or the situation create the potential for sexual maltreatment. The best predictors are past history. Therefore, persons who have sexually abused in the past are more likely to sexually abuse than those who have not. Similarly, children who have already been victimized appear to be vulnerable to future victimization (Faller, forthcoming). Obviously, factors that may play a role in potential sexual abuse also are important in predicting recurrence involving the same individuals.

Some situations, for example, foster care (see Chapter 7) or marital dissatisfaction or dissolution (see Chapter 9), may increase the probability for sexual abuse, but these circumstances do not, by themselves, cause sexual abuse. As noted in Chapter 2, the two prerequisites for sexual abuse are sexual arousal to children and the willingness to act on the arousal. Situational factors only play a contributing role.

The second type of risk—risk that sexual abuse has occurred—is discussed extensively in the previous chapter (Chapter 5). However, often the question of whether or not the child has been sexually abused is not differentiated from other types of risk: severity, harm, the likelihood of reincidence, and the question of placement. These are conceptually separate issues, and a determination of the likelihood of sexual victimization should precede any decisions regarding damage, future vulnerability, and placement. Nevertheless, in reality, mental health practitioners and others often try to make decisions about the latter without resolving the former.

These two types of decisions become blurred for two reasons. In some cases, professionals cannot determine with certainty whether or not the child has been sexually abused; yet they need to make other case management decisions, such as whether the child is safe with the alleged offender. In other instances, the failure to distinguish between the occurrence of sexual abuse and consequent case management decisions results from imprecise thinking. To emphasize these distinctions, the issue of occurrence was dealt with in Chapter 5 and other issues related to risk are addressed in this chapter. They are as follows: (1) severity of sexual abuse, (2) harm resulting from sexual abuse, (3) risk of future sexual abuse, and (4) risk of child placement.

INDICES FOR ASSESSMENT

Mental health professionals and others, including protective services and foster care workers, law enforcement personnel, attorneys, and judges, must make decisions that greatly affect the well-being of sexually abused children and their families. They must decide how much harm the victim has sustained, what the likelihood is of future sexual abuse, whether to remove the victim(s) or the offender, when it is safe to return the victim(s), when termination of parental rights is appropriate, and when to criminally prosecute the offender.

A serious impediment to making such decisions is the lack of a planned and systematic strategy for assessing cases, which in turn should guide decisions about risk and case management. The protocol that follows is structured to assist the mental health professional in gathering information necessary for assessing risk and making case decisions. Items included are those generally considered by myself and other clinicians and researchers to be central in this process.

PROTOCOL FOR ASSESSING THE SEVERITY OF SEXUAL ABUSE, HARM TO THE CHILD, RISK FOR SUBSEQUENT SEXUAL ABUSE, AND THE NEED FOR REMOVAL

I. *Type of sexual abuse* (in ascending order of risk)

A. Sexual talk

Examples:

The offender tells the child, "You have nicer breasts than your mother." The offender tells the victim, "I want to fuck you, and I know you do it with your boyfriend."

B. Exposure/voyeurism

Examples:

The offender opens up his bathrobe showing his daughter his penis as he passes her in the hall.

The offender drills a hole in the bathroom wall and watches his stepdaughter through it. He also instructs her to watch him.

C. Fondle outside clothing (perpetrator of victim or victim of perpetrator)

Examples:

The offender repeatedly rubs his daughter's clothed vaginal area when they watch television.

The offender places his stepdaughter's hand on his penis and instructs her to rub him.

D. Fondle under clothing/digital penetration

Example:

The offender has the child remove her pants and rubs her vaginal area, occasionally inserting his finger in her vagina.

E. Oral sex/genital penetration/anal penetration

Examples:

The father requires his son to perform fellatio on him.

The offender has intercourse with the 15-year-old daughter of his girlfriend.

The father puts buttery-flavored Crisco on his penis and inserts it in his 8-year-old daughter's anus.

    F. Pornography/prostitution/exploitation
       Examples:
       The mother takes pictures of her daughter and son involved in sexual acts.
       The mother and her boyfriend allow other men to have sex with her 3- and 4-year-old daughters.
       A father takes his 8-year-old daughter to parties, allows her to drink, and then lets his friends have sex with her.

II. *Characteristics of abuse situation* (each characteristic rated separately)

    A. Duration (short versus long)
       1. Short = 1 month
       2. Long = more than a month
    B. Number of times (few versus many)
       1. Few = 5 or fewer
       2. Many = more than 5
    C. Use of force (absent versus present)
       1. No force = mutual collaboration,
          seduction, bribes, other inducements
       2. Force = threats of physical harm,
          use of physical force, actual physical injury
      (each of these dimensions is actually a continuum, not dichotomous; however, to simplify scoring, each is dichotomized)

    D. Threats regarding disclosure (absent versus present)
       0. No threats
       1. Threats involving loss of affection or mild consequences
       Examples:
       The offender tells the child that the victim will get in trouble for the sexual abuse.
       The offender tells the child she will be considered a bad girl if people find out.
       The offender asserts that, if she tells, he or her mom won't love her anymore.
       2. Threats of dire consequences or serious physical harm
       Examples:
       The offender tells the child she will go to jail if people find out.
       The offender tells the child she will be put in foster care if people find out.
       The offender threatens to kill the child, her mother, or the like if she tells.

III. *Victim age* (in ascending order of risk for future abuse, however, not necessarily of harm and severity)

    A. 14-16 years
    B. 11-13 years

    C. 8-10 years

    D. 5-7 years

    E. 3-4 years

    F. 0-2 years

IV. *Perpetrator-victim relationship* (in ascending order of risk for reabuse and harm)

    A. Out-house, unrelated

        Examples:

        A baby-sitter

        A neighbor

    B. Out-house, related

        Examples:

        An uncle

        A cousin

    C. In-house, child

        Examples:

        A stepsibling

        An adolescent brother or sister

    D. In-house, unrelated adult; related female

        Examples:

        Mother's live-in boyfriend

        Aunt

    E. In-house, related uncle, grandfather, grandmother

    F. In-house, related father, stepfather, adopted father, mother, or stepmother

V. *Number of victims* (code actual number)

VI. *Number of perpetrators* (code actual number)

VII. *Functioning of nonoffending parent*

    A. Reaction to knowledge about the sexual abuse

        0. Supportive of victim

        Examples:

        Mother takes victim and goes to a relative or a domestic violence shelter when she finds out about the sexual abuse.

        Mother calls the police or protective services when she finds out about the sexual abuse.

        1. Equivocal or inconsistent reaction

        Examples:

        Initially the mother appears to believe the victim but then believes the offender when he asserts his innocence.

        Mother believes the victim but wants to keep the offender in the home, worries about who will pay the bills.

        2. Supportive of offender

Examples:

Mother says the victim is lying; the offender would never do such a thing.

Mother blames the victim, says she brought it on herself.

B. Relationship between the nonoffending parent and victim

    0. Close, nurturing relationship with open communication.

    1. Somewhat problematic relationship

Examples:

There is role reversal between victim and nonoffending parent.

Nonoffending parent has ambivalent feelings toward victim.

    2. Seriously problematic relationship between victim and nonoffending parent

Examples:

Nonoffending parent is hostile toward the child, appears to actively dislike the child.

Nonoffending parent is jealous of the child.

Nonoffending parent shows a clear preference for the offender over the child.

C. Nonoffending parent's level of dependency (upon the offender)

    0. Nonoffending parent appears very independent of the offender

Examples:

Nonoffending parent is economically independent.

Nonoffending parent has social supports that are separate from the offender.

Nonoffending parent can argue with, disagree with offender.

    1. Nonoffending parent is somewhat dependent upon offender

Examples:

Nonoffending parent can disagree with the offender in the presence of others but changes her opinion when alone with him.

Nonoffending parent has some financial resources but requires some funds from the offender.

Nonoffending parent has some job skills but is not currently working.

    2. Nonoffending parent very dependent upon offender

Examples:

Nonoffending parent totally financially dependent on offender.

Nonoffending parent has no job skills, has never worked.

Nonoffending parent never disagrees with the offender.

VIII. *Response of offender*

    0. Admits and takes responsibility

Examples:

Offender confesses to all sexual acts described by victim; expresses concern for harm to victim.

Offender states he is relieved he has been caught; he could not stop by himself.

Offender confesses and asks the victim's forgiveness.

1. Admits but does not accept responsibility

Examples:

Offender admits the sexual abuse, but says it only happened a few times, did not involve penetration, and so on.

Offender admits to part of the sexual abuse.

Offender admits, but says the victim seduced him.

Offender admits, but says it wouldn't have happened if his wife hadn't denied him sex.

2. Denies

Examples:

Offender says he would never do such a thing; sexual abusers ought to be shot.

Offender says he didn't do it, but someone else did.

3. Denies and blames victim

Examples:

Offender denies and says that the victim made this up to get her mother to throw him out of the house.

Offender denies and says that the victim has caused the family much trouble; she is a liar, she does poorly in school, and she is disrespectful of her mother; he wants her to be placed in foster care or a home for delinquent girls.

IX. *Other individual and family problems*—there are a number of individual and family problems that can play a contributing role in sexual abuse; they can also greatly exacerbate risk for future sexual abuse, increase the harm to the victim, and result in the need for removal of the victim

A. Substance abuse

There is a high correlation between substance abuse by the offender and sexual abuse (in some studies, as high as 60%; Faller, 1988; Larson and Riebel, 1978; Janzen, 1979). The substance may act as a disinhibitor for the offender, he may use chemicals to deal with guilt feelings related to the sexually abusive behavior, or both. Less dangerous, but nevertheless worrisome, is substance abuse by the nonoffending parent. An adult who is high or drunk much of the time is not in a position to protect a child. Moreover, an environment where there is chemical dependency may render a child at risk for sexual abuse or exploitation by family and nonfamily members involved in the sale or use of substances. And, in some cases, the victim is given drugs or alcohol in the course of the sexual abuse.

0. No substance abuse in family or environment

1. Substance abuse in the environment

Examples:

The family's home is suspected of being a crack house.

A lot of drinking and parties are said to go on in the home.

Alleged offender is said to deal drugs.

2. Substance abuse by the mother

Examples:

Mother has a drinking problem.

Mother is alleged to use crack.

3. Substance abuse by the offender

Examples:

Offender said to have been drunk when he sexually abused the child.

Offender known to use drugs.

4. Severe addiction of the offender

Examples:

Offender is drunk or high at least several times a week.

Offender is chemically dependent but refuses to acknowledge his problem or seek treatment.

5. Victim given chemicals during the sexual abuse

Examples:

Young girls describe having to sniff white powder before sucking men's penises.

Mother got her 13-year-old daughter drunk and then persuaded her to have sex with the mother and her boyfriend.

B. Violence

Violence by the offender is an index of absence of impulse control and absence of empathy for others, both of which are factors that increase the risk of sexual abuse. Furthermore, a violent sex offender may force a victim to submit to sexual abuse or subdue or frighten a nonoffending parent so that she cannot protect the victim. Violence toward the child by a nonoffending parent is an index of a poor relationship between parent and victim and signals possible lack of inclination to protect and lack of empathy for the victim.

0. No violence in family

1. Violence by the offender to persons outside the home

2. Spouse abuse (to nonoffending parent)

3. Child abuse by nonoffending parent

4. Offender physically abuses victim of sexual abuse

C. Mental retardation

Mental retardation on the part of the offender means that the offender is at increased risk for poor judgment and poor impulse control, factors that may enhance the propensity to sexually abuse (Faller, 1988). In addition, he may be less likely to achieve a sexual relationship with an age mate and be at greater risk for sexually abusing a child. Moreover, he will have greater difficulty than a person of normal intelligence learning new behaviors (i.e., nonabusive sex). If the nonoffending parent is mentally retarded, she will have greater difficulty being protective and appreciating what is wrong with sex between an adult and a child. Finally, if the victim is retarded, she may be more vulnerable to sexual abuse because of the paucity of other gratifying relationships and successes in her life, because she will have greater difficulty appreciating what is wrong about sex between an adult and a child, because she may be less able to communicate what she has experienced, and because her competence to accurately relate an abusive episode may be doubted. Moreover, an offender may deliberately choose a mentally retarded victim because of the child's special vulnerability and the likelihood her credibility will be doubted, should she disclose.

   0. No mental retardation in family
   1. Nonoffending parent mentally retarded
   2. Victim mentally retarded
   3. Offender mentally retarded

D. Mental illness

Few people sexually abuse children because they are mentally ill. However, when they do, they are likely to have delusions that justify their sexual involvement with children. For example, one offender believed it was necessary to explore the child's genitalia because they were infested with bugs and maggots. Women may be more likely to sexually abuse children as part of their mental illness than men (Faller, 1987). When the nonoffending parent is mentally ill, that person may not be available either psychologically (they are in their own world of psychosis) or physically (they are in the hospital) to protect the child. In addition, a mentally ill spouse may not be very sexually desirable, leading the offender to look elsewhere for sex, that is, to a child. Finally, a child who is emotionally disturbed may be more vulnerable to sexual abuse. This vulnerability may be indirectly related to the emotional disturbance, in that the illness is a consequence of traumatic experiences. These experiences can cause a child to be less attuned to the social norm violation, which sexual abuse constitutes, and/or willing to be involved in the abuse because of the attention, affection, or physical pleasure involved. In addition, the child's emotional illness may be a factor the offender considers in choosing his victims. A disturbed child may be considered more compliant and cooperative as well as less likely to be believed should she disclose.

   0. No mental illness in family
   1. Child is emotionally disturbed
   2. Nonoffending parent mentally ill
   3. Offending adult mentally ill

The Appendix at the end of the chapter is a family checklist for coding findings of this assessment tool.

USE OF THE RISK ASSESSMENT PROTOCOL FOR EVALUATION

Sexual abuse is more *severe* and victims suffer greater *harm* when the sexual behavior is more intrusive, more frequent, of longer duration, involves force, and involves more perpetrators. Similarly, severity and increased harm are associated with lack of support by the mother, denial and blaming the victim by the offender, and other problems correlated with sexual abuse: substance abuse, violence, mental retardation, and mental illness.

In general, the more severe the ratings on the dimensions in the scale, the more likely there will be a *reoffense*. More intrusive sexual abuse, more frequent victimization, victimization of longer duration, and victimization involving more children are indicative of greater intensity and/or more frequent sexual arousal felt by the offender toward children and fewer inhibitions against sexually abusing them.

The admission dimension is somewhat more complex. In general, admission and taking responsibility are factors that can diminish harm and reduce risk for reabuse. However, some offenders who feel very ashamed of their behavior, an index of reduced risk, cannot bring themselves to admit. In contrast, some abusers will admit and not see anything particularly wrong with what they did or they will blame the victim. These offenders are at higher risk for reoffense.

Removal of the victim in order to assure protection is indicated when the nonoffending parent is dependent upon and supportive of the offender, lacks positive feelings for the victim, and does not respond protectively to discovery of the sexual abuse. In contrast, if she is independent, nurturing of the victim, and protective in her reaction to the abuse, safety for the victim can be effected by removal of the offender. In some instances, the offender will agree voluntarily to leave the home. However, if the abuse has been extensive, the offender evidences no remorse, and/or the offender is in general dysfunctional, he will need to be arrested or ordered by the court to leave the home. And, even with a court order, monitoring of the family situation will be essential to make sure he does not violate the court order or insinuate himself back into the family.

A scoring system for the protocol is provided. The number that precedes the factor is its score. However, the scoring system is preliminary. That is, the system is based on my clinical experience. It has not yet been field tested and validated (i.e., demonstrated to actually be predictive of severity, harm, and/or risk with a large number of cases to which it would be systematically applied). In addition, no attempt has been made to weight the items in the protocol (for example, to determine if type of sexual abuse is more or less important than mother's unsupportive reaction in causing harm). Finally, the investigator must continually bear in mind the secrecy surrounding sexual abuse, which predisposes the victim, the offender, and others to avoid giving full information about the sexual abuse. Often a decision made early in intervention must be revised later based upon additional findings or the response of the family to intervention.

Despite these limitations, the protocol and scoring system should prove useful as a guideline for case decision making. The protocol should be used in conjunction with other input in assessing risk. A higher score is indicative of a case of greater severity, more damage to the victim, poorer prognosis, and greater need to consider removal of the victim. A score of 1-20 is low and indicative of low risk. A score of more than 40 is high and indicative of great risk.

CONCLUSION

Despite the current interest in risk assessment in child welfare, this chapter represents one of the few attempts to develop a strategy for assessing risk in sexual abuse cases. The chapter defines the different types of risk that need to be considered, delineates differences between sexual victimization and other kinds of child maltreatment that affect risk assessment, provides a protocol for assessing risk in sexual abuse, and discusses how the protocol pertains to different types of risk.

This effort is necessarily preliminary and must be understood in terms of the state of the art in sexual abuse evaluation. However, it is vital that efforts of risk assessment in sexual abuse be pursued, especially given the conclusion professionals have drawn, that sexual abuse poses grave risk to its victims.

REFERENCES

Baird, Christopher and Deborah Neuenfeldt. 1988. "Assessing Potential for Abuse and Neglect."
    National Council on Crime and Delinquency Focus. A research brief (July). Madison:
    National Council on Crime and Delinquency.

Faller, Kathleen Coulborn. 1987. "Women Who Sexually Abuse Children." *Victims and Violence* 2(4):263-76.

————. 1988. *Child Sexual Abuse: An Interdisciplinary Manual for Diagnosis, Case Management, and Treatment*. New York: Columbia University Press.

————. Forthcoming. "Children Sexually Abused by More than One Person." *Victimology.*

Janzen, Curtis. 1979. "Models of Assessing Treatment/Intervention Impact." Presented at the conference workshop, "Sexual Victimization of Children: Trauma, Trial, and Treatment," Washington, DC, November, December.

Johnson, William and Jill L'Esperance. 1984. "Predicting the Recurrence of Child Abuse." *Social Work Research and Abstracts* 20(2):21-26.

Larson, Noel Carlson and Joan Riebel. 1978. *Family Sexual Abuse: A Resource Manual for Human Services Professionals*. Minneapolis: University of Minnesota, Department of Family Practice and Community Health.

Martinez, Louis. 1987. "Illinois Presents Its Child Protection Risk Assessment Instrument." In *A Summary of the Highlights of the National Roundtable on CPS Risk Assessment and Family Systems Assessment*, edited by T. Tatara. Washington, DC: American Public Welfare League.

Pecora, Peter et al. 1986-87. "Developing and Implementing Risk Assessment Systems in Child Protective Services." *Protecting Children* 3(4):8-10, 15.

Schene, Patricia. 1987. "Remarks on the Key Points to Consider in Developing a System of CPS Risk Assessment." In *A Summary of the Highlights of the National Roundtable on CPS Risk Assessment and Family Systems Assessment*, edited by T. Tatara. Washington, DC: American Public Welfare League.

Tatara, Toshio. 1987. *Summary of the Highlights of the National Roundtable on CPS Risk Assessment and Family Systems Assessment*. Washington, DC: American Public Welfare League.

Appendix

Checklist for Assessing Severity of Sexual Abuse, Harm to Child, and Risk of Future Sexual Abuse

---

Family name _____ Case number _____

Victims _____

Offenders _____ Date _____

(To complete, circle or fill in appropriate number and add)

SCORE

I. Type of sexual abuse

    A. Sexual talk   1

        Comments:_____

    B. Exposure/voyeurism   2

        Comments:_____

    D. Fondle outside clothing   3

        Comments:_____

    E. Oral sex/genital/anal penetration   5

        Comments:_____

    F. Pornography/prostitution/exploitation   6

        Comments:_____

II. Characteristics of the abuse situation

    A. Duration

        1. Short = 1 month   1

        2. Long = more than 1 month   2

        Comments:_____

    B. Number of times

        1. Few = 5 or fewer   1

        2. Many = more than 5   2

        Comments:_____

    C. Use of force (absent versus present)

        1. No force   1

        2. Force   2

        Comments:_____

D. Threats regarding disclosure
    0. No threats   0
    1. Mild threats   1
    2. Severe threats   2
    Comments: _____

III. Victim age

    1. 14-16 years   1
    2. 11-13 years   2
    3. 8-10 years   3
    4. 5-7 years   4
    5. 3-4 years   5
    6. 0-2 years   6
    Comments: _____

IV. Perpetrator-victim relationship

    1. Out-house, unrelated   1
    2. Out-house, related   2
    3. In-house child   3
    4. In house unrelated male, related female   4
    5. In-house uncle, grandfather, grandmother   5
    6. In-house father, stepfather, adopted father, mother, or stepmother   6
    Comments: _____

V. Number of victims
    Comments: _____

VI. Number of perpetrators
    Comments: _____

VII. Functioning of the nonoffending parent

A. Reaction to knowledge about the sex abuse
    0. Supportive of victim   0
    1. Equivocal or inconsistent reaction   1
    2. Supportive of offender   2

Comments:_____

B. Relationship to victim
    0. Close, nurturing relationship   0
    1. Somewhat problematic relationship   1
    2. Seriously problematic relationship   2
    Comments:_____

C. Level of dependency (on offender)
    0. Very independent of offender   0
    1. Somewhat dependent on offender   1
    2. Very dependent on offender   2
    Comments:_____

VIII. Response of offender

    0. Admits and takes responsibility   0
    1. Admits but does not accept responsibility   1
    2. Denies   2
    3. Denies and blames victim   3
    Comments: _____

IX. Other individual and family problems

A. Substance abuse
    0. No substance abuse   0
    1. Substance use in the environment   1
    2. Substance use by nonoffending parent   2
    3. Substance use by offender   3
    4. Severe addiction of the offender   4
    5. Victim given chemicals during abuse   5
    Comments:

B. Violence
    0. No violence in household   0
    1. Offender violent outside home   1
    2. Offender violent to nonoffending parent   2
    3. Child abuse by nonoffending parent   3
    4. Offender violent to victim   4
    Comments:_____

C. Mental retardation
    0. No mental retardation in family   0
    1. Nonoffending parent mentally retarded   1
    2. Victim mentally retarded   2
    3. Offender mentally retarded   3
    Comments: _____

D. Mental illness
    0. No mental illness   0
    1. Victim emotionally disturbed   1
    2. Nonoffending parent mentally ill   2
    3. Offender mentally ill   3
    Comments: _____

TOTAL   _____

A score of 0-20 is low risk.
A score of more than 40 is high risk.

PART IV

Sexual Abuse In
Special Contexts

Chapter 7

SEXUAL ABUSE IN FOSTER FAMILY CARE

Foster family care used to be regarded as a living arrangement of unmitigated superiority for children who had been maltreated by their parents and, even at one time, a better alternative than living with a biological family without financial resources (Kadushin, 1980; Kline and Overstreet, 1972). Times have changed, and mental health professionals are now concerned with structural aspects of foster care that potentially can have detrimental effects on children. The first of these is damage to the child's attachment capability as a consequence of separation from parents and later as a result of removal from foster parents and returning home. Second, a foster family living arrangement is likely to be less stable than a biological one, because the commitment of foster parents is often not as lasting as that of biological parents. Third, once children are placed, they are prone to being allowed to languish in foster care for a variety of reasons. The most important of these is the fact that the foster care worker, who has a large caseload with continually erupting emergencies, just does not get around to serving children who are in safe and satisfactory living situations in foster care (Faller, 1986).

In recent years, mental health professionals and others have become aware that, for many children, foster care is not safe and satisfactory. In fact, there

AUTHOR'S NOTE: I would like to acknowledge the assistance provided by Patricia Ryan, Ph.D., Director of the Institute for the Study of Children and the Family at Eastern Michigan University, in the preparation of this chapter.

are detrimental effects other than attachment problems, foster care instability, and foster care drift, which children in placement can experience. One of these is sexual abuse. This chapter will discuss why maltreated children might be at greater risk for sexual abuse, will describe three types of sexual abuse in foster care, will present some data on sexual abuse in foster care, and will make suggestions for ways of preventing this type of abuse.

THE CONTRIBUTION OF THE CHILD

It is important not to blame the victim for the abuse she receives. Nevertheless, if the goal is to understand sexual abuse in foster care and intervene effectively, one must not overlook aspects of the child's functioning and behavior that may play a role in her victimization. The characteristics to be described may increase risk of victimization not only in foster care but in other contexts as well. Although other child factors also can enhance vulnerability to sexual maltreatment, the impact of having been physically and emotionally maltreated and sexually abused will be the focus of the discussion here.

The Impact of Physical and Emotional Maltreatment

Physically and emotionally abused and neglected children may be at greater risk than other children for sexual abuse in foster care. In their home situations, their physical and emotional needs have not been met. Therefore, they may not have an understanding of appropriate nurturance and care. In addition, they are likely to have unmet dependency and affective needs. Both of these characteristics may place them at increased risk for sexual abuse. The case example that follows is illustrative.

Case example: Evelyn, age 8, was placed in foster care because of long-standing physical and emotional neglect. Her mother was mentally ill and in and out of the hospital. Her father was extremely obese, had a bad back, and spent most of his time in bed. The house was filthy, with bags of garbage in every room. The family had six dogs who lived in the house and were not housebroken.

Evelyn was the youngest of three children, but the older children had been placed in care earlier. Evelyn was expected to look after herself. That is, she had to get up, dress herself, feed herself, and catch the bus for school. After school she came home, fed the dogs, and watched television. Sometimes her father fixed dinner, but often Evelyn had to prepare her meal and his.

When Evelyn came into care, she had developmental delays that appeared to have been caused by her family situation. At times, she engaged in self-stimulating behaviors, including rocking and masturbating. However, there was no evidence that she had been sexually abused. She appeared excessively friendly and quite childlike.

She adjusted well to foster care and attached quickly to her foster parents. They described her as needing lots of affection and attention, but said she was very good-natured and compliant.

She soon began to explore the neighborhood and made friends with some children who lived down the street. Because the foster parents knew and liked the parents of these children, they were happy to have Evelyn play with them after school.

About two months after Evelyn came, they became concerned because Evelyn called Tommy, the 13-year-old boy in the neighbor family, her lover. They investigated the situation and found that Tommy and two of his friends were having sexual intercourse with Evelyn. Evelyn found this to be a positive experience. She said the boys did not make fun of her like the other kids did, they gave her candy, and it felt good to do loving.

In this case, the child's developmental delays and lack of social skills probably caused her to be rejected by peers. Her naïveté and emotional deprivation made her an easy and willing target for adolescent boys.

The Impact of Being Sexually Abused on Future Vulnerability to Sexual Abuse

Sexually abused children may be at even greater risk than those mistreated in other ways for sexual abuse in foster care. The author found that 24% of a clinical sample of close to 300 sexually abused children had been victimized by more than one person. Although half had been victimized in contexts where there was more than one offender, the remainder were subjected to serial sexual abuse by different offenders (Faller, 1989). This finding and those of other writers (e.g., De Young, 1984) support clinical assumptions regarding effects of sexual abuse on future vulnerability. Furthermore, the research of Ryan and her colleagues (McFadden and Ryan, 1986; Ryan, McFadden, and Wiencek, 1987), which examined predictors of child maltreatment in foster care including predictors of sexual abuse, found that having been sexually abused or exploited previously rendered children at risk for sexual abuse in foster care involving penetration. (However, there was no comparable relationship between prior victimization and sexual abuse without penetration.)

Five ways in which sexual victimization can contribute to subsequent sexual abuse and activity will be described here. First, children who have experienced sexual abuse may have been socialized by their offenders to behave in ways that can be interpreted as invitations to sexual activity. The example that follows is one involving very young children.

> *Case example:* Nancy, 4, and Denise, 3, were sexually exploited by their mother and her boyfriend. In addition to having been sexually abused by them, they were made to undress and have their pictures taken in sexual poses with numerous men.

> Their foster mother described them as both avoidant of and provocative with her husband. When they were having their baths, they would run out of the bathroom naked and "moon" him, then retreat again to the bathroom.

> They engaged in a comparable pattern when church elders came to visit. First they hid; then they came and sat on the laps of the male elders, stroking their faces and chests and calling them "my man."

This is the kind of behavior that may be seen with very young children. Older children may wear tight clothing, clothing more suitable to adult women, or makeup. Or they may behave in ways that seem seductive (McFadden, 1986). It is important to appreciate that such behavior is a product of socialization and not a spontaneous expression of sexual desire.

Second, sexually abused children may have expectations that adults will be sexual with them. Often they learn to equate sexual behavior with affectionate behavior. They, therefore, expect adults to be sexual when showing affection. When these children fail to resist sexual overtures, it is often because they need the nurturance for which sex has become a substitute.

Third, victims' early introduction to sexual behavior results in precocious sexual awareness. Victimized children experience sexual pleasure and often orgasm at a much younger age than most children. Physical pleasure is more likely to be associated with sexual abuse if the offender has gradually introduced the child to sex and has not employed force. Especially if the victim's life is devoid of other normal childhood pleasures, the attraction of sexual behavior is enhanced.

Fourth, repeated involvement in sexual abuse may represent counterphobic behavior. De Young (1984) has described four young girls who were traumatically sexually abused and who initially evidenced marked negative reactions to these experiences and phobic responses. Nevertheless, they all were later involved in sexual interactions with older people in which they played an initiating or participating role and did not display the evidence of trauma noted earlier. She hypothesized that the reinvolvement was a form of counterphobic behavior. That is, they achieved a sense of mastery over their previous traumas by seeking out sexually abusive situations where they could be in control.

Fifth, a related dynamic that is sometimes present is identification with the aggressor. Victims overcome their feelings of vulnerability and helplessness by becoming like their abusers and sexually victimizing other, usually younger, children. Boys are more likely than girls to cope with the trauma of sexual abuse by identification with the aggressor. This is probably so because offenders against boys are more often of their sex, making such identification easier, and because boys are socialized to be sexually aggressive and girls are not.

Summary of Findings Regarding the Role of the Victim

What the discussion of the role of the victim suggests is that all kinds of maltreatment can increase a child's vulnerability to sexual abuse. Moreover, sexually abused children are probably at greater risk than children who have only suffered physical and emotional maltreatment, in large part because the insults of the sexual abuse are compounded by those of physical and emotional maltreatment. The general outcome of physical and emotional abuse and neglect is to create deficits that may result in a propensity to tolerate sexual abuse. In contrast, sexually abused children, because of their anomalous socialization and early exposure to sex, may expect, accept, and/or experience some pleasure from sexual interactions with older persons. In addition, children who have been quite traumatized by sexual abuse may nevertheless be drawn into subsequent sexual relationships with adults in order to work through their trauma. Making these sexual encounters even more difficult to understand is the fact that more than one dynamic may be involved in an incident of sexual abuse in foster care and different dynamics may operate at different times with the same victim. Nevertheless, the contribution of the child should never be viewed as the primary cause of sexual abuse.

TYPES OF SEXUAL ABUSE

Three different types of sexual abuse in foster care have been identified. These are sexual abuse by other children, opportunistic sexual abuse by a foster parent, and planned sexual abuse by a foster parent. These will be described and illustrated.

Sexual Abuse by Other Children

Foster children may become sexually involved with one another or with biological children in the foster home. It is less common to find the biological children initiating sexual contact with foster children (Patricia Ryan, personal communication, 1989). Sometimes this activity is mutual sexual exploration, but, in other instances, it involves older or more sophisticated children taking sexual advantage of younger or more naive children. A common predisposing situation is the presence of one or more sexually abused child in the same foster home.

Foster care may become a context for child-child sexual abuse because the scarcity of foster homes sometimes results in a foster family being asked to take more children than it can feasibly care for. Consequently, supervision is not adequate, and children's needs for nurturance cannot be met by the foster parents. The absence of placements may be an even greater problem where sexually abused children are concerned. Few families are willing to care for sexually victimized children at a time when they are an increasing percentage of the children coming into care (42% in Michigan; Susan Kelley, personal communication, Ann Arbor, 1988). Therefore, it is not uncommon for those families willing to foster these children to have more than one placed with them.

Because of the propensity of sexual abuse victims to act out sexually and to allow themselves to be revictimized, as described above, the presence of one or more victims of sexual maltreatment in a foster home can be a volatile situation. Moreover, as already pointed out, even those children who were victims of other types of maltreatment are at risk because of their unmet dependency and affective needs and the anomie of foster care.

The case example described below is more involved than some but is illustrative:

Case example: There were eight children living with Mrs. P. She and her husband had been regarded as model foster parents. There was an 18-year-old adopted daughter, and two foster sisters, aged 16 and 15. These girls had been sexually involved with older boys in a previous foster home. In addition, there was 12-year-old Johnny, whose father was in prison for sodomizing him and an older brother. Johnny had been at the Ps for a year and a half. Ten-year-old Vincent was the new boy; he had only been at the Ps for eight weeks. Then there was 6-year-old James. The Ps had had him since birth and had adopted him. When James had been 3, he was sodomized by a very disturbed foster brother, who also plotted to kill the Ps and steal their money. The two youngest children were Sally, 5, and her brother, Gregory, 3. These children had been at the Ps since Gregory was an infant, and the plan was for the Ps to adopt them.

Two very disruptive events preceded the sexual abuse in the P home. First, Mr. P's mother, who had Alzheimer's disease, was moved in. She was put into one of two downstairs bedrooms, the other being the P's bedroom. Prior to her advent, Sally and Gregory had slept there. On the second floor were two large bedrooms, one for boys and one for girls. Second, Mr. P died suddenly of a heart attack. Despite the tragic loss of her husband, Mrs. P did not want to give up fostering. Because all of the children except perhaps Vincent appeared attached to the Ps, the Department of Social Services decided not to move any of them and tried to give Mrs. P as much support as they could to sustain her through her grief.

Gregory told Mrs. P and then his foster care worker that James had "poked him in the butt with his wiener." Sally corroborated his story. When James was confronted, he vehemently denied that he had done anything to Gregory. However, he said that Johnny had poked him in the butt and was teaching them all to play with wieners. They would rub themselves and each other to see whose could get the biggest. James said Johnny also initiated contests to see who could pee the farthest. In addition, James said Johnny was doing things with the girls. Later James denied that Johnny had sodomized him. Although Johnny denied any sexual activities, Vincent corroborated James's assertions regarding the masturbation and urination. No further information was obtained regarding any sexual activity between Johnny and the girls or the sodomizing of James.

In this case, it is unclear whether sexual abuse would have occurred if Mr. P had not died suddenly. Nevertheless, it is clear that trying to handle eight children, all of whom had been maltreated, and a woman with Alzheimer's disease is too much for any foster parent. The risk was increased by the sleeping arrangements, which precluded adequate supervision. The dynamics of the sexual abuse of Gregory by James probably involved identification with the aggressor. It is noteworthy that Gregory was the same age as James when he was first sodomized. It is very likely that Johnny sodomized James, and the dynamics of this abuse would be similar. Although Johnny's initiation of the other boys into masturbation and his involvement with the girls may have stemmed from sexual precocity, sexual activity by 12-year-old boys is common. Its occurrence in foster care is nevertheless worrisome.

Opportunistic Sexual Abuse by Foster Parents

The term "opportunistic sexual abuse" refers to victimization by an adult who in other circumstances would be unlikely to be sexual with a child. In most cases, the offender is the foster father. This man does not have a history of sexual abuse and may be raising or have raised his own children without any sexual involvement. However, once he sexually abuses one child, he may repeat the pattern with subsequent children.

There are three characteristics of the fostering situation generally that may play a role and additional ones that are found when sexually victimized children are reabused in foster care. One of the general factors that may increase risk is the fact that the incest taboo does not operate to inhibit sexual involvement between the foster father and foster child. If the child is an adolescent, the prohibitions against sexual contact may be even weaker, and the foster father may regard this as an adulterous rather than abusive sexual liaison (Ryan, personal communication, 1989). Regardless of the child's age, the foster father may rather abruptly find himself in a situation where he is having daily, intense contact with someone else's child. He may have responsibility for such activities as bathing, disciplining, or putting the child to bed. Because the child is not his, this intimacy may be more likely to stimulate sexual arousal and/or he may be more likely to act on these feelings. Furthermore, the fairly frequent changes in family composition, which regularly require development of new parent-child relationships, may exacerbate these dynamics.

The second characteristic found generally in the foster care context relates to husband-wife dynamics and fostering. Often the woman gains more from fostering than the man. In many cases, she is the one who wants to become the foster parent, and the foster father agrees to it. The foster mother usually has greater responsibility and gains more in self-worth and a purpose for her life from fostering. The rewards she receives from being a foster parent may be greater than those she receives for being a wife. The demands may be great as well, so great that the foster mother has little time or energy left to meet her husband's needs, including his needs for nurturance and sex. He may be "left out in the cold." His use of the children for sex may reflect not only the need for emotional and sexual gratification but his anger at his wife for deserting him in favor of someone else's children.

A third and related characteristic of foster care is that, by its very nature, it results in a great deal of stress and numerous crises for the families involved. The foster parents may feel overwhelmed and unsupported, as often worker caseloads are so high that families have little contact with the professionals who are supposed to supervise them. In these emotionally draining circumstances, family members may regress and look to get their needs met by the foster children. These high-stress situations can play a role in sexual abuse by foster fathers (Ryan, personal communication, 1989). In addition, such tensions can be a factor in child-child sexual encounters. Children may react to the turmoil by being sexual with one another, and lack of adult supervision because of preoccupation with other crises may contribute to child-child sexual encounters.

Children who have already been sexually abused may be at greater risk than other children for sexual maltreatment in foster care. This heightened vulnerability arises not only from victims' behavior and attitudes but also from perceptions of the foster parent (usually the foster father). The presence of a sexually abused child in the home may lead a foster parent to consider the possibility of engaging in sex with a child when he had not considered doing so before. In fact, he may be titillated by thoughts of having sex with a child. These reactions may be enhanced by behaviors of the child, which he interprets as sexual invitations. Furthermore, because the child has already been sexually abused, the foster father may rationalize his behavior by reminding himself that he is not the first adult to have sex with the victim. He may, therefore, convince himself the abuse will not be particularly harmful. In the following case example, a number of the predisposing factors are present.

Case example: Carrie, 5, and Yvonne, 6, were placed in foster care following their reports that they were involved in group sex with their mother and father. Their first foster family asked that they be moved after two months because the foster parents could not tolerate their sexual play with each other. After supervised visits with their parents, they were usually caught in bed together engaging in mutual fondling.

Their second set of foster parents, Mr. and Mrs. T, were forewarned about their sexual acting out. The T home was a potential adoptive home for Carrie and Yvonne. Mrs. T, an "earth mother" type, appeared more eager to adopt than Mr. T. Mrs. T had been married previously and had a teenaged son. The Ts had not been able to conceive. Mrs. T was also licensed to do day care and took in several preschool-aged children.

The Ts lived in a large, old farmhouse. Carrie and Yvonne decided there were ghosts in the house and used their fear of ghosts as a reason for getting into bed with the Ts. No limits were set on this behavior. The children would wiggle down between the Ts and rub up against them. On these occasions, they would also sometimes describe their sexual abuse.

Mr. T later admitted that he found these revelations both disgusting and fascinating. He also confessed that on two occasions he was sexually aroused by the combination of their wiggly, warm bodies and their statements about sex with their parents. He said he found this to be a frustrating experience, stating he would have had sex with his wife had the children not been there.

His first sexual interaction was to allow the girls to watch him urinate and then have them touch his penis. He said that, initially when he did this, he thought it was a way to teach them not to be afraid of penises. Soon he was having them come into the bathroom with him when he had no intention of urinating. He would sit on the edge of the bathtub, take out his penis, and have them fondle him. He said that he never ejaculated during these encounters but would later masturbate while reliving the incidents or would think of them when he was having sex with Mrs. T.

In this case, it appears that Mrs. T is the one who is more invested in children. Mr. T probably felt he was the one responsible for their not having children of their own, adding to his sense of isolation. Moreover, the children were allowed to physically come between the Ts in bed. Mr. T's frustrated desire to have intercourse with his wife after having been aroused by the children is an interesting illustration of his needs not being met. His admission to being fascinated yet disgusted by the children's statements is a clear example of titillation. The children's behavior in bed may well have been a reflection of activities related to group sex with their parents.

Planned Sexual Abuse of Foster Children

Foster care, like other child-caring institutions, can be vulnerable to exploitation by those who are sexually attracted to children or desire to use them sexually for profit. Examples of other facilities that may be similarly at risk are day-care centers, camps, schools, and group-care facilities. Persons whose primary sexual orientation is to children (pedophiles), individuals who are polymorphously perverse and whose perversions include sex with children, and people intending to use children in pornography or prostitution may seek licensing as foster parents. Fortunately, this kind of misuse of foster care seems to be rare. However, it often goes on for years without detection.

Pedophiles are likely to be single male foster parents. In the polymorphous situation, there may be a couple involved, as well as others outside the family. Group sex may be practiced. An individual or a couple may be the foster parents when exploitation is the primary motive for becoming a foster parent. Sometimes a sexually abusive foster parent will encourage other like-minded people to become foster parents. One also occasionally finds a foster parent who develops a sex ring with current and former foster children and their friends.

An important issue is why an adult would choose foster care as the context for finding child sexual partners. First, foster care affords the adult a great deal of unsupervised access to the child, more, for example, than a school setting or an institutional placement. Illustrative of the role lack of supervision can play is the finding of Ryan and colleagues (1987), who found that sexual penetration while in foster care was associated with lack of contact between the worker and the child and lack of visitation between the child and the biological family. A second reason exploitative adults might choose foster care is that the child is more dependent upon the offender than in other contexts where the child goes home at night to parents. Third, the offender is likely to be aware of the unmet dependency and affective needs of abused and neglected children. These can be manipulated by the abuser to gain compliance and participation of the victim. The case example that follows illustrates some of the characteristics of this type of foster care sexual abuse.

Case example: Mr. P was an X-ray technician. He had been married for three years to a woman who had a 4-year-old son when they married. Ultimately it was learned that Mr. P's wife had divorced him after she found him fondling her son's penis. However, when this sexual abuse happened, she made no report.

Mr. P's first involvement with the Department of Social Services was after his divorce. He was a volunteer driver, taking children to various appointments, when he was not working. He then applied to be a foster parent. He faithfully attended the six orientation sessions and was regarded as a very good candidate for foster parenting. He asked that he only be given boys who were 6 years or older, stating that his single-parent status might present problems for girl children and that he did not know how to care for very young children. The Department of Social Services found these requests to be eminently sensible.

Initially, he would only take one boy at a time, and usually these placements lasted a long time, because he also asked for children who were not likely to return home. After five years as a foster parent, he had his attic finished so he could accommodate more children. He then was licensed to take as many as five boys.

He sexually abused all the boys who were placed with him. He decided to expand from one boy to several after he met a pedophile, Mr. X, who ran a child sex ring. Mr. P found Mr. X through an ad in a pedophile magazine. Mr. X persuaded Mr. P to develop his own sex ring of foster children. Mr. X then got Mr. P to take pictures of some of his boys and sell the pictures to him. As time went on, Mr. P began to make a considerable profit from the sale of these pictures. He was also persuaded by Mr. X to share his boys with him.

Mr. P was caught when one of the boys refused to return to foster care after a visit to his grandparents. When Mr. P was interviewed, he confessed and asked for help. He also described how he got involved in sexual abuse of boys. He said that he had had a couple of sexual experiences with his nephews when he was in his twenties. When he married, he did not intend to molest his wife's son, but "fell into it naturally." He was very upset when she divorced him and felt quite deprived. However, he admitted that he missed the stepson more than the wife.

He said he decided to become a foster parent so he could find a boy to replace the stepson he had lost. Nevertheless, he said that the companionship was more important to him than the sex. He described himself as shy with the first boy, waiting several months before he started to stroke the boy's body. He declared that all of the boys enjoyed their sexual activities. He also said that he gave them a lot of individual attention and that he was sure that he "gave them much more than I took away." He was quite surprised at Kevin, the boy who told, because he said that he really loved Kevin and had just bought him a new ten-speed bicycle.

In this case, although Mr. P protests that he was looking for companionship more than sex from his victims, it was clear that the motivation for becoming a foster parent was to have access to young boys. He was also involved in a progression of sexual activity beginning with single victims, then multiple victims, and finally pornography. Although he does not appear to have become involved in picture taking for financial reasons, as time went on his financial status improved markedly because of it, so much so that he could afford a ten-speed bicycle for Kevin. In addition, like many pedophiles, Mr. P has deluded himself into believing that his abuse was not that harmful and that the boys benefited greatly from their relationship with him.

RESEARCH

Although there has been some attention in the research to sexual abuse by substitute caretakers (Faller, 1989; Finkelhor et al., 1988; Halpern, 1987), foster care has not generally been the focus of these studies. In fact, the work of Ryan and colleagues (McFadden and Ryan, 1986; Ryan et al., 1987, 1988) and my research are the only two studies that could be found. Ryan and colleagues surveyed all types of maltreatment by foster parents and drew their cases from five states. The source of the data was agency records. They found 14 cases of sexual abuse not involving penetration and 13 involving penetration. Cases involving child-child sexual abuse were not defined as sexual abuse but as neglect by foster parents (Ryan, personal communication, 1989). My sample is not systematically drawn and consists of cases of sexually abused children seen for diagnosis and/or treatment by the Interdisciplinary Project on Child Abuse and Neglect (IPCAN). There are 40 children who were involved in sexual abuse in 21 foster homes. Of these 40 children, 8 were offenders. There might have been other children in the foster homes who were sexually abused, but, in order for the case to be included in the study, the victim had to be interviewed and the case validated.[1] Findings from my study will be presented and, where relevant, compared with those of Ryan and her colleagues.

Of the children, 40% were male and 60% were female. The mean age of the children was 7.6—8.3 years for boys and 7.1 for girls (n.s.). The proportion of males is higher than that of the total sample of approximately 300 victims seen by IPCAN, which is 28%; however, the age of foster care victims is virtually the same as that for the total sample (which was 7.9 years). In Ryan et al.'s cases, the proportion of victims of sexual abuse who were female was higher (85%) and the age of victims older (12.7 years). The larger proportion of male victims in my sample may relate to the inclusion of child-child encounters. The younger age of victims in my sample may also be a function of selection criteria for sending cases to an agency like IPCAN, which handles situations that are particularly difficult to diagnose; arguably, cases involving younger victims are more difficult to diagnose.

Twenty-one children in my sample were sexually abused by their foster fathers, nine by other foster children, and two by friends of the foster family. As already noted, eight of the children studied were offenders (and were involved in child-child sexual abuse). All of the latter had been sexually abused before they became perpetrators, two in foster care and the remainder in their biological families. Five were male and three female.

The most serious sexual abuse was coded for each child. Noncontact sex and fondling were the least serious, followed by oral sex, then penetration; exploitation (pornography and prostitution) was the most serious. Eighteen of the children (45%) were involved in some form of penetration; for nine (22.5%), oral sex was the most serious form of abuse; and for 13 (32.5%), the most severe form of molestation was fondling. None of the children only experienced noncontact sexual abuse, and none in the sample was involved in exploitation, although other children in some of the homes were. Ryan included oral sex in the category of sexual abuse involving penetration and, as noted above, found the sample almost evenly split between sexual abuse with penetration and without.

Cases were also categorized according to the context of the abuse: child-child sexual abuse, opportunistic sexual abuse, or planned sexual abuse. Planned sexual abuse in foster care, on the basis of these limited data, appears to be rare, two instances having been documented in my cases. Ryan and colleagues (Ryan, personal communication, 1989) found two or three possible cases. Six victims in my sample were sexually abused in planned sexual abuse. There were other victims from these two sites who were not interviewed. One of the foster homes was reportedly part of a ring of sexually abusive foster parents that exploited over 100 children. Fifteen children (37.5%) were sexually abused by adults involved in opportunistic sexual abuse, and 19 (47.5%) were involved in child-child encounters in foster care. There were differences in victim sex for the three contexts. Children involved in child-child encounters were almost equally likely to be boys as girls; victims of opportunistic abuse were more likely to be girls; and those of planned abuse, boys (chi-square = 12.9; $p = .002$).

Finally, data were collected on whether the child had been sexually abused before the abuse in foster care: 29 (72.5%) had been sexually victimized prior to placement, and 11 (27.5%) had not. Children who were subjected to planned sexual abuse were less likely than those in the other two contexts to have experienced prior victimization (chi-square = 6.1; $p = .05$). These findings are consistent with the clinical dynamics of the three types of cases described earlier in the chapter.

It is important to conclude the discussion of the research findings with a cautionary note. As has just been demonstrated, there has been very little systematic exploration of sexual abuse in foster care. The reader must appreciate that the findings discussed here are very preliminary. My sample is relatively small and consists of clinical cases, and the research findings were supplemented by only one other study, that of Ryan and colleagues.

WHAT CAN BE DONE ABOUT
THE PROBLEM?

When children are placed in foster care, it is to provide them with a living arrangement that is superior to the one from which they have been removed. The burden is on the professionals to assure that children are not further harmed in foster care. Strategies that involve training, screening, case management, and intervention that might reduce the risk of sexual abuse in foster care will be described.

Training and Guidance for Foster Parents

First, foster parents who care for sexually abused children require special training and guidance so they can address the unique needs of these children. Because sexual abuse is often not discovered until after a child has been placed, and because many parents who do not volunteer to care for sexually abused children end up doing so, all foster parents should receive this training (Ryan, personal communication, 1989). Ideally, they should receive both preparatory training and then ongoing support when caring for a sexually abused child, to address problems as they arise.

Training for foster parents can be delivered in a variety of formats. It might be part of a more general program for foster parents (McFadden, 1984; Ryan, 1984) or it might be classes focused specifically on fostering sexually abused children (McFadden, 1986). Finally, preparation and support may be provided on an informal basis to individual foster families.

McFadden (1986) has prepared a very thoughtful training program and manual for foster parents caring for sexually abused children that consists of four sessions and supporting documents: (1) the world of the sexually abused child, (2) behaviors of the child who has been sexually abused, (3) protecting the child and our (the foster) family, and (4) the foster parents' therapeutic role (McFadden, 1986).

The following outline is somewhat more detailed and is based upon my clinical experience with sexually victimized children and sexual abuse in foster care. Topics suggested are the following:

(1) An exploration of attitudes and feelings about sexuality and sexual abuse
(2) Normal childhood gender identification and sexual development
(3) Normal adolescent sexual identification and sexual development
(4) Sexual sequelae of sexual abuse
(5) Behavioral sequelae of sexual abuse

   (6) Strategies for management of sexual sequelae

   (7) Strategies for management of behavioral sequelae

   (8) Variations in victim attitudes and emotional reactions to the sexual abuse, the mother, and the offender

   (9) The causes of sexual abuse

 (10) Variations in the reactions of nonabusive parents to sexual abuse

 (11) The dynamics of relationships between sexually abused and nonabused siblings

 (12) How to handle visitation with the sexually abusive family

This sort of training program is what is hoped for. However, because resources in child welfare are limited, many communities will not be able to offer this level of support.

Nevertheless, in the absence of specialized training programs, the worker can provide individual families with guidance that can minimize the risk for sexual abuse in foster care and provide therapeutic intervention for sexually abused children. Families need, at minimum, information about the effects and sequelae of sexual abuse. Most important, they need to be made aware of the sexual behaviors of these children. Sexually abused children are likely to engage in excessive masturbation, consensual sexual interaction with other children, and behaviors that might be perceived as being seductive. In addition, sexual abuse victims are vulnerable to revictimization and becoming offenders.

Foster parents can be taught how to set limits when children engage in inappropriate sexual behavior and to make rules that will reduce the risk of child-child and other sexual abuse. An example is the following set of rules foster parents might make related to "privates":

  (1) It's okay to touch your privates, but it should be done in private, that is, in bed at night or in the bathroom.

  (2) While you can touch your privates, you should not touch anyone else's privates.

  (3) No one else should touch your privates.

  (4) You do not show anyone else your privates (except the doctor and so on).

  (5) No one else should show you his or her privates.

While rules like these might seem to make children unduly self-conscious and inhibited about their bodies, such an outcome is preferable to sexual abuse in foster care.

Other rules may also be necessary, such as restrictions related to bathing, toileting, sleeping arrangements, and nudity around the house. These might be as follows:

(1) One child in the bathroom at a time for bathing.
(2) You must wear your bathrobe to and from the bathroom.
(3) Only one child in the bathroom while toileting.
(4) Only the foster mother can assist in wiping after toileting.
(5) Only one child to a bed.

Foster parents should be encouraged to have family meetings in which the rules regarding these daily activities are discussed. As new children enter the home, the rules should be again discussed at a meeting involving all children.

Some provocative behaviors may not be appropriate for rules but are better handled by the foster parents when they arise. When children engage in inappropriate hugging, kissing, or lap-sitting, the foster parent should be instructed to interrupt the behavior and either demonstrate or describe more appropriate interaction to the child. For example, a child might be told, "Kids don't put their tongues in people's mouths when they kiss. They kiss on the cheek." Similarly, a 12-year-old lap-sitter might be told that she is too old to sit on the foster father's lap, but she can sit beside him on the couch when watching television.

Sometimes it will be appropriate to assist foster parents in developing behavioral child management interventions to extinguish inappropriate sexual interaction and foster appropriate interactions. The case example illustrates foster parent management of some of these sexual behaviors.

Case example: The Gs were new foster parents. They had two children of their own. They were asked to care for Sally, 6, who had been sexually abused by her father and her grandfather. Prior to that abuse, her mother had viciously physically abused her, and custody had been given to her father.

The first problem the Gs had with Sally was her open discussion of her abuse with school staff, classmates, neighbors, and their children. They were concerned about the effect of these disclosures on Sally's ability to make friends, on their relationships in the community, and on their children. With the assistance of their caseworker and Sally's therapist, they praised Sally for being brave and telling about the abuse, but advised her that she should limit her discussion about it to them, the caseworker, and her therapist. As far as they were able to tell, Sally stopped telling everyone she met about the sexual abuse.

However, they began to notice that Sally was unusually attentive to the toileting habits of their 2-year-old son, Jason. She would follow him into the bathroom and want to help him. She also expressed a great deal of interest in his "rootie" and wanted to know why it was so small. The foster parents explained to Sally that Jason was learning to go peepee by himself, and it was important that he do this alone. If he needed help, Mrs. G would help him. At the suggestion of the therapist, the Gs made a general rule that only one person should be in the bathroom at a time.

In addition, Mr. G expressed discomfort with the way Sally wiggled around when she sat on his lap. He felt that she was trying to locate his penis and rub her crotch on it. Initially he was instructed that he should tell her that she had to sit still if she wanted to stay on his lap. This appeared to work for a few minutes, but then she seemed to forget and start wiggling. He then was told to remove her from his lap when she resumed wiggling and tell her that she had to sit beside him if she was going to wiggle. Eventually the combination of instruction not to wiggle and removal if she started again extinguished her wiggling. She was able to sit on his lap without masturbating.

In this case, the child had a number of hypersexual behaviors that were very concerning to the foster parents. These were dealt with fairly successfully so that Sally was not involved in reabuse and the placement was not disrupted. However, ideally, the Gs should have received prior instruction in how to care for a sexually abused child, and probably their first foster child should not have been a sexually abused one with Sally's level of disturbance.

Screening Foster Parents

A question that is sometimes asked is whether it is possible to screen foster parent applicants for potential or actual sexual abusers. It appears that some sexually abusive situations could be avoided by screening, but most cannot. One problem that makes screening difficult is that there are very few predictors of sexually abusive behavior. A second problem is that family dynamics as well as individual characteristics may play a role in sexual abuse. In an attempt to understand how foster family characteristics might play a role in sexual abuse in foster care, Ryan and colleagues (1988) examined a number of factors (e.g., whether the home was in compliance with licensing standards, the total number of children in the home, prior substantiated maltreatment allegations against the family, and the foster parent holding strong religious views about discipline). They found that none of the factors they examined was related to sexual abuse of children in foster care.

There is really only one characteristic that is clearly indicative of risk of sexual abuse as a foster parent. That is having sexually abused a child in the past. Sexual abuse is regarded as a chronic condition for which there is no real cure but only enhanced capability to control (Faller, 1988; Groth, 1979). Therefore, if a person has a history of sex offenses, he or she should not be licensed as a foster parent.

Unfortunately, most applicants will not readily disclose such a history. However, it is worthwhile asking about possible sexual abuse within the larger context of an extensive personal history. In asking about intimate relationships and sexual activity, the worker can indirectly ask about sexual abuse. Revealing information may be obtained by inquiring about the oldest and the youngest sexual partner he or she has had (Faller, 1988). Depending upon the age of the respondent, an age gap of five or more years is cause for further investigation. Ryan (personal communication, 1989) suggests that letting applicants know that sexual abuse (as well as other types of maltreatment) are issues caseworkers monitor may discourage potential abusers, especially pedophiles, from pursuing licenses as foster parents. In addition, although the majority of sex offenders are male, exploration of past sexual activity should be made with potential foster mothers as well.

Because it is very unlikely that sexual abusers will be candid about their victimizing, other sources of information must be sought. Police and protective services records need to be examined. It is important not to merely rely on state abuse registers or state police records because frequently these are incomplete. An allegation of sexual abuse that has been denied will not be in the state register, but the county will usually have a record. Similarly, a local law enforcement agency may have records that the state police do not have. In addition, if the person has lived previously in another state, information from that location should be sought. Pedophiles who have lost their licenses as child care providers or who have been investigated by the police have been known to move to another state and again attempt to gain access to children. Moreover, it is often important to investigate records in addition to those of protective services and the police, for example, records of licensing agencies.

Another way a past history of sexual abuse may be uncovered is by taking a careful history of the potential foster parent's past activities with children. Persons in responsible positions related to these activities should be contacted. If these persons are not listed as references by the applicant, the licensing worker should ask why.

As part of screening, other possible correlates of sexually abusive behavior should also be explored. However, positive findings are certainly not conclusive of risk for sexual abuse. Rather, they should lead to further exploration and be weighed along with other factors in making licensing decisions.

It is important to ask if the potential foster parent was sexually abused as a child. A foster father with such a history may be more vulnerable to becoming an abuser, whereas a foster mother may be at greater risk for allowing children in her care to be sexually victimized. As with information about adult sexual activity with children, any history of childhood sexual abuse should be ascertained as the interviewer collects information about the person's general history. However, a finding of sexual abuse in childhood should not rule out foster parenthood, for many excellent and very sensitive foster parents were sexually abused as children. Nevertheless, if an applicant has been sexually abused, the licensing worker needs to explore this experience in some detail and to determine its effects. Sometimes a potential foster parent will need additional assistance to cope with this abuse, and other times it will be a contraindication for foster parenthood.

McCormack and Selvaggio (1989) have devised an instrument for detecting pedophiles who apply to be Big Brothers, which includes several questions about sexual victimization during childhood, questions that probe for social isolation, and questions that might reveal attitudes indicative of sexual attraction to children (e.g., a belief that children are innocent, a preference for the company of children). This is an unvalidated instrument but nevertheless an important first step in developing a method for systematically screening out pedophiles applying for child-care positions.

A second possible correlate of risk for sexual abuse may be having been physically maltreated or otherwise emotionally deprived as a child. Sometimes adults with such a history will lack the skills for showing affection and may manifest their caring for children in a sexual way. These adults may also be at risk for being physically abusive. However, as with a history of sexual victimization, such a finding should not automatically disqualify the applicant. Rather, it should lead the worker to explore the applicant's relationships, both with children and adults, for evidence that he or she has the ability to show affection appropriately and, with children, to set limits.

A third possible correlate of risk for sexual abuse is sexual dysfunction. Again, sexual problems should not automatically result in rejection as a foster parent. Nevertheless, the worker should bear in mind possible patterns in the sexuality of offenders and their families. The first is evidence of the offender having discomfort with adult sexual relationships. The second is hypersexuality on the part of the offender or the family, evidenced by a description of sexual activity several times a day, sometimes with multiple partners, and practice of aberrant sexual activities (e.g., group sex, voyeurism, sadomasochism, cross-dressing, and exposure). Also of concern is children observing adult sexual activities.

Other characteristics that might indicate a risk of sexual abuse, as well as being contraindications for foster parenthood, are substance abuse, criminal activity, violent behavior, and mental illness. While none of these is so directly related to sexual abuse as the factors just discussed, they all suggest deficits in the ability to foster.

Exit Interviews for Foster Children

Ryan (personal communication, 1989) suggests a client satisfaction survey for children who are being moved from one foster home to another, who are being returned home, or who are going to some other living arrangement. This practice would not prevent sexual abuse of the children being interviewed, but it could prevent future victimization. Of course, caseworkers have responsibility for ongoing assessment of children's functioning in foster care, but, for a variety of reasons, victims might be more reluctant to disclose sexual abuse while they are still residents of the foster home. A postplacement interview could focus on a range of aspects of the foster home, not merely sexual practices.

The Impact of Funding Issues on Safety in Foster Care

The absence of sufficient funding prevents the assurance of child safety in foster care. Without adequate resources, foster parents do not receive a decent wage. In fact, they barely, and sometimes do not, receive enough to meet the child's basic needs. This limits both the number and the types of people willing and able to be foster parents. Another consequence is that professionals cannot really expect the time commitment from foster parents that is necessary if they are to be part of the therapeutic process for the child. For example, it is unreasonable to expect a foster father to come to meetings if he is the sole wage earner in the family and the family is not adequately compensated for fostering.

A second major impact of inadequate funding relates to the capability of supporting foster parents. Frequently, the caseloads of child welfare workers are very large, and they do not have the time to provide the needed supervision and support for foster parents trying to deal with the special needs of sexually abused children. In addition, without funding, there will be no parenting classes, and it will be impossible to provide the resources to integrate foster parents into the treatment of the child.

Ironically, paying foster parents for their services and providing adequate support for them is much cheaper than institutional care, which is often where sexually abused children who are retraumatized in foster care ultimately are placed. Currently, however, foster parents are left with 24-hours-a-day, seven-days-a-week responsibility often for quite damaged children without adequate compensation and support. Mental health professionals must look beyond the individual sexually abused child in their advocacy and advocate for foster children in general. Taking the broader view is essential if foster care is to make a difference for children rather than being an institution at risk for iatrogenic effects.

CONCLUSION

Foster care and other substitute care arrangements may possess characteristics that increase risk for sexual abuse. First, children requiring foster care may be more vulnerable to sexual exploitation because of past physical and emotional maltreatment and past sexual abuse. However, the victim is not the major contributor to maltreatment in foster care. Structural characteristics of foster care and attributes of the foster parent and family play a greater role. These include the fact that foster care is a familylike living arrangement in which the incest taboo is not present; the relative lack of supervision of the adult-child relationship, when compared with other substitute care; possible differential gratification that husband and wife receive from fostering; and the high level of stress inherent in foster care.

Three different types of sexual abuse in foster care have been described. The first is child-child sexual abuse, which usually entails children who were previously sexually victimized becoming perpetrators in the foster care context. The second is called opportunistic sexual abuse in which an adult, usually a foster father, who does not have a previous history of sexually abusing children becomes involved in sexual activity with a foster child. Structural factors, noted above, and child behavior may lead to sexual arousal in the foster parent and then to abuse. Finally, there is planned sexual abuse in foster care in which persons seek to be foster parents with the intention of sexually abusing the children for whom they are given responsibility. These persons may be pedophiles or persons who intend to sexually exploit children for money.

Mental health professionals and others must do whatever is possible to prevent children who have already been traumatized from being further maltreated in foster care. This can be done by providing support and guidance to foster parents who are caring for sexually abused children, by screening foster care applicants for potential sexual abusers, and by advocacy for adequate funding and support for foster parents dealing with sexually abused children.

NOTE

1. For a description of the procedures employed to validate allegations of sexual abuse, see Faller (1988).

REFERENCES

De Young, Mary. 1984. "Counter-Phobic Behavior in Multiply Victimized Children." *Child Welfare* 63(4):333-39.

Faller, Kathleen Coulborn. 1986. *Case Management Using Home Based Services with High Risk Families.* Ann Arbor: University of Michigan, Interdisciplinary Project on Child Abuse and Neglect.

———. 1988. *Child Sexual Abuse: An Interdisciplinary Manual for Diagnosis, Case Management, and Treatment.* New York: Columbia University Press.

———. Forthcoming. "Children Who Are Sexually Abused by More than One Person." *Victimology.*

Finkelhor, David, Linda Williams, and Nanci Burns. 1988. *Nursery Crimes: Sexual Abuse in Day Care.* Newbury Park, CA: Sage.

Groth, Nicholas. 1979. *Men Who Rape.* New York: Plenum.

Halpern, Judith. 1987. "Family Therapy in Father-Son Incest: A Case Study." *Social Casework* 68(2):88-93.

Kadushin, Alfred. 1980. *Child Welfare Services.* 3rd. ed. New York: Macmillan.

Kline, Draza and Helen-Marie Overstreet. 1972. *Foster Care of Children: Nurture and Treatment.* New York: Columbia University Press.

McCormack, Arlene and Marialena Selvaggio. 1989. "Screening for Pedophiles in Youth Oriented Community Agencies." *Social Casework* 70(1):37-42.

McFadden, E. Jean. 1984. *Preventing Abuse in Foster Care.* Ypsilanti: Eastern Michigan University, Institute for the Study of Children and Families.

———. 1986. *Fostering the Child Who Has Been Sexually Abused: Instructor's Manual.* Ypsilanti: Eastern Michigan University, Institute for the Study of Children and Families.

McFadden, E. Jean and Patricia Ryan. 1986. "Abuse in Family Foster Homes: Characteristics of the Vulnerable Child." Paper presented at the Sixth International Congress on Child Abuse and Neglect, Sydney, Australia, August.

Ryan, Patricia. 1984. *Fostering Discipline: Instructor's Manual.* Ypsilanti: Eastern Michigan University, Institute for the Study of Children and Families.

Ryan, Patricia, E. Jean McFadden, and Peggy Wiencek. 1987. *Analyzing Abuse in Family Foster Care: Final Report* (draft). Ypsilanti: Eastern Michigan University, Institute for the Study of Children and Families.

———. 1988. "Analysis of Level of Agency Services as Related to Maltreatment in Family Foster Homes." Paper presented at the North Central Sociological Association, Pittsburgh, April.

Chapter 8

SEXUAL ABUSE IN DAY CARE

In less than five years, day care has been transformed from an acceptable solution for mothers who must find someone to look after their children while they work to a potential hazard for children because of risk for maltreatment, especially sexual maltreatment, while in day care. An important question for both parents and professionals is this: How dangerous is day care?

In a landmark national study of sexual abuse in day care, Finkelhor et al. (1988) arrived at an estimate of the incidence of sexual victimization in day care as well as a comparison of the risk of being sexually abused in day care versus at home. Taking their data from 1985, these researchers projected that sexual abuse occurred in 267 centers that year and involved 1,300 children. Although the figure seems high, it is important to appreciate that there are 229,000 licensed day-care programs in the country (Finkelhor et al., 1988). Furthermore, in the year 1985, there were 120,000 cases of sexual abuse substantiated by child protection agencies (American Association for the Protection of Children, 1987).

Based on a calculation of the relative risk of sexual abuse in day care and at home, these researchers conclude that 5.5 children per 10,000 enrolled in day-care centers are sexually abused, but 8.9 children per 10,000 under the age of 6 are sexually abused at home. Although these figures indicate that risk is greater at home, it must be remembered that children in day care are also at home.

What these statistics indicate is that, although sexual abuse in day care is not rampant, it poses a problem of significance for young children. Therefore, it is important for mental health professionals to understand its characteristics and its effects on children. As will be clear from this chapter, there are characteristics that distinguish day-care sexual abuse from other types of sexual victimization, and these characteristics and the young age of its victims result in significant harm from such maltreatment.

In this chapter the following topics will be covered: (1) what causes people to sexually maltreat children in day care, (2) the characteristics of the abuse children experience, (3) various patterns of sexual abuse in day care, (4) the immediate and longer-term effects of sexual abuse in day care, and (5) intervention.

The clinical and research literature on day-care sex abuse is sparse. However, I will make reference to my clinical and research experience with 48 day-care victims and their families as well as knowledge gained as a consultant on other day-care cases. In addition, the national study conducted by Finkelhor and colleagues (1988), noted earlier, will be relied upon. It involved 270 cases identified over a three-year period from 1983 to 1985. Another important study, that of Waterman et al. (1989a, 1989b), will also be cited, from which preliminary results are available. Subjects came from Manhattan Beach, California (including the McMartin preschool) ($n = 82$), where children were allegedly sexually abused by multiple abusers and experienced ritualistic abuse, and from a day-care center in Reno, Nevada ($n = 15$), involving one perpetrator, who admitted to the abuse. In addition, there was a comparison group of children who had not been sexually abused from Manhattan Beach ($n = 37$).

CAUSES OF ADULT
SEXUAL ABUSE OF CHILDREN

Any answer to the question about the causes of sexual abuse in day care must be preliminary because most perpetrators do not confess and receive treatment. Finkelhor and colleagues (1988) note that 83% of the perpetrators in their sample denied the sexual abuse and blamed others.

Reasons for sexual abuse in day care will be divided into two general categories: (1) unplanned sex with children and (2) planned sex with children. These and their subcategories will be discussed.

Unplanned Sex with Children

There are at least three types of unplanned sexual abuse in day care: (1) circumstantial sexual abuse, (2) naive pedophilic sexual abuse, and (3) induced sexual abuse.

(1) Circumstantial sexual abuse. Circumstantial victimization involves a perpetrator with no past history of sexual activity with children who, because of physical or life circumstances, engages in sex with a child. Physical circumstances include experiencing arousal as a result of contact with the child, seeing the child's genitals or naked body, or, in rare instances, smelling the child. For example, the child might grab and hug the offender in a way that causes sexual excitement. The adult then acts on the arousal by sexually maltreating the child.

Other life circumstances that could lead to sexual abuse of day-care children are the absence of other sexual outlets, frustration in another sexual relationship, or some life stress resulting in regression. Under such conditions, an adult who might otherwise not be sexually attracted to children might experience such feelings.

Offenders whose abuse is circumstantial are usually what Groth (1979) would call "regressed offenders"; that is, their primary sexual orientation is to peers but, in certain situations, they experience sexual desire for children. However, once the adult has experienced sex with a child, his or her perception of its gratifying qualities may lead to further sexual encounters with children.

(2) Naive pedophilic abuse. Some persons with pedophilic tendencies are unaware of them. Often they feel an affinity for children but experience this as unrelated to any sexual attraction. Frequently they prefer the company of children and report feeling more comfortable around children than adults. They regard children as uncorrupted (they see adults as corrupt), innocent, spontaneous, and nonmanipulative. They may also view children as more physically attractive than adults and more affectionate, but these feelings are not initially associated with any physiological sexual arousal.

They gravitate toward vocational and avocational roles where they can have contact with children, including positions working in day care. It is only after they are in these positions that they begin to experience sexual attraction to children. Usually they have little previous sexual experience.

I have done clinical work with one male high school student and one male college student who seemed to be naive pedophiles. The latter did not actually sexually molest any children but became aware of his sexual feelings toward little girls while working in a day-care program, and he sought help. The former sexually fondled three boys, ages 3 and 4. The only prior sexual experience he could recall was his older sister aggressively grabbing his genitals, supposedly in jest.

(3) Induced sexual abuse. Some offenders who sexually abuse in day care have no intention of doing so but are manipulated or coerced into these activities by other offenders who play leadership roles. In my experience, all

of the offenders who were induced to sexually abuse were women. However, Finkelhor and colleagues report an adolescent boy whose mother appears to have procured children and facilitated his raping them. She physically abused and perhaps sexually abused him.

Induced sexual maltreaters seem to be inadequate and dependent people. Many are single women with few social contacts. Some have a history of emotional problems. The children often ascribe less abuse to them than to the instigating offenders and declare that the instigating offenders made the women do it or told them what to do.

For example, in one case, a victim described a male offender making the two foster grandmothers take off their clothes and play "naked hide and seek." He thought they didn't want to do this and declared they were the only people in the center who "didn't put fingers in you." In another case, it appeared that the induced offenders were threatened with disclosure of past sexual acts with children if they did not continue. And in yet another situation, the police indicated that the instigating offender "had something on" the induced offender, although they did not know what this was.

Of course, where there is an offender who is induced to sexually abuse children, there is almost always another offender who planned to sexually maltreat children.

Planned Sexual Maltreatment in Day Care

Four types of planned sexual abuse in day care will be discussed: (1) calculated pedophilic abuse, (2) entrepreneurial sexual abuse, (3) sexual maltreatment by people who are child haters, and (4) ritualistic abuse.

A question that has plagued professionals concerned about sexual abuse in day care is whether persons who maltreat children are actually starting day-care centers with the intention of sexually using their charges. Because so little information is available from the perpetrators, it is difficult to know how pervasive this practice might be. However, in the Country Walk case (Hollingsworth, 1986), mentioned in Chapter 2, where a husband and wife sexually abused children in their baby-sitting service, the wife confessed. Her testimony indicated that the decision to open the business was in order to procure children for her husband to molest.

(1) Calculated pedophilic abuse. As described in Chapter 2, there are some sexual abusers whose primary sexual orientation is to children. They tend to abuse multiple children and often consciously choose to work or volunteer in settings where they can have easy access to children for sexual purposes. One choice is day care. Finkelhor and colleagues report that 29%

of the abusers in their sample were attributed pedophilic motives; however, they regard this as an overestimate because it is based upon the reports of professionals involved, some of whom had quite broad definitions of the term "pedophile." Fifteen (31%) of the children in my clinical sample appeared to have been sexually maltreated by at least one person who would be defined as a pedophile.

As noted in Chapter 2, pedophiles often have a rather narrowly defined sex object of choice. Thus a pedophile who chooses day-care-center-aged children as his object would be attracted to very young children.

On the other hand, one of the arguments put forth for the apparent explosion of sexual abuse in day care is that such programs have been targeted by pedophiles because of the pliability of young children, their inability to make a coherent statement, and the likelihood they won't be found competent witnesses in a court of law. The argument continues that, with the increasing awareness of the problem of sexual abuse and the increasing willingness to believe children's allegations, older children are risky targets. Therefore, pedophiles are choosing the younger victim, perhaps not out of preference but out of prudence.

One of the men in my sample, who appears to have been a pedophile, had a history of rape of a teenage girl as well as an open protective services case for neglect of his own two children and a history of wife-battering. He repeatedly requested to work in a day-care center to satisfy his work requirement for General Assistance and was granted that opportunity. In this capacity, he sexually maltreated at least 20 boys and girls, ages $2\frac{1}{2}$ to 5, at a day-care center sponsored by a women's advocacy organization.

(2) Entrepreneurial sexual abuse. In some cases, sexual abuse in day care is done for profit. In these cases, there are reports of the production of pornography and child prostitution. In about 10% of the cases I have seen, children described picture taking or being required to have sex with someone other than a child or a worker at the center.

It was hard to substantiate that the pictures were actually sold, and certainly they were used for other purposes. For example, at one center, several children reported that the offender took pictures and threatened to show them to the parents or the police should the children disclose the sexual abuse. Finkelhor and colleagues (1988) also report numerous cases where the children said pictures were taken but there was a similar difficulty in determining whether they were actually sold. However, they note that in one case a parent reported seeing copies of photos in Mexico.

The evidence is more persuasive in the case of prostitution. In my sample, children described both people coming to the center and also being taken to other places to have sex with strangers. In one instance, two 4-year-old girls said they were taken to a place where they had to fellate three men. In addition, they stated men gave the teacher money, and afterward the teacher bought them candy with some of the money.

One reason that unscrupulous day-care providers might be tempted into the production of pornography and offering children as prostitutes is that day care is a financially marginal institution. It is hard to make a living in day care because of the high cost of providing quality care and the low income of the clientele, that is, the adults who must use day care. By exploiting children in one's care, a shaky business could be turned into a lucrative one.

(3) Sexual abuse by people who hate children. It appears that some of the sexual abusers of children wish to do great psychological and sometimes physical harm to them. Waterman and colleagues (1989a, 1989b), when referring to the circumstances of alleged victimization at Manhattan Beach preschools, describe these abusers as intent on terrorizing the children. While such offenders may be sexually attracted to children, they must be differentiated from both naive and calculating pedophiles, who usually profess love and admiration, however distorted, for their victims.

The acts of child-hating abusers may be sadistic and accompanied by physical abuse. In some instances, the coercion is designed either to gain cooperation with the sexual acts or to prevent children from telling. However, in others, it is just gratuitous cruelty or terrorizing. For example, one child described a perpetrator pulling a rug out from under his friend as he was standing on it. The offender then laughed when his friend fell on his face and got a bloody nose. Another victim of the same offender said the man threw him across the room against the wall and then made him crawl on his knees to the man's penis and kiss it.

Moreover, some of the acts go well beyond what seems necessary to assure the children's silence. In a case involving a 2½-year-old girl, the offender claimed to have killed the center's pet rabbit and then to have made it into rabbit stew. She said she was required to eat the rabbit stew, declaring that it had bones and fur in it and tasted awful. The offender then assured her that, if she told, he would make her into stew like the rabbit.

Some of the acts do not result in physical harm but attack the victims' sense of self and self-worth. Situations where children were forced to sexually abuse their best friends or younger siblings appear to have this effect. For instance, two boys age 6 and 7, who were in an after-school program at a day-care center, allegedly were forced to have intercourse with their 3-year-old sister while she was held down by the female director of the center. Their pictures were taken as they did this. Another example was a female perpetrator who reportedly had intercourse with a 4-year-old boy and induced him to engage in cunnilingus with her. She then instructed him to go home and do these things to his mother.

(4) Ritualistic abuse. As discussed in Chapter 2, day-care centers are one context in which ritualistic abuse has been found. Generally this abuse is perpetrated by more than one person.[1] I use a narrower definition of "ritualistic sexual abuse" than some. The term is limited to situations where the sexual abuse is part of some rite that appears to have significance related to a type of religion, satanism, witchcraft, or other cult practice.

Children may report being taken to the graveyard or to a church and having sex, the sacrifice of animals and in some cases people, and the drinking of blood or other kinds of potions. Incantations and songs may be repeated. Robes may be worn. As well, emblems such as crosses, particularly upside-down crosses, signs incorporating 666, pentagrams and circles, pictures of the devil, and ritual objects may be described by victims.

It seems important to distinguish these cases, where the sex is part of some rite, from ones where offenders engage in bizarre or cruel practices for other reasons. For example, the offender may say he has extraordinary or supernatural powers but they may have no ritual significance. In one case I have seen, the offender claimed to his victim that he was stronger than the Incredible Hulk and, therefore, locking the doors to prevent him from getting the child, should he tell, would be of no avail. It would be a mistake to call this illustrative of ritualistic abuse. Similarly, the offender may use objects, such as knives, whips, or sticks, to threaten the child or insert into an orifice, but with no religious significance. There are cases, such as the one described in the section above, where the offender kills an animal but does not sacrifice it. In addition, abusers may merely dress up in costumes or masks to scare or confuse the children or to disguise themselves. Drugs do not necessarily imply ritualistic abuse. Although they can be used to create an altered state of consciousness for certain rites, they also may be used to induce compliance, or cause amnesia or confusion, so the child cannot tell a coherent story.

A tentative observation is that ritualistic abuse appears more common at church-related centers. However, this is based on a small number of cases.

Conclusions About Causes for Sexual Abuse in Day Care

A range of possible motives for sexual abuse in day care, both unplanned and planned, have been cited. These are not particularly unique to day care and can be found in other contexts where there is sexual abuse.

It seems quite likely that an individual may progress from unplanned to planned sexual activity. The most obvious instance would be the pedophile whose first sexual encounters with children are unplanned but who then consciously chooses day-care work so he can continue to have sex with little children.

Moreover, a person who is a circumstantial abuser, a naive pedophile, or an induced offender may be manipulated into such activities by any of the offenders who plan sexual victimization of children. Where this is most obvious is in the case of the induced offender who would not, under other circumstances, engage in sexual abuse of children.

Finally, a perpetrator may sexually abuse children for more than one reason. The abuser may be making money at the same time he or she is enjoying the sexual activities involving children. Similarly, an offender may engage in ritualistic practices that allow the expression of hatred for children.

EXPERIENCES OF VICTIMS

The experiences of victims of sexual abuse in day care are in some respects unique when compared with those of other victims of sexual maltreatment. Three aspects of these experiences will be discussed: (1) the sexual abuse itself, (2) other types of abuse, and (3) threats employed by the offenders. The findings are based upon my research and that of Finkelhor (1988) and Waterman (1989a, 1989b), and their respective colleagues, as well as other accounts of sexual maltreatment in day care.

The Sexual Abuse

All of the types of sexual behavior found in other situations of sexual abuse are reported in day-care cases. Thus, despite the young age of victims, a large proportion of them experience some form of sexual penetration. This may be digital penetration of the vagina or anus, penetration with objects, or genital or anal intercourse. Consequently, there frequently is physical evidence. More than a third of victims I have evaluated had some physical evidence, either documented by a physician or noted by the parents. In the cases investigated by Finkelhor and colleagues (1988), 62% of victims were physically injured during the sexual maltreatment, a very high percentage.

In addition, one of the characteristics that differentiates sexual abuse in day care is that there is proportionately more sexual activity that occurs in a group context. This includes group sex involving adults and children, children being required to have sex with one another while adults observe, and children being made to watch adults (and sometimes other children) having sex with one another. In one case I have seen, an animal was also involved. A 4-year-old girl stated that she had to fellate a dog.

As well, there are reports of sexual games involving children and adults. For example, several boys who attended the same center described being taken to a barn by three teachers. Then everyone, including the teachers, took off their clothes, and the boys were chased around the barn by one of the teachers. When they were caught, they were molested in some way. For example, one boy said the teacher poured orange pop on his penis and then licked it off. After that, the children became "it" and chased the teachers. Waterman and colleagues (1989b) had a category of sexual abuse involving sexual games and stories. Seventy-two percent of children at Manhattan Beach and 21.4% of those at the Reno center report such experiences.

Findings of sexual exploitation, that is, prostitution and pornography and ritualistic abuse, are another distinguishing characteristic of sexual abuse in day care. Each of these types of maltreatment only constitutes about 10% of the kinds of abuse experienced by victims in my sample, but the findings nevertheless are very concerning. Finkelhor and colleagues (1988) report 14% as the proportion of their cases with pornography. Furthermore, 66% of their multiple-perpetrator and 5% of their single-perpetrator cases contained some ritualistic elements.[2] Similarly, Waterman and colleagues (1989b) report that 87.7% of the children they evaluated from Manhattan Beach alleged ritualistic abuse. They contrasted these findings with those from the day-care center in Reno, where only 7.1% of victims were subjected to ritualistic abuse.

Other Abuse

In addition to sexual maltreatment, these children may also be otherwise harmed. A surprising 60% of my sample reported being abused in ways other than sexual abuse. This is surprising because the investigations focused on sexual abuse. None of these assaults resulted in severe injury, but children reported sustaining bruises and red marks, some of which were corroborated by their parents. The acts reported included physical abuse, confinement, being given drugs, poison, or medicine and being required to engage in delinquent acts. These kinds of insults were inflicted primarily by offenders who were child haters. Similarly, Waterman and colleagues (1989b) report that 78.5% of Manhattan Beach victims allegedly were subjected to abusive acts.

Threats to Victims

Finally, one of the striking characteristics of sexual abuse in day care is the extent to which offenders threaten their victims. In sexual abuse cases, coercion is used to induce children to cooperate in the sexual acts and to keep them from telling. Because little coercion is generally required to gain the compliance of such young children in sexual acts, most of the threats were to prevent disclosure.

The most common sort of threat found in my cases was a threat to kill either the victim or the victim's parents, younger siblings, or, in a few cases, grandparents. In a small number of cases in my sample, a weapon, usually a gun or knife, was used, but Finkelhor and colleagues (1988) report that in 10% of their cases a weapon was used in the sexual abuse, and in 20% the children were threatened with one. A striking 80% of the victims Waterman and colleagues (1989b) evaluated reported being threatened with death to themselves and/or others.

The following case is one in which the offender threatened death both to gain the child's cooperation with the sexual abuse and to prevent disclosure.

> *Case example:* David was a 6-year-old boy whose father was hospitalized with leukemia when David entered the center. In order to obtain David's involvement in intercourse with his 4-year-old sister, Samuel, a teacher at the center, told him that, if he didn't participate, Samuel would follow the boy's mother to the hospital and kill his father. Sometime later, the father did in fact die, and Samuel used the event to manipulate David so he would not tell. Samuel declared that he had killed David's father by shooting him through the heart, and, because of the manner of death, the father would not go to heaven. Samuel threatened David that, if he told, Samuel would shoot David, his little sister, and his mother, all through the heart so that none of them would go to heaven.

This case is more severe than most. It is apparent that Samuel is quite clever and sadistic. His threats prevented David from disclosing sexual abuse for three years.

The next most common was a threat to do bodily harm. This was most likely to be to the victim but could also be to loved ones. Finkelhor and colleagues (1988) found instances of threats to the children's pets as well. Another fairly frequent threat in my sample was to implicate the victim. This kind of coercion is sometimes found in other cases of sexual abuse, but, in the day-care center cases, some of the characteristics of the abuse and the young age of victims seemed to add to the potency of these threats. Specifically, because children were required to do things with other children and because pictures were taken, threats that blamed the victims were very compelling. For example, children were told that the pictures would be shown to the police and the children would go to jail. In addition, the offender said he would tell victims' parents about sexual acts with other children, and the parents wouldn't love the children any more.

A final unique kind of threat involved killing animals with the implication that the same would happen to the child, should she or he fail to cooperate with or disclose the sexual abuse. Reported killings occurred in only 4% of my cases. However, they were found in 14% of cases surveyed by Finkelhor and colleagues (1988), and Waterman and colleagues (1989b) report that 80% of Manhattan Beach victims stated that they endured such experiences.

A pressing question is this: Why do offenders engage in these dramatic threats? As was noted in an earlier discussion, some perpetrators wish to do serious psychological harm to their victims, and most of the threats meant to terrorize were made by these abusers. However, perhaps there is a further explanation. In sexual abuse cases involving very young, but unrelated, children, offenders are less likely to be able to rely on subtle manipulations or ones based upon the special relationship between adult and child. As a consequence, they may need to resort to extreme threats to obtain cooperation and silence.

IMPACT

Of concern to both professionals and parents is the impact of sexual abuse in day care. The following issues will be addressed: (1) the impact of the special circumstances of day-care sexual abuse, (2) initial effects of sexual abuse in day care, and (3) longer-term effects.

Impact of the Special Circumstances of Sexual Abuse in Day Care

The fact that the offenders involved in day-care sexual abuse are not within the family would suggest that the trauma would be less severe. However, the young age of the children, combined with the circumstances of the abuse, can make it very harmful. That is, the abuse occurs in a situation that may be traumatic anyway, separation of very young children from their parents for a substantial portion of their day. For many victims, this is their first experience in the world away from their parents. Moreover, although the abusers are not the parents, they are people to whom the parents have entrusted the children. Often the parents have described the day-care providers in glowing terms and have admonished their children to obey them.

However, as with other types of sexual abuse, the impact is variable. The effects of this type of sexual abuse appear to be mediated by the nature of the sexual abuse, including the number and kinds of sexual acts, the number of perpetrators, and whether the child was required to have sex with other children. In addition, the presence of other maltreatment or threats and the child's family environment mediated the impact of the sexual abuse in my sample.

With regard to the latter, families where children are sexually abused in day care differ markedly from those referred to child protection agencies for other kinds of sexual abuse. They tend to be better functioning and of higher income. Because of these factors, on the whole, the families have more resources for coping. Despite this, the impact of sexual abuse both on the family and on the child may be more overwhelming than for a family where there are many disasters and poor parenting. This is because the experience is so alien to them. When the family is overwhelmed, it affects the victim as well. It is important for mental health professionals to be sensitive to the special impact that this particular victimization has.

Finkelhor and colleagues (1988) find that similar factors mediate the impact of sexual abuse. They report that, where force was used and there was ritualistic abuse, victims had more sequelae. In addition, when the offender was peripheral to the running of the center and the perpetrator was a woman, children had fewer symptoms. Finally, there is a finding that may contradict mine: maternal impairment was a predictor of more symptoms.

Impact of Sexual Abuse in Day Care Noted
Around the Time of Disclosure

One of the very painful issues for parents is that often there were indicators that their children were being sexually maltreated preceding the actual disclosure, which they ignored or attributed to something else. A very common assumption is that reluctance to go to day care and regressive behavior, such as bed-wetting and nightmares, are a result of the child merely not wanting to be separated from her parents. Moreover, symptoms that with hindsight seem obvious indicators of sexual abuse are simply explained away. In my sample, one mother, who was a nurse, said her daughter had repeated urinary tract infections, pain on urination, and a red vagina, often indicators of sexual abuse. Yet the mother attributed these symptoms to poor hygiene. Parents may need help in dealing with guilt associated with their failure to appreciate the significance of symptoms as well as guilt related to putting their children in the hands of abusers.

In my sample, sequelae of sexual abuse were categorized into sexual acting out, sleep disturbances, physical problems (enuresis, encopresis, head-aches, stomachaches, eating problems), emotional problems, behavior prob-lems, and phobias. The average number of symptoms per child was 3.7, a very worrisome finding. However, more than half of the children had two or fewer symptoms.

One of the distinguishing findings in terms of the impact of day-care sexual abuse is its generation of phobias. In my sample, almost 40% of victims were reported to be phobic. Finkelhor and colleagues (1988) report an even larger proportion having fears (arguably a broader category than phobias), 69%. Most of the phobias in my sample could be related to the circumstances of the sexual abuse or the threats used against the children. For example, twin brothers became phobic about bugs and spiders. Later it was ascertained that they were sexually abused in a basement full of bugs and spiders. A number of children were terribly afraid of being separated from their parents. These fears were explained by two children as a conse-quence of threats to kill their parents. Probably the large proportion of children who were phobic relates not only to the special abuse experiences but also to their age. Preschool and young-school-aged children are prone to have unreasoned fears.

Other sequelae—like sleep disturbances, bowel and bladder problems, and sexual acting out—found in substantial proportions of cases probably also reflect the age of the victims. Young children are more likely to demonstrate distress by enuresis and encopresis than older ones because they may have uncertain control over these bodily functions. Similarly, their naïveté regarding the significance of sexual behavior may result in a greater propensity to demonstrate the effects of sexual abuse by engaging in sexual activity than would be seen with older and/or more sophisticated children.

Longer-Term Effects of Sexual Abuse in Day Care

It is quite apparent that the immediate effects of day-care sexual abuse can be severe. However, of greater concern to parents and professionals involved with the children is the ultimate impact of the experience. Only two studies were found that address this issue. One is the research of Waterman and colleagues (1989a, 1989b) that has already been described. The other is a study of children sexually abused at a multiple-victim/multiple-perpetrator day-care situation in southwestern Michigan (Valliere et al., 1988).

Children who were victimized at the Michigan center were compared with children in the local school system one and two years after the abuse ended, and these subjects' scores were compared with normative scores of nonclinical and clinical samples. This study utilized the Achenbach Child Behavior Checklist (Achenbach and Edelbrock, 1983), probably the most widely used instrument to assess the affects of maltreatment on dimensions of symptomatology. Parents completed the checklist, which assesses the global traits of internality/externality as well as nine more specific symptoms: depression, social withdrawal, somatic complaints, schizoid-obsessive behavior, hyperactivity, sexual problems, delinquent activity, aggressive behavior, and cruelty. General findings were that, at one year, the victims of sexual abuse looked similar to the normative clinical sample and were significantly more symptomatic than the normative nonclinical sample and the comparison children from local schools. At two years after the abuse, boy victims continued to be described as having significantly more symptoms than the two normal groups, but the girls' symptoms lessened (Valliere et al., 1988).

The research design of Waterman and colleagues (1989a, 1989b) involves two subgroups of victims who had quite different experiences as well as a comparison group. Data were collected at two time intervals, the second a year or two after the first. Ratings came from the parents, the children, and their therapists. Preliminary analyses indicate that the Manhattan Beach group continued to experience significant difficulties four to five years after disclosure of the alleged sexual abuse and after extended treatment. The comparison group was functioning the best and the Reno group falls between these two groups.

More research needs to be conducted before anything definitive can be said about the long-term impact of sexual abuse in day care. Nevertheless, the existing findings suggest that the detrimental effects can be protracted. Of particular concern are the impact on boys and the consequences of ritualistic, terrorizing abuse.

VARIATIONS IN PATTERNS

It is important for understanding and managing these cases to differentiate types of sexual abuse in day care. The typology that will be presented here is based upon my experience as well as a reading of the literature, and it must, of necessity, be preliminary.[3] In the future, as more cases are examined, other subtypes will, no doubt, emerge.[4] The variations are as follows: (1) single offender-single victim, (2) single offender-multiple victims, and (3) multiple offenders-multiple victims.

Single Offender-Single Victim

Offenders who fall into this category are usually peripheral to or not involved in the running of the day-care program. They include the following types of people: janitors at the center; bus drivers; volunteers spending a limited time there; relatives of the staff, including adolescent sons, husbands, and grandfathers; and friends of the staff, including boyfriends and neighbors.

In my experience, most of the cases involving single offenders and single victims were in family day-care homes or centers run out of or attached to the director's home. Most peripheral abusers obtain access to children by virtue of their relationship to the day-care staff. However, as Finkelhor and colleagues (1988) point out, sometimes people peripheral to the running of the center are given responsibilities for which they are unqualified because of staff shortages. For example, one case in my sample involved a handyman who was to have no contact with the children but then was used in emergencies to watch children during nap time. He gradually came to be relied on regularly to fill in when other staff did not come to work.

In my sample, most of these abusers were men and most of their victims were female (close to 90%). As already noted, peripheral offenders usually targeted one victim at a time. Thus the offender might develop a special relationship with the child, that might continue as long as the child was there. When that child was no longer available, another might be recruited.

Peripheral offenders were usually circumstantial abusers, although an adolescent offender of this type might become a pedophile. As noted earlier, Finkelhor and colleagues (1988) found less trauma associated with having been abused by a peripheral offender.

Single Offender-Multiple Victims

Abusers in these cases generally have a central role in the provision of day care. They are likely to be teachers, sometimes directors, or teacher's aides who work regular hours at the center. These cases are found in day-care centers rather than day-care homes. The offenders operate solo and, therefore, are concerned about keeping their abusive behavior secret from other staff. They are likely to victimize children when taking them to the bathroom, at nap time, and early or late in the day, when there are fewer staff around.

In my experience, most of these offenders were male, although Finkelhor and colleagues (1988) report some women in this role. In these cases, there are multiple victims. They may be male or female or both, depending upon the offender's preference. In my sample, the proportion of male and female victims was equally divided, but in some cases the offender only abused boys, in others only girls, and in yet others children of both sexes.

Although it may be an artifact of the small data set, I have found none of these offenders resorting to serious threats to prevent children from disclosing. They tended to rely on the relationship. Two of the threats noted were these: "Don't tell or I'll get in trouble," and "Don't tell, or your mom and dad won't let you come back here anymore." In yet another case, the child was given a toy soldier as a bribe to prevent disclosure, which aroused the parents' suspicion and resulted in their eliciting information about the offense from the victim.

These perpetrators are likely to be pedophiles, either naive or calculating ones. Their sexual maltreatment is not usually characterized by other harm to their victims. Although some cases involve group sex, most consist of dyadic encounters. The latter pattern may be a consequence of the need to maintain secrecy.

Multiple Abusers-Multiple Victims

Cases such as the McMartin Preschool (Crewdson, 1988; Hechler, 1988; Waterman et al., 1989a, 1989b) and Country Walk (Crewdson, 1988; Hollingsworth, 1986) are instances where children describe abuse by multiple perpetrators. In centers where multiple abusers are involved, there is much less concern about secrecy because all the staff may be involved. These are the contexts in which women are likely to be found sexually maltreating children, although there may be men in these situations as well, sometimes taking leadership roles.

Victims are both male and female. However, unlike single-perpetrator/multiple-victim cases, the sex of the victim does not depend upon the proclivities of an individual perpetrator or the center. All centers in my sample and those on which consultation was given had victims of both sexes. These are the situations in which there is group sex, and the children are required to have sex with one another. These are also the cases in which group sex games may be played.

Multiple-abuser centers are ones where there seems to be a plan by the offenders to sexually abuse children. It may be motivated by sexual attraction to children, the profit motive, a desire to harm children, or an ideology that supports ritualistic abuse. It is these cases that raise questions about offenders opening centers in order to sexually abuse children. In my experience, most of the cases where allegations of picture taking and child prostitution arise are multiple-perpetrator/multiple-victim ones.

Finally, most of the situations where children were sadistically threatened occurred in these centers. Not surprisingly, children sexually maltreated in multiple-perpetrator/multiple-victim sites evidence the most psychological trauma and symptomatology (Waterman et al., 1989a, 1989b).

INTERVENTION

Two aspects of intervention that are unique to day-care sexual abuse will be discussed. They are (1) special treatment needs for children and families and (2) how to differentiate a high-risk center from an adequate one.

Treatment Needs

In this section, the treatment needs of children and parental needs for support will be covered.

(1) Victim treatment needs. Most victims of sexual abuse in day care need some treatment. If there has been but a single incident, the behavior has not been intrusive or accompanied by coercion or threats, the child has disclosed soon after the incident, the child evidences no significant symptomatology, and the family has responded appropriately and is not severely traumatized, then short-term treatment is usually all that is needed. The treatment should focus on helping the child express her feelings about the victimization, including any anger toward the parents for entrusting the child to the abuser; what is wrong with sex between adults and children; why the abuser did it; and what to do in the future if someone attempts sexual abuse.

The importance of parental involvement in the child's treatment cannot be stressed enough. The younger the child, the less central the therapeutic role of the clinician and the more central that of the child's caretakers. This is because little children are much less individuated from their parents than older ones.

Furthermore, little children don't understand therapy and are not very cooperative with the treatment process. Often they do not want to deal with their problems when they come to therapy. They want to play. When they do need help is, for instance, in the middle of the night when they wake up because they have had a nightmare about the perpetrator or when they become frightened because their parents are going to leave them with a baby-sitter. Most therapists do not make themselves available for such occasions.

It is crucial to successful treatment outcome, in day-care center and other cases involving young children, that parents become "surrogate therapists." They need to be taught how to deal with the children's symptomatology. This includes not only phobias and sleep disturbances, mentioned above, but sexual acting out and anger at the parents for allowing them to be sexually abused.

Often the most appropriate structuring of the therapy session is to begin by allowing the child to play in the playroom while the parent is interviewed nearby. Ideally, there should be someone with the child. The discussion with the parent should center on issues that have come up since the last session and how the parent has handled them. Advice for more appropriate handling may be in order or, in some cases, role-play. The material from the parent will assist the therapist in developing the content of therapy with the child, which may be covered verbally or in activities. Then at the end of the individual session with the child, the parent may be seen again, or there may be a conjoint session with parent and child, or both. A conjoint session is a context for the therapist to model appropriate responses to the child's issues as well as to facilitate three-way communication among therapist, child, and parent.

(2) Supporting the parents. Parents of children sexually abused in day care need support. As Finkelhor and colleagues (1988) point out, often their treatment needs are ignored by the professionals and the parents themselves. This can result in family dysfunction as well as individual problems for the victim and the parents.

When the case is one involving multiple victims, parents usually have shared issues. These include feelings of guilt, disbelief related to the allegations, questions about how to help their children, concerns about how the case is being handled, and, most important, the need for mutual support. Support groups for parents whose children have been sexually abused in multiple-victim contexts are the best way to provide services for their needs. These can be short term or open ended. It is good to have a professional involved, but often parents can greatly assist one another with minimal professional input. An appropriate structure may be to have different professionals come to meetings, depending upon the issues that need to be addressed. For example, as the case moves toward criminal prosecution, the prosecutor might be invited to the group meeting. Support groups may be started by professionals and then turned over to the parents to run.

Sometimes professionals who are primarily concerned with criminal prosecution object to parental support groups because they are concerned the group will "contaminate the case." That is, parents will discuss with one another the various allegations and then question their children inappropriately about a particular sexual activity the child has not previously alleged. Or even if this type of questioning does not occur, there may be concern that the defense will make such an accusation. In my experience, most parents do not "contaminate the case," and the benefits of such groups outweigh any challenges they may elicit from the defense. For example, this kind of support can play a key role in convincing individual parents of the importance of having their children testify, despite the hazards involved.

Are There Ways of Identifying High-Risk Centers?

Obviously, a pressing question for parents who must put their children in substitute care is how to know when a setting is safe. Unfortunately, there are few guidelines that are useful. Finkelhor and colleagues (1988) found that sexual abuse occurs at all kinds of centers. These include those that are licensed and never have had licensing violations previously, as well as unlicensed centers and programs that have a history of complaints against them. In my sample, a number of the centers where sexual abuse occurred were regarded as model programs.

Finkelhor and colleagues (1988) point out that both centers and day-care homes are vulnerable. However, some parents have turned to using baby-sitters and day-care homes, rather than sending their children to centers, because they think the children will be safer.

The only guideline that I can offer has to do with parental access and participation. Parents should choose a center that has an open-door policy that will let the parent come to the center at any time, despite the disruption it may cause to the program. When feasible, a parent should pick a program that has a parental participation requirement. This means parents must spend some time, usually on a weekly basis, contributing in kind to the running of the center. This affords the parent more information about what goes on in the program and usually more say about what goes on.

CONCLUSION

Sexual abuse in day care is a phenomenon that is just beginning to be understood. However, it poses a hazard to young children and is a substantial concern for parents who must place their children in substitute care.

The more informed mental health professionals are about this problem, the more astute they will be at its diagnosis as well as in providing treatment to victims and support to their families, and the better able they will be to advise parents on how to avoid situations where their children might be at risk for sexual abuse in substitute care.

NOTES

1. I have not seen a day-care case involving a private, idiosyncratic ritual.
2. The definition employed by Finkelhor and colleagues is broader than the one employed here, however.
3. The 48 cases I have evaluated or treated personally come from 20 centers and involve 30 perpetrators, a rather small sample. However, cases where consultation was provided, as well as the findings of other clinicians and researchers, were considered in the development of this typology.
4. A more differentiated typology, which specifies seven categories of sexual abuse, has been developed by Wilson and Steppe (1986). However, some of their categories are not really sexual abuse in day care.

REFERENCES

Achenbach, T. and C. Edelbrock. 1983. *Manual for the Child Behavior Checklist and Revised Child Behavior Profile.* Burlington: University of Vermont.
American Association for the Protection of Children. 1987. *Highlights of Official Child Neglect and Abuse Reporting* (1985). Denver: American Humane Association.
Crewdson, John. 1988. *By Silence Betrayed.* New York: Harper & Row.
Finkelhor, David, Linda Williams, and Nanci Burns. 1988. *Nursery Crimes: Sexual Abuse in Day Care.* Newbury Park, CA: Sage.
Groth, Nicholas. 1979. *Men Who Rape.* New York: Plenum.
Hechler, David. 1988. *The Battle and the Backlash.* Lexington, MA: Lexington.
Hollingsworth, Jan. 1986. *Unspeakable Acts.* New York: Congdon and Weed.
Valliere, Paulette, Deborah Bybee, and Carol Mowbray. 1988. "Using the Achenbach Child Behavior Checklist in Child Sexual Abuse Research: Longitudinal and Comparative Analysis." Paper presented at the National Symposium on Child Victimization, Anaheim, CA, April.
Waterman, Jill, Rob Kelly, Jane McCord, and M. K. Oliveri. 1989b. *Supplementary Material: Manhattan Beach Molestation Study.* NCCAN Grant #90CA1179. Unpublished document. Los Angeles: University of California, Los Angeles, Department of Psychology.
Waterman, Jill, Rob Kelly, M. K. Oliveri, and Jane McCord. 1989a. "Manhattan Beach Molestation Study." Grant #90CA1179. Summary for NCCAN Grantees' Meeting, March 1989. Unpublished report, University of California, Los Angeles, Department of Psychology.
Wilson, Charles and Susan Steppe. 1986. *Investigating Sexual Abuse in Daycare.* Washington, DC: Child Welfare League of America.

Chapter 9

SEXUAL ABUSE ALLEGATIONS IN DIVORCE

Allegations of sexual abuse in divorce and custody/visitation disputes present serious problems for all professionals involved and require extraordinary care to effect judicious intervention. In these cases, accusations may be brought against fathers, stepfathers, mothers, their boyfriends, or others but most often are made against fathers. The accusers may have a variety of roles: mothers, fathers, grandparents, professionals, or victims themselves. However, in about half of these cases, the person raising the issue is the child's mother, who bases her concern on statements or behavior of the child.[1]

Unfortunately, the needs of the child, who is the alleged victim, are often ignored or become secondary in the turmoil that surrounds these cases. This turmoil is in part a reflection of the emotionally fraught dynamics of divorce. They seem to fuel the intensity of behavior and responses of family members and others who are involved.

Usually the alleged offenders and their attorneys forcefully assert that the allegations are false and may go to extraordinary lengths and expense to prove this is so. Further, there are mental health professionals who will support their claims, stating that mothers cold-bloodedly make up allegations of sexual abuse in custody disputes in order to gain exclusive rights to their children (Blush and Ross, 1986; Guyer, 1983), are women who have distorted

AUTHOR'S NOTE: I wish to thank David Corwin for his careful reading of this chapter and helpful suggestions.

perceptions of events at the time of divorce (Benedek and Schetky, 1985), or are hysterics or psychotic (Benedek and Schetky, 1985; Blush and Ross, 1986).

On the other side are the parents who believe their children have been sexually abused. They plead that they are trying only to protect their children and are not receiving a fair hearing in court. They may come with medical, protective services, or mental health evidence that supports the allegation of abuse. Probably in most cases, the court carefully considers the evidence and makes a decision that is in the child's best interest. But, in a substantial number of cases, information supportive of sexual abuse is not taken seriously or is dismissed out of hand by the court. This may result in the nonaccused parent allowing the child to be exposed to further sexual abuse. Alternatively, that parent may in effect take the law into her own hands and violate court orders. Then these parents are found in contempt of court for not allowing unsupervised visitation by the alleged offenders or for taking the children out of the court's jurisdiction without obtaining the court's permission. As a consequence, they may be jailed until they agree to comply with the court or they may lose custody of their children. Sometimes the children are given to the alleged offender, other times they are placed with relatives, and in still others they are put in foster care.

Children in these cases are often subjected not only to repeated interviews by protective services, the police, and medical personnel, as happens in other cases of alleged sexual abuse, but also to multiple evaluations by experts for the mother, experts for the father, and experts appointed by the court. There may be litigation in three separate courts: the juvenile or family court, which addresses the issue of protection; the court that has jurisdiction over the divorce; and the criminal court, which has responsibility for prosecuting the alleged offender. Involvement in these proceedings is psychologically and economically extremely taxing for the parents, but it is even more traumatic for the children. The child may be the key witness in any of these proceedings, and, even when parents attempt to shield the child, she is likely to feel responsible for the tremendous disruption in the lives of both of her parents.

In recent years, parents who believe their children have been sexually abused by an ex-spouse and are dissatisfied with the court's actions are "going underground," that is, they are taking their children and hiding. The prevalence of the problems of sexual abuse in the context of divorce and the dissatisfaction of nonaccused parents with the court's response is dramatically illustrated by the fact that there is an entire underground network of people, often persons who were themselves sexually victimized or who have had loved ones who were, who will provide sanctuary, financial support, and a chance for a new life to parents and their children on the run (Galtney, 1988).

It is important to appreciate the effects of this radical solution on both the parents involved and the children. The alleged offender may become entirely consumed with finding the child. He often appeals to the press and the public to assist in this effort. He may hire a private detective or himself pursue his ex-spouse and the child, incurring large debts or leaving behind his other responsibilities. For the fleeing parent, life is filled with uncertainty, instability, economic privation, and fear of being discovered. Such experiences are bound to have an impact on parenting ability. However, it is probably the child who suffers the most from being on the run. A young child will not fully comprehend the parent's decision to flee. She may well still be attached to the alleged offender but cannot express these feelings. She learns to fear the police, to conceal her identity or change her name, and to be suspicious of people who may turn her in. She has left behind familiar people, places, and the comforts of life. She may sleep in a different place each night in crowded conditions with little privacy. Yet she is told that all of this is for her own good and because of something that happened to her.

The case example that follows is characteristic of the course of disputed custody and visitation cases. It illustrates how children can be harmed in these situations but certainly does not represent the worst of these situations.

Case example: Mr. and Mrs. T separated when their daughters were ages 3 and 6. The reasons for the separation were Mr. T's alleged violence and Mrs. T's alleged inability to cope with household responsibilities and headaches leading to refusal of sex. Mrs. T was awarded custody of the children and Mr. T weekend visits. These visits went fairly smoothly for the first nine months.

Then Mrs. T and her mother reported the children were saying their father licked their vaginas, engaged in digital penetration, and fondled them. Initial protective services investigation yielded no definitive evidence. The father took a polygraph and passed it. The police case was closed and the protective services case was denied.

However, the children continued to make these allegations. The two children and their parents were then evaluated by an expert in sexual abuse who substantiated the allegations. The father then hired his own expert, who interviewed him and, on the basis of that interview, asserted that Mr. T was not a sexual abuser. Mrs. T then took the children out of the state for an evaluation by a nationally known team of experts who confirmed the sexual abuse. She was in contempt of court for taking the children out of state and refusing the father unsupervised visitation. The judge issued orders ex parte for her arrest and for change of custody to the father.

Upon her return to the state, the mother was arrested and spent ten days in the county jail. She was released with the agreement that there would be yet another evaluation of the children and that in the meantime she would retain custody. The proposed evaluators refused to assess the case as they said the issue of sexual abuse had already been determined. There was no litigation for the next three years, and the father had no visitation.

Five years after the original allegations, the youngest child, then 8, was in the hospital having an emergency appendectomy. Mr. T alerted the police to the mother's whereabouts, in the hospital with her daughter. She was arrested on the old contempt of court warrant. Mr. T, with the assistance of the police, took custody of the child upon her discharge from the hospital. Mrs. T remained in jail because she would not disclose the whereabouts of her other daughter. After the mother had been in jail 45 days, the father discovered the other child at school and went there with the police and received custody of her.

The judge consistently refused to hear any testimony regarding the sexual abuse and gave custody to the father. The children are unhappy and frightened there. Mr. T's new wife does not want these children, and her children do not like the T children. The mother and her parents, who had sheltered the children when their mother was in jail, are in agony.

It seems quite probable that these children were sexually abused, and it appears that the mother most certainly thought they had been. Nevertheless, the judge refused to address the issue and seems to have punished the mother for her violation of his orders by putting her in jail and by taking her children away from her. In doing so, he not only punished the mother but also the children. He also rewarded the father, who may have sexually abused the children, by giving him custody.

It is crucial that allegations of sexual abuse be handled in a way that is in the children's best interest. This requires an understanding of all the possible dynamics that may result in an allegation of sexual abuse in a divorce, the undertaking of a careful assessment that minimizes trauma to the child, and recommendations for disposition that take into account the child's needs both for safety and for relationships with her family. This chapter will address these issues and will provide empirical data on false and true allegations in custody disputes.

DYNAMICS LEADING TO AN ALLEGATION IN DIVORCE

The mental health professional should be aware that there are at least four possible circumstances that may result in an allegation of sexual abuse as a marriage is dissolving or after it has dissolved: the nonoffending parent finds out about sexual abuse and decides to divorce the offending parent, there is long-standing sexual abuse that is only revealed in the context of divorce, there is sexual abuse that has been precipitated by the marital dissolution, or the allegation is false.

Discovery of Sexual Abuse Results in Divorce

In my experience, approximately half of women who discover their husbands are sexually abusive divorce them. However, there is a great deal of variability in how these women come to this decision. In some cases, the woman learns of the sexual abuse from the children, from others in the family, or from observation. She then leaves the offender, taking the children, and files for divorce (Berliner, 1988; Corwin et al., 1987). The sexual abuse may only come to professional attention when issues of visitation with the offending parent are being decided in the divorce proceeding.

In other cases, upon discovery of sexual abuse, the woman contacts professionals, such as the police, child protective services, a minister, or a therapist. And in still others, the nonoffending parent only learns of the sexual abuse when an outside agent, such as the school, protective services, or the police, informs her. In the latter two instances, the sexual abuse is known to authorities before the woman initiates divorce action, and often these professionals are instrumental in the mother's decision to divorce.

It is somewhat ironic that, in the first instance cited, where the woman independently chose to get out of a marriage in which her children were being sexually abused, her motivations for having concerns about visitation with the offending parent are more likely to be questioned than in instances where authorities addressed the issue of sexual abuse before the filing for divorce. That is, in the former cases, it may be alleged that the mother is accusing the father of sexual abuse in order to restrict his access to the children. In the latter, the woman may have ignored sexual abuse or required persuasion by authorities to act in a protective way, indicators she may be a less capable parent. The example below illustrates one mother's process of decision making when she learned of sexual abuse.

Case example: Mrs. P, a black woman residing in a deprived inner-city environment, had three of her seven children living with her. They were Ursula, 10, Doreen, 4, and Laticia, 2. Three of the remaining children were with her mother in Louisiana, and the fourth, who was mentally retarded, was in a residential facility.

Mr. P was her second husband and the father of Doreen and Laticia. Although he did not beat Mrs. P as her first husband had, Mr. P had a hard time holding a job and he would spend money foolishly. He also expected her to wait on him. When he got an opportunity to go to Florida and work for his uncle, she encouraged him to do this. She thought that being on his own with some responsibility would help him grow up. The plan was for Mrs. P to stay behind and continue in her job as a nurse's aid for the time being, but she and the children were to join Mr. P at the end of the school year.

After Mr. P's departure, Ursula and Doreen told their mother about the pussy game Mr. P played with them. He would chase them until he caught them, throw them on the couch, and then rub their vaginas, asking "doesn't that feel good?" Sometimes he would take his penis out and masturbate. When Mrs. P first heard about the pussy game, she tried to contact her husband to get his explanation before deciding what to do. She was unable to reach him. (Later she found out that he was with another woman.) After some reflection, she concluded that her girls would not lie about such a thing and went to Legal Aid to get an attorney to file for divorce. She also informed her family and his about the allegations.

It was two years before the divorce case came to court, during which time Mr. P had not seen his daughters nor sent any child support. Mr. P had a new partner, whom he introduced as his fiancé. He claimed that Mrs. P made up the allegations because she did not want his daughters to come and visit him and his fiancé in Florida for the summer but that the girls wanted to come.

The judge interviewed the two older girls in chambers, and they described the pussy game to him. The judge made a finding that Mr. P had sexually abused his daughter and stepdaughter. Mr. P was ordered to pay back child support and was given one-hour supervised visits monthly.

In this case, the mother's initial reaction was to give the father the benefit of the doubt, but, upon reflection, she concluded that the children were telling the truth and that she wanted to end the marriage. That decision might not have been so easy if he had been in the home at the time or had been a more desirable partner. Her choice of informing family members, who might also have children endangered by Mr. P, rather than going to the police, may reflect reservations black families have about involving such agents in their lives.

Sexual Abuse Revealed During Divorce

Early clinical literature describes "classical incest" as a pattern of father-daughter incest that persists for years. It is only reported by the victim when she reaches adolescence and is able to free herself of the incestuous relationship, or it is revealed when the couple divorces (Berliner, 1988; Faller, 1988). Thus it would appear that clinicians observed as early as the 1960s that sexual abuse that has been long-standing might not surface until marital breakup.

The reasons for revelation at this time can be several. The child may at that time feel safe enough to report sexual abuse, which has been ongoing, because the perpetrator is then out of the picture and no longer able to punish her for the disclosure (Berliner, 1988). Second, the mother may have consciously or unconsciously avoided looking into certain behavior that was present during the marriage, but, as the marriage dissolves, she is able or willing to consider the implications of these observations. Third, the mother may have known about the sexual abuse during the marriage but was fearful of making it known or chose to tolerate it because there were other benefits in the marriage.

In the example below, the reason for the mother acknowledging the possibility of long-standing sexual abuse of her four children was probably the second one mentioned.

Case example: Mrs. N had left her second husband, who was the father of her three younger children and the stepfather of the oldest, because she said he was strange and had crazy spells. She indicated that she was concerned about sexual abuse because some things that happened during the marriage now worried her. She stated when her youngest daughter, Jane, was 2, she asked her mother to rub her vagina. When her mother refused, the child said that her daddy did that and it feels good. Mrs. N also reported discovering her 4-year-old daughter, Sally, masturbating and putting her fingers in her vagina. When Mrs. N told her not to do that, the child replied that her father said it was okay and showed her how to do it. Mrs. N said that during the marriage she had worked nights and would come home and find her husband in the bed with their children, Eric, 5, and the two girls. On one occasion, the girls had their nightclothes off. However, at the time, she thought nothing of it because the weather was hot. Frequently her husband slept in the nude.

At the time Mrs. N made these reports, she was also concerned because the children had been involved in a lot of sexual play, including oral sex. Interviews with the children confirmed sexual abuse of the three younger children. The stepson, who was 12, denied any involvement. However, the three children described him taking part in group sex with them and their father.

In this case, the mother made a number of observations that might be indicative of sexual abuse but only clearly realized their implications after she had made a decision to get out of the marriage and indeed after she had extricated herself from a relationship where she was constantly worrying about her husband's depression and unpredictable mood swings.

Sexual Abuse Precipitated by Divorce

Divorce is usually a traumatic experience for all parties, husband, wife, and children. In this context, behavior not exhibited under other circumstances may develop. This may include sexual abuse. The offending party may be either the mother or the father, although, as with other types of sexual abuse, the abuser is more likely to be a male.

There may have been behavioral indications of sexual attraction to children during the marriage, but these urges appear to have been held in check by the structure of the marriage. For example, the offending parent may have engaged in an unusual amount of touching and caressing of the child, may have engaged in tongue kissing, or may have slept with the child. In addition, there may be reports of the father experiencing erections when wrestling or involved in other body contact with the child or while bathing with the child.

One of the consequences of divorce is the loss of marital structure. Often, there is no longer another adult around to monitor the parent's behavior. The parent has unsupervised access to the child during visitation or as a custodial parent. Rules that regulate where children and parents sleep, when they go to sleep, and with whom they bathe may no longer exist. This situation may lead to the expression of sexual feelings toward children.

There are two other dynamics that may contribute to sexual abuse as a marriage dissolves. The parent, who becomes the abuser, may feel a tremendous emotional loss with separation from the spouse. In my clinical experience, the offending parent is usually not the instigator of the divorce and often is bewildered and overwhelmed by the marital demise. In this vulnerable psychological state, the parent turns to the child to get his emotional needs met, and because this parent has some sexual attraction to children, the relationship becomes sexual. Second, the parent who becomes an abuser often is very angry at the spouse for destroying the marriage and for other perceived or actual transgressions. The parent may not have the opportunity to directly express that anger or may have such an opportunity but find it insufficient to satisfy the need for retaliation. The child then becomes the vehicle for the expression of anger toward the partner. Because of the intensity of these feelings, physical injury may result from the sexual mal-treatment.

It is also important to be aware that the offender is in such a state of emotional turmoil that he may not be able to control his sexually abusive behavior even when he is aware that his ex-spouse, protective services, or the court is monitoring his contact with the child. Therefore, reincidences are not uncommon in this type of sexual abuse, even when the visits are partially supervised. In some cases, these reincidences may be interpreted by mental health experts as a way of keeping the ex-spouse involved and, in other cases, they may be seen as a cry for help.

The following case example is fairly typical of sexual abuse arising in the context of divorce:

Case example: Mr. and Mrs. X had been married ten years. They were both stockbrokers. Initially they were both highly successful and had a typical dual-career marriage. They wanted children but thought this would not be possible after Mrs. X's second miscarriage. However, she conceived for the third time and, after a difficult pregnancy, delivered a healthy baby girl, Alice. Mrs. X had to return to work when Alice was 6 weeks old or else face a major career setback. This was very difficult for her as her boss refused to take her parental duties into account, frequently scheduling noon meetings, when Mrs. X planned to go home and nurse Alice, and weekend work sessions. Mr. X at this time left the stockbroking business and opened a manufacturing company with other members of his family, using capital supplied by Mrs. X.

He was described as a devoted father, although the only care of Alice that interested him was bathing. He typically took baths with her, often spending an hour in the bath playing with her. He did not heed Mrs. X's assertions that this was inappropriate and continued to insist on his bathing time with Alice.

His business venture was unsuccessful, and he had to declare bankruptcy. Alice was 3 at the time. Initially, he searched for other jobs but felt that the ones he was offered were not good enough. He became preoccupied with a scheme to start another business. He spent long days at home working on these plans. He wanted to invest the family savings in this business, but Mrs. X refused to allow this.

A housekeeper cared for the child until the X's could no longer afford her. Mr. X then had the responsibility of caring for Alice and the house. Mrs. X would return from work to a messy house, a dirty child, and no dinner. Often Mr. X remained in his pajamas the entire day. Mrs. X threatened to divorce her husband if he did not find a job. He blamed her for his situation, saying that if she would let him use the savings then he would have a job. She refused him sex. He became physically violent with her, throwing her up against the wall and pulling her hair. This behavior took place in front of Alice.

Mrs. X filed for a divorce, and Mr. X left the home, moving in with his parents. He returned to the house on several occasions. He begged for reunification, but he also threatened to assault Mrs. X and attempted to break in. The police were called.

Nevertheless, because Mr. X had always been good with Alice, Mrs. X allowed him liberal visits. Then Alice began to return from visits with a red and sore vagina. Eventually Alice described to her mother her father "rubbing her tushie and trying to put his dinky in her." Mrs. X took her to the county sexual abuse expert, who confirmed, based upon Alice's statements, that she had been sexually abused by her father. The expert filed a report with protective services.

Mrs. X took the expert's report to the circuit court, which had jurisdiction over the divorce and visitation, and demanded the father's visits be stopped. They were suspended while another evaluation was conducted of Alice and her parents by an expert in disputed custody cases. That expert found both parents to be very self-absorbed people and no evidence on the child's psychological tests that she had been sexually abused.

The father's visits were reinstated. Upon return from the first visit, Alice stated her father had rubbed her tushie, and there was medical evidence consistent with repeated fondling.

The family was then ordered to be evaluated by a second, more prominent expert in sexual abuse. The father failed to keep his appointment. However, the expert found evidence from the interview with the child that she had been sexually abused by her father and no evidence, based upon the interview with the mother, that she had fabricated the allegation. When the father was told the results of the evaluation by his attorney, he physically assaulted his attorney and fired him.

The expert in child custody asked to see the child again and was granted permission. She found evidence of inappropriate sexual interaction between the child and the father.

 The court ordered that the father's visits be supervised by the friend of the court. However, he failed to visit his daughter and sought a new attorney to litigate the matter further.

Mr. X's bathing behavior with his daughter could be evidence of his physical and sexual attraction to her. Clearly he was heavily invested in her and likely took solace in that relationship as he perceived his wife to be unsupportive, sexually rejecting, and destructive of his efforts to become gainfully employed again. Evidence of his anger at his wife is found in his violence, uncharacteristic of his behavior earlier in the marriage. The violence escalated after the separation but was accompanied by pleas for reunification, evidence of how bereft he felt by the loss of his wife. This is also a case where, despite the supervision of the court, Mr. X reabused his daughter on the first visit after reinstatement of visitation.

False Allegations in the Context of a Divorce and/or Custody or Visitation Disputes

The context of divorce appears to yield larger proportions of false accusations than other situations where sexual abuse is alleged. Most false allegations come from adults rather than from the alleged victims (Berliner, 1988; Faller, 1988; Jones and McGraw, 1987).

The larger proportion of false allegations in this context can be understood by contrasting it with other types of cases. In most cases of intrafamilial sexual abuse, a major issue is convincing nonabusive family member(s) that the perpetrator did abuse the child. A mother may find it very difficult to believe that someone to whom she is married could sexually victimize her children. Quite the opposite situation may occur when parents are divorcing. These adults may be convinced that their ex-spouses are capable of almost anything, including sexual abuse. Therefore, the adult may overreact to suspicious occurrences rather than underreacting to them.

There are several variations in this pattern. First, under the stress of divorce and its aftermath, parental perceptions may become distorted (Benedek and Schetky, 1985). They often perceive their ex-partners as very pathological persons. Occasional drinking episodes become redefined as chronic alcoholism. A desire for certain sexual activities or for more frequent sexual activity are labeled perversion. A single incident of the use of physical force in an argument may result in the ex-spouse being labeled a batterer. Having developed a distorted view of the ex-partner, the parent may conclude that anyone who is an alcoholic, a pervert, or a batterer would also sexually abuse a child. Alternatively, the child may say something like, "daddy touched me," "daddy hurt me," or "daddy takes baths with me," which leads the parent with the distorted perception to conclude that the child is describing sexual abuse. In addition, these parents may have distorted perceptions of the child in relationship to the ex-spouse. For example, when the child returns from a visit and doesn't seem particularly disturbed, the parent may conclude the child has been drugged or brainwashed by the alleged offender. Because the ex-partner has such a disturbing effect on the parent, it must be the same for the child, and, if not, the ex-spouse must have manipulated the child in some devious way.

Second, the parent or others may observe behavior by the child that could indicate sexual abuse but could as well have other explanations. Typical examples are resistance to visits with the alleged abuser, having nightmares before or after the visits, wetting the bed, masturbation, or engaging in other unusual behaviors related to visits or the alleged abuser. These behaviors could be precipitated by the stress related to the divorce, the fear of losing the custodial parent if the child evidences loyalty to the alleged abuser, or an appreciation that the custodial parent would welcome negative reactions to or comments about the alleged abuser. Even masturbation may not be related to sexual abuse. Masturbation is normal among children (and adults). Only excessive masturbation is regarded as possibly symptomatic of sexual abuse, but who is to say what is excessive? Furthermore, self-stimulation feels good, and children may need to comfort themselves in a divorce situation. Especially if their parents are too preoccupied to comfort them, they may resort to self-comfort in the form of genital stimulation.

Third, parents may correctly perceive that their children have been sexually abused but incorrectly attribute it to their ex-partners. The child may evidence precocious sexual knowledge, engage in sexual behavior, or present with physical evidence of having been sexually abused. In three cases I have recently evaluated, it was clear based on medical or behavioral evidence that the child had been sexually abused, and the mother was convinced the estranged father was the perpetrator. However, after a careful evaluation, it appeared that, in two cases, the stepfathers, and in one, a boyfriend, had sexually abused the children, not the fathers. In a fourth case, precocious sexual knowledge came from other children.

Finally, the parent may consciously lie in making the allegation. These situations appear to be quite rare (Nicholson and Bulkley, 1988; Faller, 1988; Jones and McGraw, 1987; Thoennes, 1988). In my experience, lies are more common about the new partner of the ex-spouse than the ex-spouse him- or herself, although they are quite rare in both cases. They appear to be motivated by the desire to get the accused parent out of the lives of the child and the nonaccused parent. Consciously fabricated allegations may also be made as counterallegations by an accused parent.

In the example below, there is evidence both of distortion and of attributing the sexual abuse to the wrong party.

Case example: Mrs. L made accusations that her ex-husband, Mr. M, was sexually abusing their 4-year-old daughter, Kathy, on visits. She became concerned because her daughter had a sore vagina and said her daddy had hurt her "down there." Mrs. L also described him as an alcoholic and said he had "Vietnam veteran's syndrome."

Kathy was interviewed and said that her daddy had touched her and her stepbrother. She could give no detail beyond this. Mr. M's visits were cut off and a protective services investigation was undertaken. Mr. M's three stepchildren were interviewed but denied any sexual abuse by their stepfather.

Mr. and Mrs. L, Mr. and Mrs. M, and Kathy were sent to a multidisciplinary team for evaluation. Even before asked, Kathy told the interviewer in a rote fashion that her daddy had touched her and that she had told her mother. She said her daddy was bad. No further detail was forthcoming. Somewhat later in the interview, she was asked about her stepfather, Mr. L, and described in detail sexual abuse by him. She said that he sat her on the kitchen table and took off her panties. He put his finger in her hole and then he put his peter in her hole. This hurt and it made blood come out. She said her mom was at the store and her little brother was outside. She had told her mother but her mother said her real daddy did this. She also said that her stepfather hit her little brother with a belt and that he had pushed her little brother down the stairs. Kathy added that she was a bad girl. She got lots of whuppins and had to spend a lot of time in her room.

Interviews with the four adults and assessments of the interaction between Kathy and the two sets of adults yielded the following information. Mr. M, Kathy's father, appeared to be quite intelligent and to have a good relationship with her. He could also describe his stepchildren in detail and seemed to understand them. His wife said their relationship with him was good. Mr. M had been in Vietnam, but did not appear to be suffering from posttraumatic stress disorder. He said when he had been married to Mrs. L, he used to have parties with his work mates, and they drank lots of beer. When Mrs. L was his wife, she had an affair with his best friend and left him. He drank more after that, but drinks little now. Mrs. M appeared warm and nurturing and interacted very appropriately with Kathy.

Mr. L was found to be character disordered, and he reported a history of being wrongly accused of raping a 4-year-old girl. He had recently been fired from his job after repeated absences and a fight with his boss. He did not interact with Kathy at all during the family interaction session and described her in very negative terms. Mrs. L did interact with Kathy, but this consisted of Mrs. L complaining about coming to the evaluation and making negative comments about Mr. M. She appeared to be a very dependent woman who had a tendency to distort reality. She said that Mr. M had it in for her; he had reported her for neglect and had told the friend of the court that she was a prostitute. Mrs. L had been reported twice for neglect, but not by Mr. M. He had described to the court worker how their marriage had ended but had not said Mrs. L was a prostitute.

At the end of the interviews, the evaluators were not sure whether Kathy had been sexually abused or by whom, but they thought her relationship with her father and stepmother should be fostered. They recommended gradually increasing visits with the father and his family and careful monitoring of the situation.

Six months later, while Kathy was having an extended summer visit at her father's, she began to complain of sexual and physical abuse by her stepfather. There was another protective services investigation. Custody was switched to the father with visitation with the mother.

On two separate visits to the mother, she made reports to the friend of the court that Kathy was being sexually abused by her father. Upon return from a visit with her mother, Kathy had physical evidence of forced penetration and implicated her stepfather.

An evaluation by an expert in sexual abuse was initiated. Kathy's statements about her stepfather were graphic and she denied any involvement with her father. She also again described injury to her brother, age 2. He was assessed and current injuries and old scars were found. The expert concluded that Kathy had been sexually abused and that victimization by the stepfather but not the father was most consistent with the evidence.

This is obviously a complicated case. However, it appears that Mrs. L's perceptions of her ex-husband are somewhat distorted and there is a paranoid quality about them. Examples of the former are her description of him as an alcoholic and suffering from "Vietnam veteran's syndrome." Of course, his functioning may have been much worse when the marriage dissolved. Paranoia is suggested by her belief that he is the source of the protective services referrals. Mrs. L seems to have rightly perceived that her daughter had been sexually abused but to have had a need to believe it was her ex-husband rather than her current husband who was the abuser.

STRATEGIES FOR EVALUATING ALLEGATIONS

Evaluations of allegations of sexual abuse differ from evaluations for custody and visitation decisions. As noted in Chapter 5, at the heart of the investigation of an allegation of sexual abuse is the child interview, and, assuming the allegation is confirmed, the interviews with the offending and nonoffending parents serve to determine why the sexual abuse took place, what intervention is appropriate, and what the treatment prognosis is. In contrast, investigations to determine custody and visitation put much greater emphasis on parent-child attachment and what is seen in parent-child interaction. In addition, evaluators of the latter respond to child custody statutes, which generally set forth multiple criteria to be considered in making custody decisions, for example, the capacity to provide the child with education and religious guidance, the ability to provide materially for the child, the length of time the child has been with that parent, and the physical and mental health of the parent (Committee on the Family, Group for the Advancement of Psychiatry, 1980). When there is an accusation of sexual abuse, emphasis is on protecting the child, whereas resolution of a custody dispute is often a compromise that gives something to each parent. In cases where both are issues, determining whether the child has been sexually maltreated must take priority.

Strategies for sexual abuse evaluation in cases where there is a divorce and a custody/visitation dispute differ somewhat from those described in Chapter 5, which lays out a general framework for assessing an allegation. The interview with the alleged victim is still the primary tool for determining whether or not there has been sexual abuse (Berliner, 1988; Bresee et al., 1986; Corwin, 1988). However, there are additional techniques that may be useful in disputed custody/visitation cases, and there will be some differences in emphasis. Special considerations and approaches for custody/visitation disputes will be discussed concerning three areas: the victim interview, the interview with the nonaccused parent, and assessment of the parent-child relationship.[2]

The Child Interview

As in other cases, the statements and/or behavior of the child will be the primary determining factors in assessing the allegation. The evaluator will be looking for data in the three areas discussed in Chapter 5, the child's ability to describe the context of the victimization, the child's account of the sexual abuse itself, and the child's emotional state when recounting the maltreatment. However, the interviewer will be more alert to the possibility of a coached allegation than in other cases. There are four ways in which this child interview may differ from child interviews in other cases.

First, in this type of a case, the evaluator will want to minimize possible pressure on the child to make a false statement. In most sexual abuse cases, the evaluator takes pains to see that the child is not influenced to conceal sexual abuse. This may be done by not having the alleged offender there when the child is seen and by having the child accompanied by a supportive adult. In divorce cases, there is concern that the victim not only might be coerced not to disclose but might also be influenced to assert something that is not true. It is as important to prevent undue influence on the child as it is to avoid the discreditation of the evaluation because of perceived influence. Therefore, it may be appropriate to have a neutral party, such as the child's therapist, school counselor, the child protection worker, or a family friend, bring the child to the evaluation. However, logistically, this may be difficult. If the evaluator must choose one parent to bring the child, it should be the nonaccused parent. The reason for this is that, so far, clinical and research findings indicate that an offender trying to influence a child not to tell is a much more common phenomenon than an accusing parent influencing a child to make a false allegation. There is an additional consideration if the child is young or anxious. Having the child brought by someone other than a parent may be inappropriate and counterproductive because it results in additional trauma to the child and inhibits disclosure.

Even when the nonaccused parent accompanies the child to the evaluation, she should not be in the room when the child is questioned about the sexual abuse. This can be accomplished by having the parent there for the initial part of the interview, when general topics are covered or the evaluator plays with the child, and then having the parent leave before the issue of sexual abuse is addressed.

However, there will be times when this approach does not work, and the evaluator must keep the parent in the room or have the parent return. For example, the child may be too anxious or refuse to talk to the interviewer but, nevertheless, may indicate something has happened. The interviewer may then ask the child if she thinks it would be easier to talk with the parent there.

Second, it may be appropriate for the interviewer to try in a nonaccusatory way to determine if anyone has suggested to the child what to say. For example, the evaluator may ask the child what mom said about coming here today and whether she said anything about what the child should say. However, the fact that the child says that her mother said for her to tell the evaluator that "daddy put his fingers in her peepee" should not lead to a conclusion that the allegation is false. Rather, it should be a cue to ask an additional question, "Is that what happened to you or not?" and, if the response is affirmative, to ask for further details.

Third, in disputed custody/visitation cases, the evaluator will focus even more than in other cases on the alleged victim's ability to provide detail. Therefore, a simple statement that "he touched me" will not be sufficient to confirm the case. Descriptions of the sexual acts, an indication of sexual knowledge beyond that expected for the child's developmental stage, and an account told from a child's viewpoint should be sought. Further, the child's ability to describe the specifics of the context of the abuse will assist the evaluator in deciding whether the child is attributing the abuse to the correct perpetrator. The absence of detail about the abuse or the context could signal a coached allegation.

Fourth, it is important to consider questioning the child about adult figures in her life other than the accused. Therefore, despite the fact that the allegation is about the father, if there is a stepfather or if the mother has a boyfriend, the child should probably be asked about him as well. There are three reasons for doing this. First, as already noted in this chapter, mothers may correctly perceive that their children have been sexually abused but wrongly attribute it to the father. Second, sometimes the children themselves will indicate they have been sexually abused but will attribute it to someone who is less valued or less feared than the actual perpetrator. The less valued or feared person could be the father. Third, there may be multiple perpetrators. In some situations, women choose several partners who are sexually attracted to children.[3] Therefore, in stepfather cases, there may be a biological father who first sexually abused the children (Faller, 1988). As well, it seems that for some men the knowledge that a child has been sexually abused may trigger sexual responses in them, although they had not previously sexually maltreated children.

Interview with the Nonaccused Parent

The interview with the nonaccused parent is the aspect of the assessment where most adjustments must be made when allegations of sexual abuse come in the context of a divorce and/or custody/visitation dispute. Assuming this is the person alleging the sexual abuse, the evaluator will want to pay careful attention to the basis of those concerns, the reaction of this parent to the possibility of sexual abuse, and the parent's functioning.

Therefore, the evaluator will want to hear exactly what made the parent think the child might be sexually abused (Bresee et al., 1986). Often a chronology of signs of possible victimization is useful and can be elicited by asking the parent to begin with the first observation that led to concern and follow with subsequent incidents.

Compelling evidence will be observations of the child engaging in sexual behavior and an account that the child said this behavior was learned from or done with the offending parent, specific statements by the child regarding sexual activities with the alleged offender, and physical indicators of sexual abuse documented by a physician.

Unpersuasive findings are parental reports of statements by the child that could refer to experiences other than sexual abuse, reports of nonsexual symptomatic behavior, and reports of inappropriate activity by the accused parent that is not sexual. Examples of the first might be the child saying "daddy hurt me" or "I don't like daddy; he's bad." Nonsexual symptoms might include the child not wishing to go for visits, having nightmares, wetting the bed, doing poorly in school, having problems with peers, displaying behavior problems, and experiencing mood changes. Finally, the parent may report concerns about the child's relationship with the alleged offender because, for example, the child does not have a set bedtime on visits, is watching R-rated movies, is not eating nutritious meals, is sleeping with the alleged offender, or is bathing with that parent. The latter two examples are worrisome but not, by themselves, indicators of sexual abuse.

The case example that follows is one where the parent gives quite persuasive information.

> *Case example:* Mrs. T, at the direction of protective services, brought her 4-year-old son, Mike, to be evaluated for possible sexual abuse by his father. When asked what first made her think he might have been sexually abused, she recounted the following incident. Mike had one of his friends from nursery school over to spend the night. They were taking a bath together, and Mrs. T caught Mike licking the anus of his friend. She asked him what he was doing, and he said playing a game. She then asked where he learned the game, and he said from his dad. His dad did this to him and had him do it to other people when he visited.

In this case, the mother gave graphic and specific details of the incident that triggered her concern. She seems to have very good reason to think her son has been sexually abused.

In addition to the observations that led to thoughts the child might have been sexually abused, the nonoffending parent's reaction to this information may be important in ruling out the likelihood that she or he manufactured the allegation. Typically, coming to believe that someone has sexually abused a child takes time, that is, the initial reaction to a report about someone close or close to the child is disbelief. If the nonaccused parent reports not believing the alleged offender would do such a thing, reports thinking the child was mistaken, or asks the evaluator to confirm that the abuse didn't occur, then it is unlikely this parent is making up the allegation. In contrast, if the adult reports her initial reaction was that she "knew it all along," or it would be just like the alleged offender to sexually maltreat a child, this may signal some distortion by the reporter. Of course, it is important to examine the individual situation to see if the immediate conclusion that the alleged offender must have done it is justified. If the alleged offender has previously sexually abused children, then such a conclusion may be very appropriate.

There are a number of aspects of the nonoffending parent's functioning that may shed some light on the truth or falsehood of the allegation. However, it must be emphasized that findings in these areas are not conclusive of a false allegation. They merely assist the evaluator in understanding why the allegation was made if the interview with the child does not yield evidence supportive of sexual abuse. Moreover, to further muddy the waters, positive findings (that is, problems) in the functioning of the accusing parent may be consistent with the dynamics of sexual abuse as well as those of a fabricated allegation.

If, based upon the child interview, the evaluator thinks perhaps the mother has coached the child to make a false allegation, it is necessary to assess the mother to see if she has the type of personality that would be consistent with falsely accusing someone of sexual abuse. The evaluator will be looking for deficits in superego functioning, a severely impaired superego being consistent with making a false accusation of sexual abuse. Therefore, if the accusing parent appears psychopathic or severely character disordered, there is a possibility the person made up the allegation. However, the finding that the mother has very impaired superego functioning does not rule out sexual abuse. Such an adult may be at increased risk of marrying a sexual abuser.

A childhood history on the part of the mother of unresolved sexual victimization is another characteristic that may play a role in a false allegation. The childhood experience may result in distortions of events or hypervigilence (Bresee et al., 1986; Jones and McGraw, 1987), so that sexual maltreatment is imagined. However, sexual victimization can also signal increased vulnerability to having children who are sexually abused. A woman who has been sexually abused may feel uncomfortable with normal adult sexual relationships and choose a partner who does not make sexual demands upon her because his primary sexual attraction is to children. In addition, a woman with a background of sexual victimization may not be as sensitive to risk situations as other woman and unwittingly place her children at risk.

Some authors have described mothers who make false allegations as hysterics (Benedek and Schetky, 1985; Blush and Ross, 1986). The argument they make is that these women overreact to signs that *may be* indicators of sexual abuse, or they distort what they observe and wrongly assume the child has been sexually abused. This appears to be true in a few cases. However, caution must be used in drawing this conclusion. Most mothers are upset when they think their children have been sexually abused. One would be concerned about them as parents if they were not. Moreover, being in the process of a divorce is likely to cause adults who ordinarily cope well to become quite distraught. Therefore, a parent who is both caught in a divorce and has discovered her child has been sexually abused may look hysterical.

To conclude, in custody and visitation disputes, it is useful to alter somewhat the evaluation of the mother, assuming she is the accusing parent, but findings must be interpreted with care and in light of the results of the child interview.

Assessing the Parent-Child Relationship

Finally, understanding the quality of the parent-child relationship is important for disposition of these cases, regardless of whether sexual abuse is found. There are those who argue that an accusation of sexual abuse can be decided based upon the interaction between the child and the parents (Steven Cook, personal communication, Ann Arbor, 1985; Green, 1986; Guyer, 1983). They assert that children who are making a false allegation may have a symbiotic relationship with the accusing parent and will turn to that person for guidance during the interview. Further, they state that sexual abuse is unlikely if the interaction between the alleged offender and the child appears to be appropriate. According to these professionals, children who have been sexually abused will interact in a sexual or provocative way with the abusive parent or, alternatively, will be frightened and will avoid the offender. There are even a few evaluators who believe that the child and the alleged abuser should be brought together and the child be asked to repeat the allegations to the offending parent (Benedek, 1987; Green, 1986), although they do not agree about how to interpret the child's response.

The limitations of what can be learned from observing the parent-child interaction will be addressed first. This will be followed by a discussion of the advisability of having a confrontation between the child and the accused parent, including one that involves asking the child to repeat the accusations.

I caution evaluators against making too much of what is seen in a circumscribed time frame in the presence of the evaluator. This is not to discount what is observed but to appreciate its limitations. What will be seen is one type of interaction between parent and child, but certainly not the only type, and perhaps not interaction that is typical of the parent-child relationship. The evaluator's presence is likely to have an effect. A child may feel safe in the presence of another adult or inhibited in that context. In many cases, an observed interaction between parent and child will be the first contact for many months because visits have been curtailed following an allegation of sexual abuse. Therefore, the evaluator may see an interaction distorted by the absence of contact. The interaction may also be influenced by the custodial parent's opinion of the alleged offender, especially if there has been a hiatus in visits. The result may be expressed fear of the alleged offender or spontaneous engagement with the person, depending on the child's reaction to the circumstance of contact. Moreover, the accused parent will certainly be alert to the significance of how he relates to the child in the presence of the evaluator and will probably be on his best behavior.

It is also worth bearing in mind that there will be many aspects to the parent-child relationship other than the sexual abuse. These may be displayed during the evaluation, rather than the sexual aspect. Moreover, the differences between an appropriate parent-child relationship and a sexualized one may be quite subtle; interaction that could have a sexual potential may be misunderstood as implying a good parent-child relationship. Furthermore, the parent may be quite invested in the child, a positive attribute; however, that investment may result in the parent looking to the child to get a variety of needs met, including sexual needs. In addition, it is not uncommon for a parent who is sexually abusive to have the capability of being nurturing. Often the sexual interaction between adult and child evolves from appropriate hugging, caressing, and kissing. Moreover, many sexual abusers are quite adept at playing appropriately with their children. This may be because they are more comfortable with children than with adults and function on a regressed, childlike level.

Therefore, I do not rely on observations of parent-child interaction in determining whether or not a child has been sexually abused. Such observations will tell the evaluator something about the parent-child relationship, but not all there is to know.

There is disagreement among experts in sexual abuse about whether to include an interview between the child and the alleged offender as part of the evaluation in cases where there is a divorce and custody/visitation dispute (Corwin, 1988). Some evaluators include it and others do not. I do not routinely do an assessment of the relationship between the child and the accused by observing their interaction. The reason for this is that the child may perceive such an encounter as a betrayal. If the child has trusted the evaluator enough to disclose sexual abuse, and then the evaluator requires the child to face the abuser, the child may experience this as a violation of that trust. The child was led to believe that it was safe to tell and then suddenly discovers it was not. Children who have been sexually abused already have fears that adults will betray them, and the evaluator then exacerbates that problem. This will probably be true even when the sexual abuse is not directly discussed, but it most certainly will be the outcome if the child is required to confront the offender with the abuse. It is curious that some writers think this confrontation appropriate despite the fact that, in other sexual abuse cases, it is considered counterproductive because it usually leads to denial of actual sexual abuse. Moreover, in therapy, such a confrontation may be a treatment goal, but it usually requires a great deal of work and preparation.

Finally, there may be other ways of ascertaining the quality of the relationship between the child and the alleged offender. One is by asking the children what they like about the parent, what they dislike, whether they want to see that parent and under what circumstances. A less desirable approach is asking the nonoffending parent; this is less desirable because the view may be biased. However, if the nonoffending parent says the relationship in the past was good, then there is good justification for maintaining and facilitating it. There may also be others who can provide useful information, for example, other relatives, therapists, neighbors, and teachers.

STRATEGIES FOR PROTECTING THE CHILD

If there is no significant indication of sexual abuse as a result of a careful assessment, then the decision about custody should be based on criteria in the child custody statute, and visitation with the noncustodial parent (assuming this is the accused parent) should be liberal and unsupervised. However, if there has been a lot of turmoil surrounding the accusation, initially short and perhaps even supervised visits should precede unsupervised and liberal contact. Often the accused parent can be persuaded of the efficacy of this gradually increased access both out of empathy for the child and as a way of protecting himself against renewed allegations.

If sexual abuse is found, a number of strategies can be considered, and there is a lack of consensus in the field about what is preferable. In my opinion, it is rarely in the child's best interest to totally sever contact with the abusive parent. Cases where that might be appropriate are those where the parent is dangerous or where contact is markedly traumatic for the child. A dangerous parent would be one who is a compulsive sexual abuser, who endeavors to molest the child even in the context of supervised visits, or who is likely to physically harm the child, the nonoffending parent, or a person supervising the visits. A determination that the visits are markedly traumatic to the child should be made by a neutral party, and several visits should be attempted before such a decision is made. Even when a decision to sever contact is made, there may come a time in the future when some contact with the offender is deemed to be in the child's best interest.

The reasons for a practice of trying to preserve the child's relationship with the offending parent are several. First, as noted earlier, there are many aspects to the relationship other than the sexual abuse, and these may well be worthy of preservation. One way of viewing this is that no parent is perfect, yet one does not sever the relationship because of this. Sexual abuse can be viewed as one of many parental problems that children must be protected against, but the existence of problems in the relationship does not rule out contact. A second reason for maintaining the relationship is that it affords the child an opportunity to work through feelings about the sexual abuse as well as the divorce. Third, access will encourage a realistic view of the offending parent. Without the contact, the child is likely to come to view the parent as either all bad or all good. Either perception is problematic.

Another possible disposition is no contact with the child until the offending parent has successfully completed treatment. In the abstract, this sounds like a sensible approach. However, problems may arise. Often the offender does not follow through on treatment and de facto relinquishes his relationship with the child. A different problem is that the offender may be pronounced cured when his problem has not been addressed. This is likely to happen when his treatment is divorced from any input from the victim, the nonoffending parent, or other professionals involved with the family. It may also occur when the offender is admonished to go out and get treatment on his own and chooses someone unskilled in therapy for sex offenders or even denies to the naive therapist that he sexually abused the child. Therefore, as with other sex abuse treatment, contact between the offender's therapist and others in the family or their therapists is important.

A third possible disposition is supervised visits with the offender. Under ideal circumstances, the offender will also receive therapy. As a rule, these visits should be short and should not include overnights. The choice of a person to supervise will be very important and may prove an obstacle to visitation. Relatives provide the most flexibility and allow for more extended visits. However, two problems may arise with relative supervision. If they are the nonoffending parent's relatives, the offender may find his relationship with them too difficult to allow for comfortable visits. On the other hand, if the relatives are the offender's, they may disbelieve or discount the importance of the sexual abuse and not provide the victim with adequate protection. As noted earlier, with this type of sexual abuse, there may be risk of subsequent maltreatment, despite the involvement of the court and the vigilance of agencies and the nonoffending parent. One situation where reabuse may happen is when visits are supervised by the offender's relatives.

Additional potential supervisors of visits are persons from agencies who have responsibility for case management in cases of child sexual abuse. These may be agents of the friend of the court and protective services. In some cases, a therapist involved with the family may furnish supervision of visits. The advantage of these people as supervisors is that they are neutral and, therefore, likely to be acceptable to both parents, and they will be protective. The major disadvantage is the limited time they have available and the fact their involvement may be time-limited.

Or there could be a jointly agreed-upon supervisor. This might be a friend of the family, a professional or paraprofessional who is moonlighting, or someone else. Problems that may occur in this arrangement are that the parents usually must pay for this service and sometimes the person withdraws the service, particularly if there is a lot of hostility or other difficulties around contact.

Finally, the issue of visit supervision may be resolved if the offender acquires a new partner. That person may become the supervisor of visits. While the new partner shares with the offender's relatives the vulnerability of not being sufficiently protective, that partner's presence may decrease the potential for future sexual abuse because the offender's needs are being met by the new partner.

Unsupervised visits are rarely recommended in this type of sexual abuse because the risk for reincidence appears quite high. Liberal access would only be resumed after the offender has successfully completed a course of treatment. Even then, contacts should be carefully monitored, and extended and unsupervised access gradually introduced.

In addition to cases where sexual abuse is found and cases where it is not found, are those where evaluators just cannot tell whether or not the child has been sexually abused. For a variety of reasons, these appear to occur at higher rates in custody/visitation disputes. The first is the young age of many victims (Faller, forthcoming-b; Hewitt, forthcoming; MacFarlane, 1986; Paradise et al., 1988). MacFarlane first called attention to the very young age of some alleged victims in divorce situations and to the fact that, because of this, it may not be possible to determine whether or not the child has been sexually abused. The author has found that the mean age at evaluation for a sample of children sexually abused by a noncustodial father was 5.4 years. This was significantly younger than the age of victims of sexual abuse by biological fathers in intact families (8.7 years) and stepfathers (9.9 years) (Faller, forthcoming-b). The second reason for inconclusive findings regarding sexual abuse is that children may be evaluated multiple times, and there is a concern that their accounts may be contaminated by this process. The third is the concern that they may have been pressured to say they were sexually abused when they were not.

A considerable dilemma is what to do regarding contact with the alleged offender when the results of evaluation are inconclusive. Recently, Hewitt (forthcoming) has written a very sensible article that describes a strategy employed with seven cases of preschool children where the results of evaluations were inconclusive. She suggests the following: a meeting with the child to develop a list of acceptable and unacceptable touching from the child's viewpoint; a meeting with the nonaccused parent to give her an opportunity to develop a similar list, to deal with her anxieties around resumed visits, and to teach her ways of asking nonleading questions and seeking help, should further concerns arise about sexual abuse; a meeting with the alleged offender to elicit a list of appropriate and inappropriate touching from him; a meeting with the nonaccused parent and child to clarify appropriate and inappropriate touch and the child's strategy for telling should there be any inappropriate touching; and, finally, a carefully orchestrated meeting between the child and the alleged offender in which they go over the list of appropriate and inappropriate touching and the alleged offender gives the child permission to tell should anyone, including himself, engage in bad touching. The evaluator then supervises several subsequent visits. Following that, unsupervised visits are gradually introduced, but there are meetings with the child alone to allow the child to disclose any inappropriate behavior on visits. Hewitt recommends involvement for at least a year and cites follow-up data on five cases, none of which had additional referrals for sexual abuse by the alleged offender.

RESEARCH ON FALSE ALLEGATIONS

As already noted, there are those who have declared that false allegations are widespread in disputed custody cases and that mothers are using this charge as a way of gaining sole custody of their children (Ager, 1987; Benedek, 1987; Blush and Ross, 1986; Renshaw, 1987; Schuman, 1986). These claims must be taken seriously; it is important to examine the empirical data that support or disconfirm these assertions.

When Jones and McGraw (1987) examined 576 protective services referrals for Denver County in 1983 (described in Chapter 5), they found that 6% of the allegations made by adults and 2% of those made by children were fictitious. Of the false allegations by adults, a large proportion were accusations that were made in the context of a custody/visitation dispute. Troubled by the high percentage of false allegations involving custody disputes, Jones went to a source of cases having a larger proportion of divorce and custody/ visitation disputes, the Kempe National Center for the Prevention and Treatment of Child Abuse and Neglect (Jones and Seig, 1988). Twenty cases involving divorce/custody disputes were identified between 1983 and 1985. Of those cases, 70% were considered reliable reports, 20% were considered fictitious, and 10% were uncertain.

Paradise et al. (1988) reviewed sexual abuse cases from Children's Hospital of Philadelphia over a 10-month period and six cases from the clinical practice of the first author. They selected 31 cases involving an allegation against a biological parent—12 cases with custody/visitation disputes and 19 without. The substantiation rate for the former group was 67% and for the latter, 95%. The children in disputed custody cases were significantly younger (5.4 years) than those in the other biological parent cases (7.8 years).

I have evaluated 97 allegations of sexual abuse where there were questions of custody and/or visitation, the overwhelming majority of which were referred by protective services, the guardian ad litem, or by joint agreement of both parents. Of these, 79 (81%) were deemed to be valid. Of those cases that could not be validated, 8 were found to be invalid and 10 inconclusive. In these cases as a whole, 69 involved charges against biological fathers; 3, charges against mothers; 10, stepfathers; 3, mothers' boyfriends; 7, other relatives; and 5, unrelated persons. No relationship was found between the role of the alleged offender and whether or not it was deemed a false allegation.

A much larger study has been conducted by the Association of Family and Conciliation Courts Research Unit (1988). It involved 9,000 cases where there was a divorce and a custody dispute. Cases came from 12 different states, with intensive examination having been completed in cases from eight court jurisdictions. Out of the 9,000 disputed custody cases, only 1.5% (169 cases) involved allegations of sexual abuse. In almost half of these cases, mothers were making allegations against fathers. In the remainder of cases, fathers made allegations against mothers, stepfathers, or mothers' boy-friends; either parent charged another family member, such as an uncle or a stepsibling; or someone other than the parents made the allegation.

The researchers used the protective services disposition on the case or the findings of an evaluator chosen by the divorce court as indicators of the validity of the case. In a fourth of the cases, the allegation of sexual abuse was not addressed. Of the remaining cases, for half, sexual abuse was determined to be likely, for about one third, unlikely, and for 17%, the assessors could not tell. Of those cases in the abuse-unlikely category, in only 8 cases (out of 9,000 cases where there were custody disputes) was the allegation felt to be malicious.

Benedek and Schetky (1985) have cited 18 cases of allegations of sexual abuse, 10 (56%) of which were not confirmed. In all cases where allegations were deemed to be false, they were made by mothers. However, false accusations were determined to be the result of distortions in perception rather than consciously constructed fabrications. In understanding these findings, the case selection process is important. According to Benedek (1987), her process was as follows. When asked to evaluate and provide testimony on a case (usually by the accused), she requests past investigative reports, evaluations, and previous court testimony. If, after reviewing the material, she believes the sexual abuse to have taken place, she informs the accused and refuses to work on the case. Conversely, if she believes the abuse is questionable or unfounded based upon the material supplied, she agrees to serve as an evaluator and expert witness.

Green (1986) describes 4 out of 11 cases (36%) that he determines to be false and then, on the basis of these four cases, describes characteristics of false allegations. His article occasioned a challenge by Corwin et al. (1987), in part because one of the cases he deemed to be false was that of a boy whom two of the authors of the Corwin article, on the basis of careful exploration and physical evidence, thought might well have been sexually abused. Green's article also led to a letter calling into question its conclusions. The letter appeared in the *Journal of the American Academy of Child Psychiatry* (March 1988) signed by 19 experts in child sexual abuse.

Schuman (1986) cites seven cases that he judges to be false, and Kaplan and Kaplan (1981) report on a single case. Blush and Ross (1986) and Guyer (1983), who assert that most allegations made in the context of divorce are false, do not present any data.

How should these findings and the fact they do not necessarily agree be evaluated? In making an assessment of the validity of the research and clinical reports, it is important to take into account sample size, sample biases, and criteria employed to determine whether an allegation is true or false. The largest sample is that of the Association of Family and Conciliation Courts Research Unit—9,000 cases. A further strength of the study is that it is drawn from several courts in 12 different states and, therefore, should be representative of the full range of cases where there are custody disputes. The fact that it relies upon decisions of protective services workers and court-appointed evaluators as opposed to experts in sexual abuse may account for a lower substantiation rate than that of Jones and Seig (1988), Green (1986), Paradise and colleagues (1988), or myself. Arguably, the findings of the experts in sexual abuse are a more accurate reflection of the true incidence of false and valid reports of sexual abuse in this context.

The samples of Paradise and colleagues, Jones and Seig, Benedek and Schetky, Green, and mine are clinical samples of cases evaluated by experts and, therefore, may not represent the full range of allegations in custody disputes. Indeed, as already noted, I have a selection procedure that is likely to screen out false cases, whereas Benedek and Schetky have criteria that would screen them in. These differences no doubt play a role in the different levels of substantiation. Studies with such a small sample size as Benedek and Schetky's, Green's, and Schuman's, and certainly those reports citing one case or presenting no data, cannot be given much weight at all (Berliner, 1988; Sink, 1988). Finally, as noted in Chapter 5, a major dilemma in determining the proportion of true and false allegations is the lack of agreement about the criteria for differentiating a true from a false allegation. Those with higher substantiation rates rely more heavily on the child's statements and behavior, whereas those with lower rates place more weight on other material, such as parental psychiatric diagnosis, observations of parent-child interaction, or the results of a confrontation between the child and the alleged offender.

Despite these differences in findings, some conclusions can be drawn from the research. First, it appears that a substantial percentage of allegations (between half and three-fourths) made in divorce situations are confirmed. Second, allegations of sexual abuse are a relatively infrequent charge in custody disputes. Finally, cases where the accusation is deemed to be a calculated lie are very rare.

CONCLUSION

The problem of sexual abuse allegations in custody/visitation disputes is complex. Such charges have the potential of being very damaging to children, regardless of their validity. Children must deal not only with the trauma of divorce but with the additional impact of an allegation and/or experience of sexual abuse.

NOTES

1. For the sake of readability, the masculine pronoun will be used for the accused parent and the feminine for the nonaccused parent. However, I recognize that in a number of cases a woman is accused, and a man does the accusing. The term "accusing parent" is not used because the person making the allegation in many instances is someone other than a parent, often the alleged victim or a professional who has involvement with the victim.

2. No suggestions for changes in the interview of the alleged offender are offered. As in other cases, he will be interviewed to assess whether he has the propensity to sexually abuse and to obtain his view of the allegation. The only authors who have suggested that there are any characteristics of an innocent accused parent in divorce cases are Blush and Ross (1986). The traits they note are also ones found to be characteristic of some incestuous fathers.

3. In my research on a sample of 275 victims, 24% were found to be victims of more than one abuser (Faller, forthcoming-a).

REFERENCES

Ager, Susan. 1987. "Daddy Hurt Me." *Free Press Magazine*, February 22.

Association of Family and Conciliation Courts Research Unit. 1988. *Allegations of Sexual Abuse in Custody and Visitation Disputes.* Denver: Association of Family and Conciliation Courts.

Benedek, Elissa. 1987. Court Testimony. E. Morgan v. E. Foretich, V. Foretich, D. Foretich. Alexandria, Virginia, United States District Court, February 18.

Benedek, Elissa and Diane Schetky. 1985. "Allegations of Sexual Abuse in Child Custody and Visitation Disputes." In *Emerging Issues in Child Psychiatry and the Law.* New York: Brunner/Mazel.

Berliner, Lucy. 1988. "Deciding Whether a Child Has Been Sexually Abused." In *Sexual Abuse Allegations in Custody and Visitation Cases*, edited by E. B. Nicholson and J. Bulkley. Washington, DC: American Bar Association.

Blush, Gordon and Karol Ross. 1986. *Sexual Allegations in Divorce: The SAID Syndrome.* Unpublished manuscript, Mt. Clemens, MI.

Bresee, P., G. Stearns, B. Bess, and L. Packer. 1986. "Allegations of Child Sexual Abuse in Child Custody Disputes: A Therapeutic Assessment Model." *American Journal of Orthopsychiatry* 56(4):560-68.

Committee on the Family, Group for the Advancement of Psychiatry. 1980. *Divorce, Child Custody, and the Family.* San Francisco: Jossey-Bass.

Corwin, David. 1988. "Early Diagnosis of Child Sexual Abuse—Diminishing the Lasting Effects." In *The Lasting Effects of Child Sexual Abuse*, edited by G. Wyatt and G. Powell. Newbury Park, CA: Sage.

Corwin, David, Lucy Berliner, Gail Goodman, Jean Goodwin, and Susan White. 1987. "Child Sexual Abuse and Custody Disputes: No Easy Answers." *Journal of Interpersonal Violence* 2(1):91-105.

Faller, Kathleen Coulborn. 1988. *Child Sexual Abuse: An Interdisciplinary Manual for Diagnosis, Case Management and Treatment.* New York: Columbia University Press.

———. Forthcoming-a. "Children Who Are Sexually Abused by More than One Person." *Victimology.*

———. Forthcoming-b. "Young Age of Victims of Intrafamilial Sexual Abuse." *Victimology.*

Galtney, Liz. 1988. "Mothers on the Run." *U.S. News and World Report,* June 13, pp. 22-32.

Green, Arthur. 1986. "True and False Allegations of Sexual Abuse in Child Custody Disputes." *Journal of the American Academy of Child Psychiatry* 25(4):449-56.

Guyer, Melvin. 1983. Class presentation, University of Michigan Law School, Ann Arbor.

———. 1988. "False Allegations of Sexual Abuse." Presented at the Workshop for the Michigan Academy of Forensic Psychiatry.

Hewitt, Sandra. Forthcoming. "Therapeutic Case Management of Pre-School Cases of Alleged But Not Substantiated Sexual Abuse." *Child Welfare.*

Jones, David and E. M. McGraw. 1987. "Reliable and Fictitious Accounts of Sexual Abuse to Children." *Journal of Interpersonal Violence* 2(1):27-45.

Jones, David and A. Seig. 1988. "Child Sexual Abuse Allegations in Custody or Visitation Cases: A Report of 20 Cases." In *Sexual Abuse Allegations in Custody and Visitation Cases,* edited by E. B. Nicholson and J. Bulkley. Washington, DC: American Bar Association.

Kaplan, S. L. and S. J. Kaplan. 1981. "The Child's Accusation of Sexual Abuse During a Divorce and Custody Struggle." *Hillside Journal of Clinical Psychiatry* 3:81-95.

MacFarlane, Kee. 1986. "Child Sexual Abuse Allegations in Divorce Proceedings." In *Sexual Abuse of Young Children,* edited by K. MacFarlane and Jill Waterman. New York: Guilford.

Nicholson, E. Bruce and Josephine Bulkley, eds. 1988. *Sexual Abuse Allegations in Custody and Visitation Cases.* Washington, DC: American Bar Association.

Paradise, Jan, Anthony Rostain, and Madelaine Nathanson. 1988. "Substantiation of Sexual Abuse Charges When Parents Dispute Custody or Visitation." *Pediatrics* 81(6):835-39.

Renshaw, Domeena. 1987. "Child Sexual Abuse: When Wrongly Charged." *Encyclopedia Britannica Medical and Health Annual,* pp. 301-3.

Schuman, David. 1986. "False Allegations of Physical and Sexual Abuse." *Bulletin of the American Academy of Psychiatry and Law* 14(1):5-21.

Sink, Frances. 1988. "Studies of True and False Allegations: A Critical Review." In *Sexual Abuse Allegations in Custody and Visitation Cases,* edited by E. B. Nicholson and J. Bulkley. Washington, DC: American Bar Association.

Thoennes, Nancy. 1988. "Sexual Abuse Allegations in Custody Disputes." Presentation given at the National Conference on the Victimization of Children, Anaheim, CA, April.

INDEX

ABOUT THE AUTHOR

KATHLEEN COULBORN FALLER (M.S.W., Ph.D.) is Associate Professor in the School of Social Work and Co-Director of the Interdisciplinary Project on Child Abuse and Neglect, University of Michigan. She is the author of *Social Work with Abused and Neglected Children* (Free Press, 1981) and *Child Sexual Abuse: An Interdisciplinary Manual for Diagnosis, Case Management and Treatment* (Columbia University Press, 1988). She conducts research and engages in clinical work with sexually abused children and their families.

NOTES

NOTES

NOTES

NOTES

NOTES